XSLT

⟨XSLT⟩

Working with XML and HTML

Khun Yee Fung

♠ Addison-Wesley

Boston • San Francisco • New York • Toronto • Montreal
London • Munich • Paris • Madrid
Capetown • Sydney • Tokyo • Singapore • Mexico City

The publisher offers discounts on this book when ordered in quantity for special sales. For more information, please contact:

Pearson Education Corporate Sales Division
One Lake Street
Upper Saddle River, NJ 07458
(800) 382-3419
corpsales@pearsontechgroup.com

Visit us on the Web at www.awl.com/cseng/

Library of Congress Cataloging-in-Publication Data

Fung, Khun Yee.
    XSLT : working with XML and HTML / Khun Yee Fung.
       p.   cm.
    Includes bibliographical references and index.
    ISBN 0-201-71103-6
    1. XML (Document markup language)   2. HTML (Document markup language)   I. Title.

QA76.76.H94 F86 2000
005.7'2—dc21   00-048514

Text printed on recycled paper.
1 2 3 4 5 6 7 8 9 10—DOC—0403020100
First printing, December 2000

This book is dedicated to the gang in the Warp Core Room:

Kuni Katsuya,

Glen Kim,

Edward Borejsza, and

Zoltan Fulop;

and to the developers:

James Eberhardt and

Susan Celentano.

Contents

Contents

5   Paths   89

6   Transformation   137

7   Control   161

8   Constructing the Result Tree   181

Contents

> PART III

12 A Case Study   239

Contents

> PART IV

13 Transforming to XML and Text   289

> Appendixes

A Tools and Resources   313

Contents

Preface

This book is about XSLT, or **XSL Transformations** (XSL stands for Extensible Stylesheet Language), which is a language developed by W3C[1] that can be used to transform XML documents. XSLT is so versatile that it can transform one kind of XML document to another kind of XML document, to an HTML document, or to a text document.

This book is for anybody who wants to use XSLT to transform XML documents to HTML documents. We will look at what XSLT is all about, how it is used for transformation to HTML, and especially how to write the XSLT documents for the transformation. Although XML to HTML is the focus of this book, the principles of transformation do not change whether you want to transform XML documents to HTML, XML, or text. Once you know how to produce HTML documents, you will possess the knowledge to produce the other two types as well.

---

1. World Wide Web Consortium, the consortium that specified HTML and XML, among other markup languages.

The Main Specifications

Before we get into XSLT, we must become familiar with its four core specifications: XSLT, XML, XML Namespace, and XPath. All four specifications are W3C recommendations; in other words, they are standards for the Web and the final authority for XML, XSLT, XPath, and XML Namespaces. These specifications are available at `http://www.w3.org/TR`. Because we will be using HTML as the primary output document format, you may want to look at the HTML specifications as well. They are also available at this site.

The Learning Curve

Although XSLT has concepts that require some programming fundamentals, it is not necessary to have a programming background. In other words, it is typical of the technologies that Web developers encounter and use every day. The definitions and examples should help you grasp the nonprogramming concepts.

This book was written in plain English, with as little computer jargon as possible. However, since you occasionally need to consult the specifications related to XSLT, I have used that terminology in the book.

XSLT Processors

To perform examples in this book, an XSLT processor program is needed. I use the XSLT processor written by James Clark to verify the examples. This XSLT processor can be obtained from James Clark's Web site: `http://www.jclark.com`. You can certainly use a different XSLT processor if you wish to.[2]

Appendix A lists URLs that will help you find other tools to write XML and XSLT documents.

Conventions Used in This Book

Concepts and terms are set in **boldface** type the first time they are used. Examples and code are set in the `typewriter` font. File names are set in *italics*. The ⎵ symbol is used to make the invisible space character visible.

---

2. There is a chance XT may be retired shortly after this book is published. If so, I suggest you check the Xalan XSLT processor at `http://xml.apache.org`.

Organization

This book is organized into four parts and three appendixes. Part I provides you with the features of XML and XSLT that you will use most of the time. Part II describes the concepts of XSLT and XPath in more depth. Part III presents the usage of XSLT. Part IV discusses transformation to XML and text documents. The appendixes include online resources, character sets and encoding schemes, and a reference for XSLT and XPath, with many examples for the elements and functions in different circumstances.

Part I

The first three chapters discuss the most frequently used 20 percent of XML and XSLT. You will be able to handle 80 percent of XSLT work in your daily life as an XSLT developer. Chapter 1, "Introduction," explains the importance of XML and the role of XSLT in the scheme of things. Chapter 2, "XML," is a simple introduction to XML. Chapter 3, "Introduction to XSLT," introduces you to XSLT. The most frequently used features are discussed here, with three related examples.

Part II

The chapters in Part II explain how the transformation is constructed. Once you understand the transformation, you should have no problem writing XSLT documents to produce your desired result. Chapter 4, "XML Documents as Trees," displays the XML document as a tree. Chapter 5, "Paths," explains the all-important concept of location path. These are expressions that allow you to refer to elements, among other things, in XML documents. Chapter 6, "Transformation," explains the transformation process in XSLT, which uses templates for matching the XML documents. This is the foundation for understanding how XSLT provides a versatile tool to transform XML documents to HTML. Chapter 7, "Control," explains control elements in XSLT that allow you to manipulate XML documents. Chapter 8, "Constructing the Result Tree," shows you how to create the output document that you need for your project. Chapter 9, "Combining Templates," explains how templates can be combined together for reuse. Chapter 10, "Extensions," discusses the extension mechanism in XSLT.

Part III

The two chapters in Part III examine the usage aspects of XSLT. Chapter 11, "Idioms and Tips," discusses some of the hard and not-so-hard lessons I learned in various XSLT projects. Chapter 12, "A Case Study," discusses the process and the XSLT documents necessary to design a Web site using XML and XSLT.

Part IV

Part IV deals with transformation to XML and text documents. Chapter 13, "Transforming to XML and Text," presents examples of transformations from one XML document type to another XML document type. It also explains how to produce text documents with XSLT.

Appendixes

Appendix A, "Tools and Resources," lists some of the URLs for XML and XSLT resources online. Appendix B, "Character Sets and Encoding Schemes," provides a simple explanation of character sets and encoding schemes. Appendix C, "XSLT and XPath Reference," provides examples for the elements and functions in XSLT. Once you understood the basic XSLT concepts, you will consult Appendix C often.

Acknowledgments

I thank Kuni Katsuya and Glen Kim for being there when the idea for the book first came up. I thank Lucilla, Susan, and (Young) Brian for being the guinea pigs in my XSL tutorial. I thank David Faria for reading one of the first drafts.

I thank my family for supporting me while I worked 7 days a week, more than 12 hours a day. I thank Melissa for her love and support, even though I have been mentally absent for so long. I thank Opheliar for reading the first draft of the manuscript and offering helpful suggestions.

PART I

⟨ 1 ⟩

Introduction

This is why when you do something,
the beginning is simple;
but it always becomes complex and difficult after that.
—*Zhuang Zi*

There are high hopes for the success of XML (Extensible Markup Language). If XML is accepted—and it looks that way right now—it will provide us with a unified notation for the structure to text documents, a universal definition for the structure of classes of documents, and a common ground on which applications can interoperate.

Most of these documents will be used to exchange information among computer applications. In other words, XML will be used mostly as the notation for document exchange. But XML can also be used to define documents meant for presentation—for example, XHTML (Extensible HyperText Markup Language), a redefinition of HTML in XML. XHTML documents can be rendered in the same way as an HTML document.

XML documents that are not XHTML documents, however, must be presented in other ways. One way is to first transform an XML document to HTML, rendering an HTML document. This method does not require any changes to the Web browsers, and it happens to be the theme of this book.

In this chapter, we will look at what XML is and why it is so important. We will also look at how to present XML documents and how XSLT is used in the

3

process. Finally, we will examine the possible positions of XSLT in the Web publishing pipeline.

1.1   What Is XML?

XML has a set of syntax rules on how to mark up text documents and data. These markups supply the structure of the document or data. Marking up a text document means adding more characters to the document, but since XML was designed with human readability in mind, this verbosity is a small price to pay.

XML's versatility and ability to define many kinds of text documents with wildly different structures make it a candidate for the universal notation of structured text documents. Only a few years since its recommendation, the universality of XML is becoming a reality.

XML is more versatile for structured text than is GIF for graphics. GIF is only useful for bitmapped images; in consequence, other formats are still needed for other types of graphics, for example, vector graphics, movies, and so forth.

But if XML is used, almost all structured text files can be represented in XML. When a new class of text documents with a different structure is needed, a new class of XML documents to handle the new structure can be created. This means almost no proprietary tool development will be necessary to handle the format XML documents, hence easy interoperability for applications that exchange text documents and broad industrial experience with XML documents.

1.2   The Importance of Extensive XML Documents

When XML documents become widespread, good tools will be developed because such tools will be necessary to handle XML documents correctly and efficiently. And the tools are a good investment because there will no longer be a need to handle many notations. There will be no reason not to use XML documents for exchange; the most basic interoperability problem will have been solved.

The other significant impact of ubiquitous XML documents is that good minds will concentrate on XML. There will be heavy concentration on XML because it will be unnecessary to learn competing notations. There will be as many XML documents as HTML documents, probably more.

1.3   The Difference between XML and HTML

XML documents and HTML documents have a similar syntax, but on the abstraction level, they are very different. The HTML specification defines a class of documents to represent text documents with embedded hypertext links and presentation elements. The tag <TD> has a specific meaning as defined in the HTML specification.

On the other hand, XML can be used to define text documents with very different structures. XML does not define the meaning of the structure of a class of documents defined in XML or of individual elements. The tag <book> in an XML document does not have a predefined meaning in the XML specification.

The designer of a class of XML documents is responsible for assigning meanings to the structure of the class and for communicating this meaning outside XML. For example, the set of XSLT documents is a class of documents defined in XML. The structure of XSLT documents is defined in XML, whereas the meaning of the XSLT elements is explained in the XSLT specification. Therefore, you can use XML to define a class of documents just like HTML for display purposes (as has been done by W3C with XHTML).

In summary, XML provides a notation to define classes of documents where the members of the same class share the structure and semantics. HTML, on the other hand, is a class of documents designed for presentation of text documents with hyperlinks.

1.4   Presenting XML Documents

One obvious question when dealing with an XML document is how is it presented in a Web browser? All Web browsers know how to render HTML documents, but how do they render XML documents?

Actually, this is the same as asking how a plain text document is rendered by a Web browser. A Web browser simply shows the characters in a main text file, unless an application has been designated for handling plain text files; in that case the designated application is responsible for displaying the plain text file in whatever way it desires. A Web browser that understands the XML notation will probably show you the structure of an XML document. It may show you only the character data after stripping the markups or even just as it shows a plain text document. But how do we present an XML document in a Web browser?

1.4.1   *Rendering XML Documents*

There are three basic ways to present an XML document in a Web browser: (1) associate a CSS document with an XML document; (2) transform the XML document to XSL (Extensible Stylesheet Language), a language with features that allow you to specify precisely how the output should look; and (3) transform the XML document to HTML (and later on, XHTML).

Associating a CSS file with an XML document is the same as associating a CSS file with an HTML document. The styling of the XML document is performed in the Web browser on the client side. You can also transform an XML document into an XSL document first, using XSLT for the transformation. In fact, this is the primary design goal of XSLT—to handle all transformation needs of XSL. Most probably this transformation will be performed on the client side—the same as CSS. Although you can transform the XML document on the server side, the nature of XSL and the size of the resulting document strongly suggest transformation on the client side. These two approaches, if they are performed on the client side, require the client to have an engine for CSS styling or to have an XSLT processor and an XSL renderer.

Finally, you can transform the XML document on the server side to an HTML document and then ship it to the client for display. The advantage of transforming an XML document to an HTML document before shipping it to a Web browser is, of course, the universal ability of HTML rendering in the browsers. The disadvantage of transforming to HTML documents is that the original XML document will not be available to the Web browser, which will not know the structure of the XML documents used to obtain the HTML document.

1.5   The Role of XSLT

XSLT's original purpose was to transform XML documents to XSL documents. As defined right now, however, XSLT can do much more. It can also transform to HTML, plain text files, and text files with structures not defined in XML.

On the other hand, XSLT is not the only way to transform XML documents. A general programming language like C, C++, or Java can also be used. XSLT has the advantage of being more lightweight than these languages.[1] It is meant for transformation and is well-equipped as a language to perform this main

---

1. Most of the time, XSLT is interpreted. However, Sun Microsystems has come up with a compiler to compile XSLT documents to Java's intermediate code.

design goal. It allows us to write programs that are much smaller than in a general programming language.

1.6   XSLT in the HTML Publishing Pipeline

Suppose we wanted to present an XML document in the user's Web browser. There are quite a few components the document will go through to become an HTML document ready to be displayed in the Web browser. We call these components an HTML publishing pipeline.

The XML document can get in the Web server in many ways. The document can be created manually using an editor, it can be the output of a program, or it can be part of an XML database. How it gets there, however, is not relevant for our purposes.

We can transform the XML document into an HTML document in the Web server and then send it to the Web browser. In other words, the XML document can be fed to an **XSLT processor** to convert it to an HTML document according to the instructions in an XSLT document. When the HTML document is received by the Web browser, the browser will not know that the original document is an XML document. The browser does not need to know anything about XSLT or how it transforms the original XML document. It simply displays the HTML document it receives.

It is also possible to ship the XML document to the Web browser. Accompanying the XML document is an **XSLT document** with the instructions for transforming the XML document to an HTML document. In this instance, when the Web browser receives the XML and XSLT documents, it has to apply the XSLT document to the XML document to obtain the HTML document as the result. The browser must know how to perform the transformation, and it must have an XSLT processor in it. The advantage is that the browser has both the XML and the final HTML documents. The browser can transform the XML document multiple times, so this can be a significant advantage.

Whether the transformation is performed on the server side or on the client side, an XSLT document with the instructions for the transformation is needed. How to write the XSLT document is the focus of this book.

1.7   Summary

We have briefly examined XML, XSLT, and their relationships. The important point is the impending ubiquity of XML documents and XSLT's role in transforming XML documents to other kinds of XML documents, HTML documents, and other formats.

Of course, this book focuses on the transformation of XML documents to HTML documents. For this transformation, XSLT can be used on both the server side and client side. Although the environments will be different for the two uses, the design of the XSLT documents is identical.

1.8   Looking Ahead

You don't need to know all the details about XML to use this book, but you must know the basics. The next chapter provides a simple introduction to XML.

⟨2⟩

XML

We will now look at the different parts of an XML document, with emphasis on the parts that are important in XSLT.

2.1 URI

Before we look at the basic XML document structure, there is a term we need to discuss: URI. URI is the abbreviation for Uniform Resource Identifier. A URI can be a URL (Uniform Resource Locator) or a URN (Uniform Resource Name). You are probably familiar with URLs. URNs are used to identify resources permanently, even when the resource may not be accessible anymore. As a consequence, an intermediary is probably required to implement URNs.

A URL is always a URI but the reverse may not be true (because a URN is not a URL, and a URI can be a URN as well as a URL). In XSLT documents there are URIs that are fixed by the specifications. For instance, you will often see the URI `http://www.w3.org/1999/XSL/Transform`. It refers to the URI representing the namespace used by XSLT.

2.2   The Basic XML Document Structure

All XML documents have the same basic structure. In the beginning of an XML document is the **XML declaration**, followed by the **XML document type declaration**, and then the **document element** (or the **root element**[1]) of the document.

The XML declaration, if there is one, must be the first thing in an XML document, but an XML document can have comments after the XML document type declaration as well as inside and after the document element.

The following is a simple XML document.

```
<?xml version='1.0'?>
<!DOCTYPE doc SYSTEM 'simple.dtd'>
<doc>
  <!-- Inside the <doc> element -->
  <title>A simple XML document</title>
</doc>
<!-- The end of the XML document -->
```

2.2.1   *The XML Declaration*

The XML declaration is the tag `<?xml version='1.0'?>`, which may also specify the character encoding scheme used in the document. (See Appendix B for a simple explanation of character sets and encoding schemes.) For instance, if the encoding scheme used in the XML document is ISO 8859-1, then the tag looks like `<?xml version='1.0' encoding='ISO-8859-1'?>`. The XML declaration is a special tag not accessible from an XSLT document. If the character encoding scheme is not specified, then it is assumed to be UTF-8.[2]

The XML declaration is optional, but if there is one, it must be the first thing in an XML document. When possible, provide the XML declaration for XML documents.

---

1. Because the word *root* has another meaning in this book, we will use *document element* from now on.

2. If you are creating XML documents and they have to use a particular encoding scheme, make sure your editor is familiar with that encoding scheme. If you are editing English text, an editor that can handle ASCII is fine as long as you use only characters defined in ASCII.

2.2.2   *The XML Document Type Declaration*

The XML document type declaration, which comes after the XML declaration, is optional. It contains **markup declarations**, or it points to a document that contains markup declarations.

Markup declarations define the structure of a class of documents. They can be contained directly within the XML document type declaration, or they can be in a **document type definition (DTD)** file. We will not go into markup declarations here since they are not crucial in using XSLT.

If the XML document type declaration is present and the XML document satisfies the markup declarations defined in the XML document type declaration, the XML document is said to be a **valid** XML document.

The XML document type declaration also specifies the document element. The XML document type declaration starts with `<!DOCTYPE`. It is not accessible in an XSLT document and is ignored by the XSLT processor. Here is a simple example of an XML document type declaration.

```
<!DOCTYPE personnel SYSTEM "personnel.dtd">
```

The string `personnel` after the word `DOCTYPE` is the name of the document element of the XML document. The string `SYSTEM` specifies that the URI following it is a system-dependent URI. The string `personnel.dtd` is the URI that points to the DTD document. What this usually means is that the DTD is in a file called `personnel.dtd`. How this file is obtained is system dependent.[3] In other words, the XML document type declaration is as follows: The document element is called `personnel`; the markup declarations are in the document called `personnel.dtd`; and how this document is obtained is system dependent.

2.2.3   *The Document Element*

All XML documents start with one element that is the document element of the XML document. For instance, for the XML document

```
<?xml version='1.0'?>
<a>
  <b/>
</a>
```

---

3. An HTTP URI can be specified so that the DTD does not have to reside on the same machine as the XML document that refers to it.

the **a** element is the document element. XML allows only one document element in a document.

The other elements and all the character data are contained inside the document elements.[4] For example, the **b** element is nested inside the **a** element. Outside the document element you can only have comments (explained in Section 2.8) and processing instructions (explained in Section 2.7).

2.3   Valid Names in XML

A valid name in XML is a string that starts with a letter, a - character, or a : character. If the name has more than one character, starting from the second character the name must contain only letters, digits, combining characters, extender characters, and the characters ., -, _, or :.[5]

Letters can be from alphabets other than the Latin alphabet. Digits do not necessarily have to be Arabic. In this book, all letters used in the names will be from the Latin alphabet (*a* to *z* and *A* to *Z*), and all digits are Arabic (*0* to *9*).

2.4   Elements

In XML, every element must have a start-tag and an end-tag; even empty elements (elements with no content) must have end-tags. Empty elements can be written in two forms. Form one has the start-tag and end-tag combined, for example,

```
<top/>
```

and in form two, the start-tag and the end-tag are separate.

```
<top></top>
```

Be careful not to have any characters between the two tags, not even space characters or carriage returns.

---

4. Although you can have whitespaces (the carriage return, linefeed, space, and tab characters) after the document element.

5. You should only use the colon character (:) for namespaces. (See Section 2.4.3 for information about namespaces.)

2.4.1 Nesting Elements

In XML, start-tags and end-tags of elements must nest properly. This nesting of elements is correct

```
<a><b></b></a>
```

but this nesting is incorrect

```
<a><b></a></b>
```

because a and b overlap.

2.4.2 Attributes

Attributes in XML must have values. The values must be quoted, using single or double quote marks. There is no exception. Therefore,

```
<OPTION SELECTED>
```

is not acceptable (or, in XML terminology, **well formed**[6]) XML. Also,

```
<TD WIDTH=10>
```

is not well formed, as the attribute value 10 is not enclosed in quotes. Instead, the first example should be written as

```
<OPTION SELECTED='SELECTED'>
```

and the second example as

```
<TD WIDTH='10'>
```

2.4.3 Namespaces

Because XML allows us to define our own classes of documents, it is easy to have name clashes. A name clash happens when the same name is used by two classes of documents. This is not a problem as long as the two classes of documents are not mixed together, but if they are used at the same time, it becomes a problem. For example, a name clash happens if the name "title" is

---

6. A valid XML document is an XML document that satisfies the markup declarations in its XML document type declaration. A **well-formed** XML document, on the other hand, is an XML document that fulfills all the syntactic rules: an element must have a start-tag and an end-tag, elements must nest properly, and so on. Well-formedness is a necessary condition for validity as well.

used for both a class of documents for books and another class of documents for aristocracy, and then you have to write an XSLT document for presenting books written by authors who have aristocratic titles.

The way to distinguish identical names from different classes of documents in the same XML document is to use the concept of a namespace. Then, for the two "title" names, we can make one into "the `title` element from the class of documents for books" and the other "the `title` element from the class of documents for aristocracy."

To refer to a namespace in an element or attribute, you use a prefix. For instance, the namespace of the `book:title` element is represented by the prefix `book`. The prefix is delimited by the `:` character from the element or attribute.

Namespaces are identified by URIs. Before a prefix is used to represent a namespace, it must be declared to associate with the URI identifying the namespace. Namespace declarations look a little different from ordinary attributes.

There are two parts in a namespace declaration: the prefix and the URI identifying the namespace. The following example presents an element with a namespace declaration that declares a namespace with the prefix `xsl`.

```
<xsl:stylesheet
    xmlns:xsl='http://www.w3.org/1999/XSL/Transform'>
```

The URI identifying the namespace is

```
http://www.w3.org/1999/XSL/Transform
```

and any element contained in the `xsl:stylesheet` element, including the `xsl:stylesheet` element itself, that has an `xsl` prefix is considered to be in this namespace.

```
http://www.w3.org/1999/XSL/Transform
```

The prefix can be thought of as an alias of the URI. The prefix does not apply outside the element it is declared. In the previous example, the prefix can be `xsl` or `x` or something else (although `xsl` is clearly much easier to recognize than `x`). Using the prefix `x`, an equivalent declaration is

```
<x:stylesheet
    xmlns:x='http://www.w3.org/1999/XSL/Transform'>
```

If you have a namespace declaration in an element, the scope (the range where the prefix is in effect) of the namespace declaration is the element and its content. In this document

```
<xsl:stylesheet
    xmlns='http://www.w3.org/1999/XSL/Transform'
    version='1.0'>
  <xsl:output method='html'/>
</xsl:stylesheet>
```

the scope of the xsl prefix is the stylesheet element and everything it contains.

If within the scope of a namespace prefix, all elements are from that namespace, then the namespace prefix can be omitted. A namespace without a prefix is called the **default namespace**. To declare the default namespace in an element, simply omit the prefix from the namespace declaration.

This is an example of a default namespace declaration.

```
<bookitem xmlns='http://www.jmedium.com'>
  <book><title>The Black Book</title></book>
</bookitem>
```

The bookitem, book, and title elements are all in the namespace identified by the URI http://www.jmedium.com.

It is possible to override a prefix. Simply associate it with another namespace URI, and the prefix becomes the prefix for the new namespace—for example,

```
<?xml version='1.0'?>
<items xmlns='http://www.items.org'>
  <book xmlns='http://www.jmedium.com'>
    <title>The Joy of Idling</title>
  </book>
  <pencil>
    <kind>Soft</kind>
  </pencil>
  <pens:pen xmlns:pens='http://www.pens.org'>
    <pens:location>Germany</pens:location>
    <country>Germany</country>
  </pens:pen>
</items>
```

The scope of the default namespace identified by http://www.items.org is the items element and everything contained in it. However, inside the items element, the default namespace is declared in the book element again. The default namespace is now identified by the URI http://www.jmedium.com. But the scope of this new default namespace declaration does not go beyond the book element. The first default namespace is still in force for the pencil element and everything the pencil element contains.

We also have the `pens` prefix declared in the `pen` element. Its name-space URI is `http://www.pens.org`. However, the `country` element inside the `pens:pen` element is still in the first default namespace (with URI `http://www.items.org`).

Using namespaces, you can mix and match elements and attributes from different places and still be able to identify which element is from which class of document.

There are two other points to remember: First, when we talk about the name of an element with a prefix, the name includes the prefix. The part of the name after the prefix and the colon character will be called the **local name** of the element. Second, when two elements have the same local name, the two elements can only be distinguished by comparing the URIs of their prefixes, even if the two prefixes are different. In other words, when you compare `x:title` and `y:title`, be sure to check the URIs of x and y. If the URIs are the same, these two elements are the same elements, even though the prefixes are different.[7]

2.5   Character Data

XML documents contain character data and markup. Anything that is not markup is character data in an XML document. Control characters that are not also whitespace[8] characters are not allowed in XML documents. Whitespace characters are the space character, the linefeed character, the carriage return character, and the tab character.

Some legal characters must be escaped in an XML document. For instance, the character < must be escaped using the entity reference `&lt;` or character reference `&#60;`. If many characters need to be escaped, then a better way is to include a **CDATA** segment instead. For instance, an element in an XML document may look like this.

```
<example>
An example of an empty element is
<![CDATA[<top/>]]>
</example>
```

---

7. As we go to press, a debate on what it means to compare two namespace URIs is still raging. The result of the debate will be quite significant. Fortunately, we will not have to face this problem explicitly in this book.

8. Or, if you prefer, "white space." Both forms are used in the specifications.

CDATA segments in an XML document are replaced by their character data before the XML document is given to an XSLT processor. As a result, you will never have to worry about CDATA segments in your XSLT documents, unless you want to use them in the XSLT document itself.

2.5.1 *Character References*

A character reference represents a character in the Universal Character Set (UCS).[9] For instance, the character < cannot be used anywhere in an XML document other than as part of a tag unless it is inside a CDATA segment or a comment. If this character is needed in an attribute, the character reference < can be used instead.

There are two ways to specify the numeric value (the **code point**, as used in the standard) of a character. You can use the decimal number—for example, the space character is —or you can use the hexadecimal (base 16) number. The same space character can be referenced as , with the letter x specifying that the number is a hexadecimal number.

2.6 Entities

Most entity references[10] in an XML document are replaced by the entities they refer to before the document is handled by an XSLT processor.

2.7 Processing Instructions

Processing instructions are tags that begin with <? and end with ?>. The first word after the prefix <? is called the **target** of the processing instruction. The rest of the tag up until the suffix ?> is the **value** of the processing instruction, sometimes called the data.

Here is an example of a processing instruction.

```
<?java class='java.io'?>
```

The target of this processing instruction is java, and the rest of the instruction up to the ?> is the value of the processing instruction.

---

9. See Appendix B for a discussion of UCS.
10. For example,   is an HTML entity reference.

2.8   Comments

A comment in an XML document is enclosed by the prefix `<!--` and the suffix `-->`. The group of characters between the prefix and the suffix is the value of the comment. Any combination of characters except the string `--` can be contained in a comment. The character before the closing `-->` characters cannot be a `-` character. As the string `--` is not allowed inside a comment, a comment cannot be nested inside another comment. This is a simple example of a comment.

```
<!-- This is a comment -->
```

Comments can be present in almost any place in an XML document. The places that they are not allowed are before the XML declaration and inside an element tag—that is, between the `<` character and the `>` character of a tag. Comments cannot be inside a CDATA segment, either, as they will be treated as character data inside the segment.

2.9   The Root of an XML Document

Although the other name of the document element is the root element, the document element does not contain everything in an XML document. For instance, it does not contain the XML declaration, the XML document type declaration, and comments before and after the document elements. We will call the feature that contains everything in an XML document the **root** of the XML document.

2.10   Summary

In this chapter we examined the main XML features that will be used in this book. If you are used to handling HTML documents, it shouldn't take long to learn XML. However, keep these points in mind.

> Empty elements must have end tags as well. So, an equivalence of the HTML `<BR>` element looks like `<BR/>` in XML.

> Attribute values must be quoted. You must write `<td width='10'>` in XML, even though you can write `<td width=10>` in HTML.

> All elements must end with an end-tag. So you can expect the `<p>` element to be closed for you in HTML, but you must close it yourself with a `</p>` tag in XML.

> Most character entity references in HTML are not defined in XML. But you can always check the entity definitions to find out how to refer to these entities in an XML document. The URL for the character entity definitions in HTML 4.01 is `http://www.w3.org/TR/html4/sgml/entities.html`.

> XML is case-sensitive. The elements `<p>` and `<P>` are two different tags in XML.

If you remember these points, you should be fine with XML.

2.11   Looking Ahead

We now know enough about XML to talk about how to transform an XML document to HTML using XSLT. In the next chapter, we will look at the XSLT features used most frequently to transform two XML documents into three sets of HTML documents.

⟨ 3 ⟩

Introduction to XSLT

This is indeed a useless tree.
This is why it has grown to such height.
The wise should take this as an example.

—*Zhuang Zi*

Many people observe that the most frequently used features of a computer tool (including a programming language) are usually only a small portion of the tool. This is called the 80/20 rule, meaning that usually 20 percent of the features of a tool will be used 80 percent of the time. This rule certainly rings true because from our experience, a small subset of the features of a tool are usually used over and over again, whereas the other features—the majority—are used infrequently or not at all.

Another principle of the 80/20 rule is that the most frequently used features are usually the most basic features of a tool. In other words, the 20 percent most frequently used features are also the most basic features of a tool. If these two observations are true, we should be able to learn the basic 20 percent of the features of a tool and be effective 80 percent of the time.

Even if the rule is not accurate, however, it is certainly a good idea to start from the most used features of XSLT, which is what we are going to do in this chapter. We will look at three related examples to present the most frequently used features of XSLT.

3.1 The Meeting Room Booking Documents

We'll start with two examples of XML documents, which are part of a meeting room booking system. One XML document contains all the bookings of the meeting rooms, and the other contains information about the meeting rooms.

3.1.1 *The Bookings Document*

The bookings document contains all the bookings of all the meeting rooms. All bookings, their dates, their purposes, their attendees, their organizers, and so forth are in this document. This is a part of the document containing the bookings.

```xml
<?xml version='1.0'?>
<bookings>
  <lastUpdated date='20000623' time='1317'/>
  <room name='Red'>
    <date>
      <year>2000</year>
      <month>June</month>
      <day>23</day>
      <meeting>
        <period>
          <from>1300</from>
          <to>1330</to>
        </period>
        <bookedBy>John Smith</bookedBy>
        <attendees>
          <attendee><individual>Jennifer Platt</individual></attendee>
          <attendee><group>NewBieNetGroup</group></attendee>
          <attendee><individual>Peter Shanahan</individual></attendee>
          <attendee><individual>Susan Zak</individual></attendee>
        </attendees>
        <meetingTitle>Project Status</meetingTitle>
        <purpose>The client is not very happy about the pace of
        development. This meeting is booked to find out the actual
```

```
          status of the project before we get back to the
          client.</purpose>
          <bookedAt date='20000413' time='1004'/>
          <reminder><email>jsmith@peacockpaint.com</email></reminder>
        </meeting>
        <!-- the rest of the meeting for the day -->
      </date>
      <!-- the rest of the days with meetings -->
    </room>
    <!-- the rest of the meeting rooms -->
  </bookings>
```

The document element is the `bookings` element. It in turn contains a `last-Updated` element. It also contains one `room` element for each meeting room. Each `room` element contains one `date` element for each day the room has a booking. Each `date` element contains elements providing the year, the month, and the day. It also contains one `meeting` element for one meeting booking for the day. Each `meeting` element contains a `period` element to provide the meeting time, a `bookedBy` element for the person who booked the meeting room, an `attendees` element containing a list of `attendee` elements, a `meetingTitle` element for the title of the meeting, a `purpose` element for the purpose of the meeting, a `bookedAt` element for the time the meeting was booked, and finally, whether a reminder is needed and how it is done.

The meanings of the elements can be more or less guessed from the names of the elements. Let us call the document *bookings.xml*.

3.1.2   *The Meeting Room Document*

The second document contains the description of the meeting rooms. Here is part of the document.

```
<?xml version='1.0'?>
<rooms>
  <room name='Red'>
    <capacity>10</capacity>
    <equipmentList>
      <equipment>Projector</equipment>
    </equipmentList>
  </room>
```

```
<room name='Green'>
  <capacity>5</capacity>
  <equipmentList>
  </equipmentList>
  <features>
    <feature>No Roof</feature>
  </features>
</room>
<!-- the rest of the meeting rooms  -->
</rooms>
```

The document element is **rooms**. It contains a set of **room** elements, each of which contains a **capacity** element, an **equipmentList** element, and possibly a **features** element. We will call the document *rooms.xml*.

3.1.3   *The Task*

Our job is to transform these XML documents to the following three kinds of HTML documents:

1. HTML documents that show the meetings booked for one particular day, for all meeting rooms, on the same page.
2. HTML documents that show the availability of meeting rooms for one particular day, for all meeting rooms, on the same page.
3. One document for each meeting room for one particular day, showing its availability in graphics, its meeting room features, and all the meetings booked on that day for the meeting room.

The user will choose which day the HTML documents should show.

Suppose the user chooses June 23, 2000 as the day to show all three HTML documents. The first kind of HTML document is shown in Figure 3.1, the second kind is shown in Figure 3.2, and the third kind is shown in Figure 3.3.

As Figures 3.1, 3.2, and 3.3 show, XSLT alone will not produce attractive HTML documents. Right now our only concern is generating the correct content. Once you know how to produce the correct content, you can use your creative talent to make the HTML documents more beautiful.

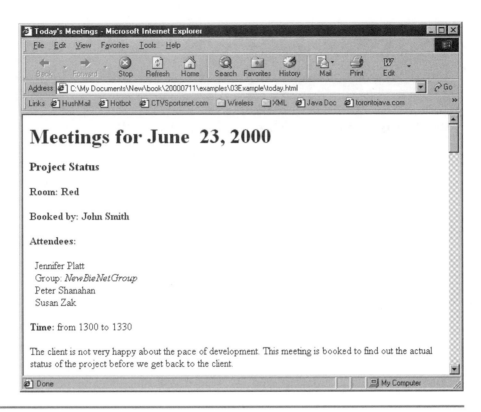

FIGURE
3.1   Meetings booked for all meeting rooms for June 23, 2000

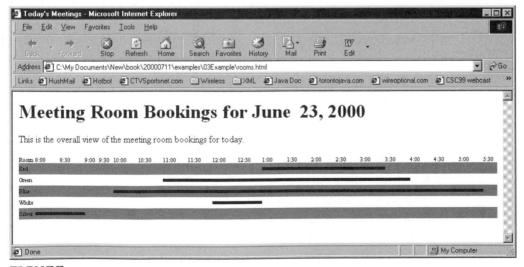

FIGURE
3.2   Availability of all the meeting rooms for June 23, 2000

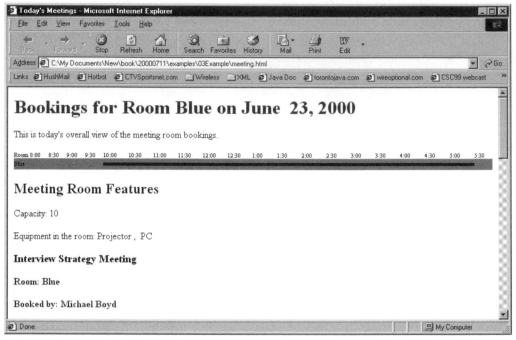

FIGURE

3.3   Features, bookings, and availability of the Blue meeting room for June 23, 2000

3.2   Designing XSLT Documents

Before we discuss how XSLT documents should be designed, let us look at some examples of very simple documents that you can use to build up your XSLT knowledge. Then we will design XSLT documents for the three kinds of documents in Figures 3.1, 3.2, and 3.3.

3.2.1   *The Simplest XSLT Document*

XSLT documents[1] form a special class of XML documents. As all XML documents have one document element, all XSLT documents have one as well. The document element of an XSLT document is the `xsl:stylesheet` element. This is the simplest XSLT document.

---

1. The generic word *document* is used in the book, but XSLT documents are really programs, not just any documents. On the other hand, when XSLT is used with XSL, the document is a stylesheet.

```
<?xml version='1.0'?>
<xsl:stylesheet
  version='1.0'
  xmlns:xsl='http://www.w3.org/1999/XSL/Transform'>

</xsl:stylesheet>
```

The `xsl:stylesheet` element must have the mandatory `version` attribute.
Currently, only one value is accepted: `1.0` for version one of the XSLT specification. The namespace prefix `xsl` is also declared in here.

We will call it *minimal.xsl*, and you can try it on *bookings.xml*

```
xt bookings.xml minimal.xsl
```

assuming that the XSLT document is called *minimal.xsl* and you use the XT
XSLT processor by James Clark on the command line. Part of the result is shown
here.

```
<?xml version="1.0" encoding="utf-8"?>




␣␣␣␣␣␣2000
␣␣␣␣␣␣June
␣␣␣␣␣␣23


␣␣␣␣␣␣␣␣␣␣␣1300
␣␣␣␣␣␣␣␣␣␣␣1330

␣␣␣␣␣␣␣␣␣John Smith

␣␣␣␣␣␣␣␣␣␣Jennifer Platt
␣␣␣␣␣␣␣␣␣␣NewBieNetGroup
␣␣␣␣␣␣␣␣␣␣Peter Shanahan
␣␣␣␣␣␣␣␣␣␣Susan Zak

␣␣␣␣␣␣␣␣Project Status
.
.
.
```

As you can see, the result is not an HTML document. This document is simply *bookings.xml* with all the markups stripped. This is not exactly what we had in mind, but you have now written your first XSLT document.

Now, let us look at XSLT documents that produce HTML documents that can be displayed in Web browsers.

3.2.2   *Generating HTML Elements*

Suppose we want to generate this HTML document.[2]

```
<!DOCTYPE HTML PUBLIC "-//W3C//DTD HTML 3.2 Final//EN">
<HTML>
<HEAD>
<TITLE>The Meeting Room Booking System</TITLE>
</HEAD>
<BODY>
<H1>The Meeting Room Booking System</H1>
</BODY>
</HTML>
```

Here's the XSLT document that generates the HTML document.

```
<?xml version='1.0'?>
<xsl:stylesheet version='1.0'
    xmlns:xsl='http://www.w3.org/1999/XSL/Transform'>

  <xsl:output method='html' indent='yes'
      doctype-public='-//W3C//DTD HTML 3.2 Final//EN'/>

  <xsl:template match='/'>
    <HTML>
      <HEAD>
        <TITLE>The Meeting Room Booking System</TITLE>
      </HEAD>
      <BODY>
        <H1>The Meeting Room Booking System</H1>
      </BODY>
    </HTML>
  </xsl:template>

</xsl:stylesheet>
```

---

2. The HTML version is not relevant to this discussion. You can use the DOCTYPE for HTML 4.0.

Let's call this document *static.xsl*. The differences between this XSLT document and the minimal XSLT document are as follows:

> The new document has an `xsl:output` element. This element contains the public identifier for the HTML public ID. It also specifies the output method—`html` in this case.

> The new document has an `xsl:template` element. It has the value / for its `match` attribute. This element contains all the HTML elements in the output document.

The `xsl:output` Element

The `xsl:output` element in the new document specifies that (1) the output document is an HTML document, (2) indentation should be done, and (3) the document type of the output HTML document is to be HTML version 3.2.

The `xsl:template` Element

The `xsl:template` element in the document matches the root, not the root element (see Section 2.9 for an explanation of the root of a document), of a document. It indicates that intention by specifying the value of the `match` attribute to be /, the root of an XML document. A template that matches the root of a document is significant because the transformation process always starts from a template that matches the root.

Our new XSLT document does not do much more than copy to the output document the content of the template matching the root. That is what the XSLT processor does for HTML elements in a template: It copies them to the output document.[3]

What about the minimal XSLT document that does not have a template that matches the root? In that case, the XSLT processor uses the hidden **default template** that matches the root. Default templates are templates defined by the XSLT processor to ensure that all elements will be matched somehow. It only uses the default template when such a template is not specified. Because no template that matches the root in *minimal.xsl* is specified, the XSLT processor uses this default template. However, it is always a good idea to include a template that matches the root. You never know whether the default template will do what you expect. Besides, the template that matches the root is the perfect place to put the `<HTML>` element.

---

3. Actually, it does that for all elements not in the XSLT namespace. But if you are producing HTML documents, you probably want the non-XSLT elements to be HTML elements.

FIGURE
3.4   The output from *static.xsl*

Running *static.xsl*

You can try *static.xsl* with *bookings.xml* like this.

```
xt bookings.xml static.xsl
```

You can also try it with *rooms.xml*.

```
xt rooms.xml static.xsl
```

The output HTML document always looks the same regardless of which XML document is used. Why? In *static.xsl*, we have only the template that matches the root of an XML document. The processor, if it only inspects the root, cannot distinguish the roots of two XML documents. Because we do not consider the rest of the XML document after the match, the same HTML document is produced, whatever the input (or **source**) XML document is. When we start processing the other elements of the source document, we will be able to produce different HTML documents.

You can probably visualize the HTML document in a browser. If you can't, look at Figure 3.4.

3.2.3   *Showing the* lastUpdated *Element*

Let's try something more interesting. Suppose we put the last updated date of the bookings document in an HTML document. Specifically, our goal is to generate this HTML document.

```
<!DOCTYPE HTML PUBLIC "-//W3C//DTD HTML 3.2 Final//EN">
<HTML>
  <HEAD><TITLE>Our Simple HTML Document Example.</TITLE></HEAD>
  <BODY>
    <H1>Last Updated: 20000623</H1>
  </BODY>
</HTML>
```

Using our previous XSLT document as the base, the XSLT document we want to write looks like this.

```
<?xml version='1.0'?>
<xsl:stylesheet version='1.0'
    xmlns:xsl='http://www.w3.org/1999/XSL/Transform'>

  <xsl:output method='html' indent='yes'
    doctype-public='-//W3C//DTD HTML 3.2 Final//EN'/>

  <xsl:template match='/'>
    <HTML>
      <HEAD>
        <TITLE>Our Simple HTML Document Example.</TITLE>
      </HEAD>
      <BODY>
        <H1><!-- Do something to get the value of the date
             attribute of the lastUpdated element. --></H1>
      </BODY>
    </HTML>
  </xsl:template>
</xsl:stylesheet>
```

The value we are interested in can be described in this way: The value of the `date` attribute of the `lastUpdated` element of the `bookings` element of the root. In XSLT,[4] the same value is expressed as

```
/bookings/lastUpdated/@date
```

This says, the `date` attribute of the `lastUpdated` element of the `bookings` element of the root. Notice how we start from the end of the expression and

---

4. More correctly, in XPath (the XML Path Language), described in detail in Chapter 5.

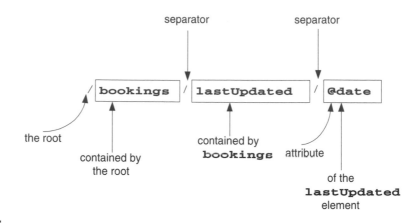

3.5   The XSLT expression dissected into its parts

work to the beginning. You can start from the beginning and work to the end but it is more of a mouthful that way.

The symbol @ means "attribute." Other than the first / character, the other / characters are only separators for the different steps of the expression. Figure 3.5 dissects the expression above.

Actually, the initial / (for the root) is redundant here. When you are in the template matching the root of the document, the current item of the XML document being inspected (or your context[5]) is the root. So you can say something like the value of the `date` attribute of the `lastUpdated` element of the `bookings` element of the context. As your context is the root, this is the same as the expression we used previously. In XSLT it is as follows:

```
bookings/lastUpdated/@date
```

Obtaining the Value of the `date` Attribute

We have specified the value we are interested in. How do we get the value? In XSLT, to get the value of an attribute or an element, you can use the `xsl:value-of` element. In our case, the element looks like this.

```
<xsl:value-of select='bookings/lastUpdated/@date'/>
```

---

5. We use this word loosely in this chapter. It will be defined in more detail in Chapter 5.

It means get the value of `bookings/lastUpdated/@date` as a string. If you want it to be inside an `H1` element in the HTML document, use this.

```
<H1><xsl:value-of select='bookings/lastUpdated/@date'/></H1>
```

You can mix HTML and XSLT elements together. The XSLT processor copies all the HTML elements to the result and processes only those elements that are in the XSLT namespace.

The whole XSLT document now looks like this.

```
<?xml version='1.0'?>
<xsl:stylesheet version='1.0'
    xmlns:xsl='http://www.w3.org/1999/XSL/Transform'>

  <xsl:output method='html' indent='yes'
    doctype-public='-//W3C//DTD HTML 3.2 Final//EN'/>

  <xsl:template match='/'>
    <HTML>
      <HEAD>
        <TITLE>Our Simple HTML Document Example.</TITLE>
      </HEAD>
      <BODY>
        <H1>
          <xsl:value-of select='bookings/lastUpdated/@date'/>
        </H1>
      </BODY>
    </HTML>
  </xsl:template>
</xsl:stylesheet>
```

The result is shown in Figure 3.6. It's not very exciting, but we now know how to find the value of something and how to put the value in the resulting HTML document.

3.2.4 *Processing Multiple Occurrences*

It is satisfying that we now know how to get the date *bookings.xml* was last updated, but, after all, there is only one `lastUpdated` element in *bookings.xml*.

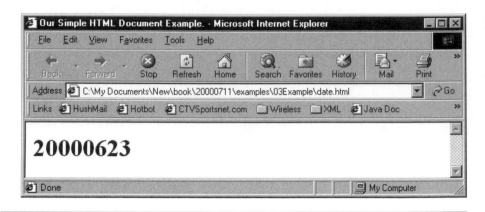

FIGURE

3.6

The last update date of *bookings.xml*

But what if we want to list the names of the meeting rooms (from the file *rooms.xml*)? In other words, how do we generate this HTML document?

```
<!DOCTYPE HTML PUBLIC "-//W3C//DTD HTML 3.2 Final//EN">
<HTML>
  <HEAD>
    <TITLE>Our Simple HTML Document Example.</TITLE>
  </HEAD>
  <BODY>
    <H2>The Red Room</H2>
    <H2>The Green Room</H2>
    <H2>The Blue Room</H2>
    <H2>The White Room</H2>
    <H2>The Silver Room</H2>
  </BODY>
</HTML>
```

The skeleton of the XSLT document looks like this.

```
<?xml version='1.0'?>
<xsl:stylesheet version='1.0'
    xmlns:xsl='http://www.w3.org/1999/XSL/Transform'>

  <xsl:output method='html' indent='yes'
      doctype-public='-//W3C//DTD HTML 3.2 Final//EN'/>
```

```
<xsl:template match='/'>
  <HTML>
    <HEAD>
      <TITLE>Our Simple HTML Document Example.</TITLE>
    </HEAD>
    <BODY>
        <!-- find all the room elements contained
          in the rooms element. -->

          <!-- Handle each room element and show the value
            of its name attribute. -->
    </BODY>
  </HTML>
</xsl:template>

</xsl:stylesheet>
```

There are two XSLT expressions in the skeleton that we have to design. The first is the expression to find the room elements contained in the rooms element. The second is the expression to get the value of the name attribute of a room element. The first XSLT expression is rooms/room. It refers to the room element(s) contained in the rooms element in the context. The second XSLT expression is @name. It refers to the name attribute of the element that is the context. We already know how to get the value of the name attribute of a room element. We can use xsl:value-of as in our previous example.

```
<H2>The <xsl:value-of select='@name'/> Room</H2>
```

How do we get all the room elements in the rooms element and handle each separately? We can use the xsl:for-each element.

```
<xsl:for-each select='rooms/room'>
   <!-- do something with one room element -->
</xsl:for-each>
```

What this element means is for each of the room elements contained in the rooms element contained in the context, do something.

Combining this xsl:for-each element and the code to show the value of the name attribute of the room element, we get this.

```
<xsl:for-each select='rooms/room'>
  <H2>The <xsl:value-of select='@name'/> Room</H2>
</xsl:for-each>
```

35

Now we have the following XSLT document.

```
<?xml version='1.0'?>
<xsl:stylesheet version='1.0'
    xmlns:xsl='http://www.w3.org/1999/XSL/Transform'>

  <xsl:output method='html' indent='yes'
      doctype-public='-//W3C//DTD HTML 3.2 Final//EN'/>

  <xsl:template match='/'>
    <HTML>
      <HEAD>
        <TITLE>Our Simple HTML Document Example.</TITLE>
      </HEAD>
      <BODY>
        <!-- find all the room elements contained
             in the rooms element. -->
        <xsl:for-each select='rooms/room'>
          <!-- Handle each room element and show the value
               of its name attribute. -->
          <H2>The <xsl:value-of select='@name'/> Room</H2>
        </xsl:for-each>
      </BODY>
    </HTML>
  </xsl:template>

</xsl:stylesheet>
```

The HTML document in a Web browser is shown in Figure 3.7.

3.2.5   *Basic Matching*

The xsl:for-each element is a very useful element in XSLT. However, the previous example is usually written as follows:

```
<?xml version='1.0'?>
<xsl:stylesheet version='1.0'
    xmlns:xsl='http://www.w3.org/1999/XSL/Transform'>

  <xsl:output method='html'
      indent='yes'
      doctype-public='-//W3C//DTD HTML 3.2 Final//EN'/>
```

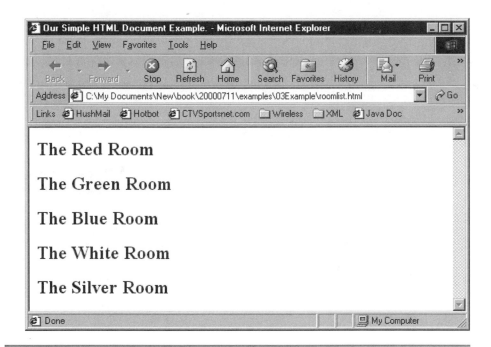

FIGURE
3.7

The list of meeting rooms in *room.xml*

```
<xsl:template match='/'>
  <HTML>
    <HEAD>
      <TITLE>Our Simple HTML Document Example.</TITLE>
    </HEAD>
    <BODY>
      <xsl:apply-templates select='rooms/room'/>
    </BODY>
  </HTML>
</xsl:template>

<xsl:template match='room'>
  <H2>The <xsl:value-of select='@name'/> Room</H2>
</xsl:template>

</xsl:stylesheet>
```

Both this XSLT document and the previous version produce the same HTML document (for this input). But this new version has flexibility that the previous example does not.

37

The new version uses a new element, `xsl:apply-templates`. In the document, this element first finds all the `room` elements that are contained in the `rooms` element and then applies the templates that match the `room` elements. In the new version, there is a new template in addition to the template that matches the root. This new template has `room` as the value of the `match` attribute. In other words, it matches a `room` element. When it matches a `room` element, it outputs an `H2` element.

Why is it more flexible? It's because the new template in fact matches any `room` elements. The template can contain presentation elements for `room` elements no matter where and when a `room` element is encountered. In this way, the presentation of `room` elements is in one place. When it comes time to modify the presentation of the `room` element, only this one place needs to be modified.

3.2.6   *Going Through Contained Elements*

We can omit the `select` attribute in `xsl:apply-templates`. For the previous example, let us modify `xsl:apply-templates` to remove the `select` attribute as follows:

```
    .
    .
    .
<BODY>
   <xsl:apply-templates/>
</BODY>
    .
    .
    .
```

The `xsl:apply-templates` element without the `select` attribute applies templates for the elements, character data, comments, and processing instructions contained by the element with which we are working—in this case, the `rooms` element.

If you use `xsl:apply-templates` without the `select` attribute to *rooms.xml*, the output looks similar but not identical. The differences are the whitespaces in the results. The context at the location of the `xsl:apply-templates` element is the root. When the `xsl:apply-templates` element is processed, the contents of the root are processed one by one. In this case, the root contains only the document element `rooms`, but there is no explicit template defined for the `rooms` element. When there is no explicit template that matches an element, the default template for elements is used and simply reapplies templates for the elements, character data, and so on contained by that element. The elements contained in the `rooms` element are the `room` elements. There is a template defined for the `room` elements. So this template is applied, with the same result as in the previous XSLT documents.

The XSLT processor also applies templates for the character data in the `rooms` element. Since we do not have an explicit template for character data, the XSLT processor uses the default template for character data, which copies the character data to the result. That is why we end up with more whitespaces in the second XSLT document than in the first; all the whitespaces are also sent to the output.

What about the `lastUpdated` element? The default template is also applied for this element, but because there is nothing in the element, nothing is output. The default template for attributes produces nothing.

Again, this way of writing an XSLT document is quite flexible. You can add the last updated date to the output by simply adding an additional template like this.

```
<xsl:template match='lastUpdated'>
  <H3>Last Updated: <xsl:value-of select='@date'/></H3>
</xsl:template>
```

Just add the template to the previous document. Then, apply the XSLT document to *bookings.xml*, and the result is as follows:

```
<!DOCTYPE HTML PUBLIC "-//W3C//DTD HTML 3.2 Final//EN">
<HTML>
  <HEAD>
    <TITLE>Our Simple HTML Document Example.</TITLE>
  </HEAD>
  <BODY>
    <H3>Last Updated: 20000623</H3>
    <H2>The Red Room</H2>
    <H2>The Green Room</H2>
    <H2>The Blue Room</H2>
    <H2>The White Room</H2>
    <H2>The Silver Room</H2>
  </BODY>
</HTML>
```

If we go through the whole matching process for the `xsl:apply-templates` element again, everything will be the same as before, except when the `last-Updated` element is encountered. We have an explicit template for the element, the template is applied, and the additional H3 element is added to the output. The XSLT document now looks like this.

```
<?xml version='1.0'?>
<xsl:stylesheet version='1.0'
    xmlns:xsl='http://www.w3.org/1999/XSL/Transform'>

  <xsl:output method='html'
      indent='yes'
      doctype-public='-//W3C//DTD HTML 3.2 Final//EN'/>

  <xsl:template match='/'>
    <HTML>
      <HEAD>
        <TITLE>Our Simple HTML Document Example.</TITLE>
      </HEAD>
      <BODY>
        <xsl:apply-templates/>
      </BODY>
    </HTML>
  </xsl:template>

  <xsl:template match='lastUpdated'>
    <H3>Last Updated: <xsl:value-of select='@date'/></H3>
  </xsl:template>

  <xsl:template match='room'>
    <H2>The <xsl:value-of select='@name'/> Room</H2>
  </xsl:template>

</xsl:stylesheet>
```

If you run the XSLT document for *rooms.xml*, the Last Updated line is missing from the result, but the rooms are still there. As *rooms.xml* does not have a lastUpdated element, the template for that element is never applied.

This shows how flexible XSLT can be when used to process multiple XML inputs with similar structure. Although we designed the XSLT document for *rooms.xml*, it can actually be used for *bookings.xml*. This flexibility comes from the templates defined in the XSLT document. If you use xsl:for-each elements instead, you would not be able to use it for *bookings.xml* because /rooms/room cannot be matched in *bookings.xml*.

3.2.7   *Showing All Meetings for All Days*

We are now ready to design XSLT documents for the three types shown in Figures 3.1, 3.2, and 3.3. First, let's produce the HTML document that shows all meetings on all days with meetings booked. For each meeting, we want the output to be like this.

```
<H2>June 23, 2000</H2>
<H3>Project Status</H3>
<H4>Room: Red</H4>
<H4>Booked by: John Smith</H4>
<H4>Attendees:</H4>
  Jennifer Platt<BR>
  Group: <I>NewBieNetGroup</I><BR>
  Peter Shanahan<BR>
  Susan Zak<BR>
<P><B>Time: </B>from 1300 to 1330</P>
<P>The client is not very happy about the pace of
development. This meeting is booked to find out the actual
status of the project before we get back to the
client.</P>
```

The original XML for *bookings.xml* looks like this.

```
  .
  .
  .

<room name='Red'>
  <date>
    <year>2000</year>
    <month>June</month>
    <day>23</day>
    <meeting>
      <period>
        <from>1300</from>
        <to>1330</to>
      </period>
      <bookedBy>John Smith</bookedBy>
      <attendees>
        <attendee><individual>Jennifer Platt</individual></attendee>
        <attendee><group>NewBieNetGroup</group></attendee>
        <attendee><individual>Peter Shanahan</individual></attendee>
        <attendee><individual>Susan Zak</individual></attendee>
      </attendees>
```

```
            <meetingTitle>Project Status</meetingTitle>
            <purpose>The client is not very happy about the pace of
            development. This meeting is booked to find out the actual
            status of the project before we get back to the
            client.</purpose>
            <bookedAt date='20000413' time='1004'/>
            <reminder><email>jsmith@peacockpaint.com</email></reminder>
        </meeting>
     .
     .
     .
```

We know we will look at all **room** elements, so we will define a template for it. We know that we will look at all the **date** and **meeting** elements as well, and we will define a template for each of them. These templates will handle all the other elements without their own templates.

The First Step

After defining the skeleton of the templates, the XSLT document looks like this.

```
<?xml version='1.0'?>
<xsl:stylesheet version='1.0'
    xmlns:xsl='http://www.w3.org/1999/XSL/Transform'>

  <xsl:output method='html'
      indent='yes'
      doctype-public='-//W3C//DTD HTML 3.2 Final//EN'/>

  <xsl:template match='/'>
    <HTML>
      <HEAD>
        <TITLE>All Meetings.</TITLE>
      </HEAD>
      <BODY>
        <xsl:apply-templates/>
      </BODY>
    </HTML>
  </xsl:template>

  <xsl:template match='room'>
    <!-- Template for the room element -->
  </xsl:template>
```

```
<xsl:template match='date'>
  <!-- Template for the date element -->
</xsl:template>


<xsl:template match='meeting'>
  <!-- Template for the meeting element -->
</xsl:template>


</xsl:stylesheet>
```

We'll call this the skeleton document of meeting list.

The Second Step

The template for the `meeting` element obviously contains most of the information shown in the output. With your XSLT knowledge, you will have no problem coming up with the following template (you can almost guess what `xsl:choose` means).

```
<xsl:template match='meeting'>
  <H3><xsl:value-of select='meetingTitle'/></H3>
  <H4>Room: <!-- How to get the room name? --></H4>
  <H4>Booked by: <xsl:value-of select='bookedBy'/></H4>
  <H4>Attendees:</H4>
  <xsl:for-each select='attendees/attendee'>
    <xsl:choose>
      <xsl:when test='group'>
          Group: <I><xsl:value-of select='group'/>
          </I><BR/>
      </xsl:when>
      <xsl:otherwise>
          <xsl:value-of select='individual'/><BR/>
      </xsl:otherwise>
    </xsl:choose>
  </xsl:for-each>
  <P><B>Time: </B>from <xsl:value-of select='period/from'/> to
     <xsl:value-of select='period/to'/></P>
  <P><xsl:value-of select='purpose'/></P>
</xsl:template>
```

The only new element here is the `xsl:choose` element, which has at least one `xsl:when` element inside; you can have more. You can also have an optional `xsl:otherwise` element. The meaning of the `xsl:choose` element in the previous template is as follows. If there is a **group** element contained by an **attendee** element, then output

```
  Group: <I><xsl:value-of select='group'/>
  </I><BR/>
```

Otherwise, output

```
  <xsl:value-of select='individual'/><BR/>
```

The **xsl:choose** element chooses one of many alternatives. It must contain at least one **xsl:when** element, although it can have more than one.

The XSLT processor evaluates the **test** attribute of the **xsl:when** elements. The first **xsl:when** element for which the **test** attribute evaluates to the Boolean value **true** will be processed. The other **xsl:when** elements and the **xsl:otherwise** element will simply be ignored. If none of the **xsl:when** elements has a true **test** attribute, then the **xsl:otherwise** element will be processed.

You might also ask what the mysterious ** ** is about. This is simply the nonbreaking whitespace character identical to ** ** in HTML. Since ** ** is not defined in XML, the actual character code for the character must be used.

Replace the template for the **meeting** element in the skeleton document with this template. Use it to transform *booking.xml*. With whitespaces removed, the output looks like this.

```
<!DOCTYPE HTML PUBLIC "-//W3C//DTD HTML 3.2 Final//EN">
<HTML><HEAD><TITLE>All Meetings.</TITLE></HEAD><BODY>
</BODY></HTML>
```

What's wrong? Remember that when no template matches an element, the default template is used. The default template applies templates for the elements, character data, and so forth contained in the element. In this case, as the default template is activated where no template matching the **bookings** element is found, it applies templates for the **lastUpdated** element and the **room** elements. The default template is again used for **lastUpdated**, and nothing comes out of it. The default template is not applied to the **room** elements, because a template for **room** elements is defined.

But the template matching **room** elements does not contain anything. The template, therefore, does nothing. Because there is no further action, the whole transformation process stops after the **room** elements have been handled.

The lesson is, if you don't want to do anything for an element but you want to do something for the elements contained in the element, continue the transformation process by using an `xsl:apply-templates` element without a `select` attribute. Since the template for the `room` element does not continue the transformation process, the template matching the `meeting` elements does not even have a chance of being applied.

The Third Step

So the solution is to add a simple `xsl:apply-templates` to the templates for the `room` and `date` elements like this.

```
<xsl:template match='room'>
  <xsl:apply-templates/>
</xsl:template>

<xsl:template match='date'>
  <xsl:apply-templates/>
</xsl:template>
```

Try it again. This time the result is almost what we expected. A partial output is shown here.

```
<!DOCTYPE HTML PUBLIC "-//W3C//DTD HTML 3.2 Final//EN">
<HTML><HEAD><TITLE>All Meetings.</TITLE></HEAD><BODY>
      2000
      June
      23
      <H3>Project Status</H3>
        <H4>Room: </H4>
        <H4>Booked by: John Smith</H4>
        <H4>Attendees:</H4>
            Jennifer Platt<BR>
            Group: <I>NewBieNetGroup</I><BR>
            Peter Shanahan<BR>
            Susan Zak<BR><P><B>Time: </B>from 1300 to
      1330</P><P>The client is not very happy about the pace
        of development. This meeting is booked to find out the
        actual status of the project before we get back to the
        client.</P>
   .
   .
   .
```

The Fourth Step

There are two problems with the output, one expected, one not. The known problem is the missing room name, which we'll talk about later. The unknown problem is the formatting of the date. We want to format the date so that it looks like this.

```
<H2>June 23, 2000</H2>
```

The template for the `date` element must be modified. First, format the `year`, `month`, and `day` properly.

```
<H2><xsl:value-of select='month'/> <xsl:value-of
    select='day'/>, 
  <xsl:value-of select='year'/></H2>
```

Because we have handled these elements, we have to prevent them from being handled again, which is what will happen if we do not specify the `select` attribute for the `xsl:apply-templates` element in the template for the `date` element. To exclude these elements, specify the `select` attribute to have the value `meeting`. Then, only the `meeting` elements contained by the `date` element will be matched. The whole template for the `date` element now looks like this.

```
<xsl:template match='date'>
  <H2><xsl:value-of select='month'/> 
      <xsl:value-of select='day'/>, 
      <xsl:value-of select='year'/></H2>
  <xsl:apply-templates select='meeting'/>
</xsl:template>
```

The Fifth Step

How do we get the name of the meeting room deep inside the `meeting` element? Specifically, how do we get the value of the `name` attribute of the `room` element containing the `date` element containing the `meeting` element? When the template for `meeting` is applied, our context is a `meeting` element. To get to the element containing this `meeting` element, use the XSLT expression `..` (the **parent** of the context). For example,

```
<H4>Room: <xsl:value-of select='../year'/></H4>
```

gives you

```
<H4>Room: 2000</H4>
```

The value 2000 is the value of the year element. To go one more level up, use

```
../..
```

Since this is really just the room element, we can ask for the name attribute.

```
../../@name
```

Therefore, when our context is the meeting element, the room name can be obtained as follows:

```
<H4>Room: <xsl:value-of select='../../@name'/></H4>
```

Finally, we have the XSLT document for listing all meetings for all meeting rooms for all days with meetings booked. We are just steps away from showing meetings on a particular day.

3.2.8   Showing Meetings for a Specific Day

Producing an HTML document showing only the meetings for a specific day poses two problems: (1) finding the specific day and (2) finding meeting elements that are for the specific day.

Specifying a Day

XSLT has an element that allows you to pass string values from the command line.[6] This element is called xsl:param.

For our purposes, we want to show meetings on a specific year, month, and day. We define three xsl:param elements as follows:

```
<?xml version='1.0'?>
<xsl:stylesheet version='1.0'
    xmlns:xsl='http://www.w3.org/1999/XSL/Transform'>

  <xsl:output method='html'
        indent='no'
        doctype-public='-//W3C//DTD HTML 3.2 Final//EN'/>
```

---

6. Normally, if you are using an XSLT processor from the command line, you must specify the values on the command line. But the vendor of an XSLT processor can use any other method. From now on, when I refer to passing values on the command line, I mean by whatever method chosen by the vendor of the XSLT processor.

```
<xsl:param name='year'/>
<xsl:param name='month'/>
<xsl:param name='day'/>
   .
   .
   .
</xsl:stylesheet>
```

Call the XSLT document that transforms *bookings.xml* to an HTML document
that shows all the meetings on a specific day *daymeeting.xsl*.

To set the value of the year param to 2000, the value of the month to June,
and the day to 23, the following command line is used (if you are using xt):

```
xt bookings.xml daymeeting.xsl year=2000 month=June day=23
```

We can put the values of the parameters back as follows:

```
<?xml version='1.0'?>
<xsl:stylesheet version='1.0'
    xmlns:xsl='http://www.w3.org/1999/XSL/Transform'>

  <xsl:output method='html'
       indent='no'
       doctype-public='-//W3C//DTD HTML 3.2 Final//EN'/>

  <xsl:param name='year'/>
  <xsl:param name='month'/>
  <xsl:param name='day'/>

  <xsl:template match='/'>
    <HTML>
      <HEAD>
        <TITLE>Put back the parameters.</TITLE>
      </HEAD>
      <BODY>
        <H4>Year = <xsl:value-of select='$year'/></H4>
        <H4>Month = <xsl:value-of select='$month'/></H4>
        <H4>Day = <xsl:value-of select='$day'/></H4>
      </BODY>
    </HTML>
  </xsl:template>

</xsl:stylesheet>
```

(To get the value of a parameter called `var`, prefix the symbol $ in front of it, as in `$var.`)

Choosing Specific Elements

Now that we know how to assign values to parameters on the command line and how to get the values of parameters, we must find out how to select elements based on some criteria. In the document that we use to show all meetings on all days, the template for the `room` element looks like this.

```
<xsl:template match='room'>
  <xsl:apply-templates/>
</xsl:template>
```

Since the `room` element contains only `date` elements, this is equivalent to

```
<xsl:template match='room'>
  <xsl:apply-templates select='date'/>
</xsl:template>
```

with the differences in the amount of whitespace in the output documents.

To specify the criteria that (1) the value of the `year` element contained in the `date` element should equal `$year`, (2) the value of the `month` element contained in the `date` element should equal `$month`, and (3) the value of the `day` element contained in the `date` element should equal `$day`, the following XSLT expression can be used:

```
<xsl:apply-templates
  select='date[year=$year and month=$month and day=$day]'/>
```

The expression `date[year=$year and month=$month and day=$day]` means the date elements that have their `year` element the same as the value of the `year` parameter, the value of their `month` element the same as the value of the `month` parameter, and the value of their `day` element the same as the `day` parameter. Let's change the template for the `room` element to include this expression.

```
<xsl:template match='room'>
  <xsl:apply-templates
    select='date[year=$year and month=$month and day=$day]'/>
</xsl:template>
```

If the day we ask for does not have any meetings booked, the HTML document looks like this.

```
<HTML>
<HEAD>
<TITLE>Today's Meetings</TITLE>
</HEAD>
<BODY>
<H1>Meetings for June 
            23, 2001</H1>
</BODY>
</HTML>
```

This is fine for our purposes.

We have finished an XSLT document that can be used to transform *bookings.xml* to HTML documents showing meetings for a particular day, specified on the command line. Let us call this document *today.xsl*. We only have two more XSLT documents to write now.

3.2.9   *Decisions*

The second kind of HTML document contains a table showing the availability of time slots for the meeting rooms. To make it easy to separate adjacent meeting rooms, the background color of the rows of the table alternates between gray and white. To produce this effect, we have to be able to count the number of elements selected by the `select` attribute of the `xsl:apply-templates` element or the `xsl:for-each` element.

The Skeleton

First, let us look at the skeleton of the XSLT document we are writing.

```
<?xml version='1.0'?>
<xsl:stylesheet version='1.0'
    xmlns:xsl='http://www.w3.org/1999/XSL/Transform'>

  <xsl:output method='html' indent='yes'/>

  <xsl:param name='year'/>
  <xsl:param name='month'/>
  <xsl:param name='day'/>

  <xsl:template match='/'>
```

```
<HTML>
  <HEAD><TITLE>Today's Meetings</TITLE></HEAD>
  <BODY>
    <H1>Meeting Room Bookings for <xsl:value-of
        select='$month'/> <xsl:value-of
        select='$day'/>, <xsl:value-of
        select='$year'/>
    </H1>
    <xsl:apply-templates/>
  </BODY>
</HTML>
</xsl:template>

<xsl:template match='bookings'>
  <P>This is the overall view of the meeting room
    bookings for today.</P>

  <TABLE cellspacing='0' cellpadding='0'>
    <TR>
      <TD><FONT SIZE='-2'>Room</FONT></TD>
      <TD><FONT SIZE='-2'>8:00</FONT></TD>
      <TD><FONT SIZE='-2'>8:30</FONT></TD>
      <TD><FONT SIZE='-2'>9:00</FONT></TD>
      <TD><FONT SIZE='-2'>9:30</FONT></TD>
      <TD><FONT SIZE='-2'>10:00</FONT></TD>
      <TD><FONT SIZE='-2'>10:30</FONT></TD>
      <TD><FONT SIZE='-2'>11:00</FONT></TD>
      <TD><FONT SIZE='-2'>11:30</FONT></TD>
      <TD><FONT SIZE='-2'>12:00</FONT></TD>
      <TD><FONT SIZE='-2'>12:30</FONT></TD>
      <TD><FONT SIZE='-2'>1:00</FONT></TD>
      <TD><FONT SIZE='-2'>1:30</FONT></TD>
      <TD><FONT SIZE='-2'>2:00</FONT></TD>
      <TD><FONT SIZE='-2'>2:30</FONT></TD>
      <TD><FONT SIZE='-2'>3:00</FONT></TD>
      <TD><FONT SIZE='-2'>3:30</FONT></TD>
      <TD><FONT SIZE='-2'>4:00</FONT></TD>
      <TD><FONT SIZE='-2'>4:30</FONT></TD>
      <TD><FONT SIZE='-2'>5:00</FONT></TD>
      <TD><FONT SIZE='-2'>5:30</FONT></TD>
    </TR>
```

```
          <xsl:apply-templates select='room'/>
      </TABLE>
  </xsl:template>

  <xsl:template match='room'>
    <TR>
      <TD>
        <FONT SIZE='-2'><xsl:value-of select='@name'/></FONT>
      </TD>
    </TR>
  </xsl:template>

</xsl:stylesheet>
```

We will use a table to present the meeting rooms. This XSLT document does not do much other than set up the headers for the table. If you apply it to *bookings.xml*, you get the output shown in Figure 3.8.

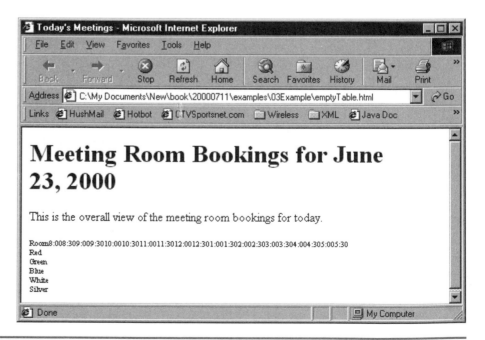

FIGURE ____

3.8   Availability of meetings for the day June 23, 2000

Changing the Background Colors

When the `room` elements are collected by the `xsl:apply-templates` element, each of them is assigned a number starting from 1. This is called the **position** of the element in the collection. To alternate the background colors, we assign gray rows to rooms whose positions are odd numbers and white to the rooms whose positions are even numbers.

In XSLT, the position of the context in the current collection is obtained by using the function `position()`. To check whether a number is even, divide the number by 2; if the remainder is 0, then the number is even. In other words,

```
<xsl:choose>
  <xsl:when test='position() mod 2 = 0'>
    <!-- the position is even -->
  </xsl:when>
  <xsl:otherwise>
    <!-- the position is odd -->
  </xsl:otherwise>
</xsl:choose>
```

The `xsl:choose` element means if the position is even (the first `xsl:when` element), then do something; if not (the `xsl:otherwise` element), do something else.

One room occupies one row of our table. The template for the `room` element can now be modified to this.

```
<xsl:template match='room'>
  <TR>
    <xsl:choose>
      <xsl:when test='position() mod 2 = 0'>
        <!-- the position is even -->
      </xsl:when>
      <xsl:otherwise>
        <!-- the position is odd -->
      </xsl:otherwise>
    </xsl:choose>
    <TD>
      <FONT SIZE='-2'><xsl:value-of select='@name'/></FONT>
    </TD>
  </TR>
</xsl:template>
```

To add the BGCOLOR attribute to the TR element, use the xsl:attribute element. It will add an attribute to the output element containing this element. Because it is contained in the TR element in our XSLT document, it will add the attribute to the TR element. Using this element, the template above becomes the following:

```
<xsl:template match='room'>
  <TR>
    <xsl:choose>
      <xsl:when test='position() mod 2 = 0'>
        <xsl:attribute name='BGCOLOR'>white</xsl:attribute>
      </xsl:when>
      <xsl:otherwise>
        <xsl:attribute name='BGCOLOR'>gray</xsl:attribute>
      </xsl:otherwise>
    </xsl:choose>
    <TD>
      <FONT SIZE='-2'><xsl:value-of select='@name'/></FONT>
    </TD>
  </TR>
</xsl:template>
```

Omitting the headers of the table, the output document looks like the one in Figure 3.9.

```
<HTML>
  <HEAD>
    <TITLE>Today's Meetings</TITLE>
  </HEAD>
  <BODY>
    <H1>Meeting Room Bookings for June 
            23, 2000</H1>
    <P>This is the overall view of the meeting room bookings for
today.</P>
    <TABLE cellspacing="0" cellpadding="0">
      <TR> <!-- omitted --> </TR>
      <TR BGCOLOR="gray"><TD><FONT SIZE="-2">Red</FONT></TD></TR>
      <TR BGCOLOR="white"><TD><FONT SIZE="-2">Green</FONT></TD></TR>
      <TR BGCOLOR="gray"><TD><FONT SIZE="-2">Blue</FONT></TD></TR>
      <TR BGCOLOR="white"><TD><FONT SIZE="-2">White</FONT></TD></TR>
      <TR BGCOLOR="gray"><TD><FONT SIZE="-2">Silver</FONT></TD></TR>
```

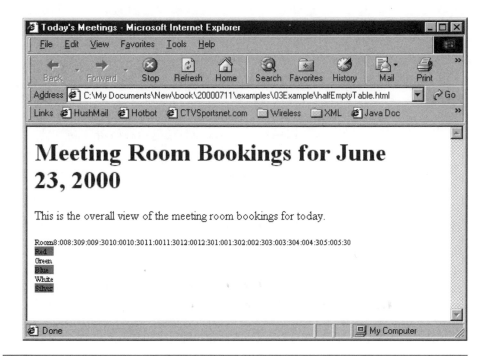

FIGURE
3.9   Availability of meetings for the day June 23, 2000, with only meeting rooms

```
        </TABLE>
      </BODY>
    </HTML>
```

Now we have to find out which time slot is empty and which time slot is occupied.

Repeating

Our next step is to go through each time slot for each room. If the time slot is booked, link to the image called *black.gif*. If the time slot is available, do nothing. The time slot may be in the middle of a long meeting, so be careful.

We will only consider time slots from 8 A.M. to 6 P.M. Each time slot is half an hour, so altogether there are 20 time slots for one day. The logic for finding whether a time slot is occupied is quite simple: If there is a meeting that starts earlier or at the time slot and ends later than the time slot, then the time slot is occupied. If there is no such meeting, then the time slot is empty.

Again, for each time slot, we will use an `xsl:choose` element to select *black.gif*. The `xsl:choose` element looks like this.

```
<xsl:choose>
  <!-- the value of an attribute must be on the same line.
      I break it up to get it to fit on the page -->
  <xsl:when
      test='period[from &lt;= $timeSlot and
            to &gt; $timeSlot]'>
    <TD><img src='black.gif' width='42' height='5'/></TD>
  </xsl:when>
  <xsl:otherwise>
    <TD width='42'> </TD>
  </xsl:otherwise>
</xsl:choose>
```

The entity reference `&lt;` is used inside an attribute because the literal `<` is not allowed inside an attribute. The expression is really `period[from <= $timeSlot and to > $timeSlot]`. This is fine for one time slot, but we have 20 time slots. To handle the 20 time slots, let us assume that we always want both time slots of an hour to be shown (so, for example, we will never start at 8:30 or end at 5:30). For any hour, the preceding code segment can be expanded to this.

```
<xsl:choose>
  <!-- the value of an attribute must be on the same line.
      I break it up to get it to fit on the page -->
  <xsl:when
   test='period[from &lt;= $timeSlot and
         to &gt; $timeSlot]'>
    <TD><img src='black.gif' width='42' height='5'/></TD>
  </xsl:when>
  <xsl:otherwise>
    <TD width='42'> </TD>
  </xsl:otherwise>
</xsl:choose>
<xsl:choose>
  <!-- the value of an attribute must be on the same line.
      I break it up to get it to fit on the page -->
  <xsl:when
      test='[from &lt;= $timeSlot + 30 and
            to &gt; $timeSlot + 30]'>
```

```
    <TD><img src='black.gif' width='42' height='5'/></TD>
  </xsl:when>
  <xsl:otherwise>
    <TD width='42'> </TD>
  </xsl:otherwise>
</xsl:choose>
```

The first `xsl:choose` element is for the top of the hour, the second for the bottom of the hour. We add 30 to the time slot because the bottom of the hour always starts with 30 and the top of the hour always starts with 00. For instance, `0800` is 8:00 o'clock, and `0830` is 8:30.

Now all we have to do is call this code segment 10 times for each room. A code segment like this can be put into a template as well. Instead of having a `match` attribute, the template will have a `name` attribute. The template will be called by its name rather than applied by the elements it matches.

Let us call the template `onePeriod`.

```
<xsl:template name='onePeriod'>
  <xsl:param name='timeSlot'/>
  <!-- the code segment here -->
</xsl:template>
```

The `xsl:param` contained inside the template specifies that the template has one parameter. The parameter is the hour to be shown.

The place to call the template is obviously right after the name of a room has been output, in the template for the `room` element.

```
<xsl:template match='room'>
  <TR>
    <xsl:choose>
        .
        .
        .
    </xsl:choose>
    <TD><FONT SIZE='-2'><xsl:value-of
                           select='@name'/> </FONT></TD>
    <xsl:call-template name='onePeriod'>
      <xsl:with-param name='timeSlot' select='0800'/>
    </xsl:call-template>
    <xsl:call-template name='onePeriod'>
      <xsl:with-param name='timeSlot' select='0900'/>
    </xsl:call-template>
    <xsl:call-template name='onePeriod'>
```

```
          <xsl:with-param name='timeSlot' select='1000'/>
        </xsl:call-template>
        .
        .
        .
        <xsl:call-template name='onePeriod'>
          <xsl:with-param name='timeSlot' select='1700'/>
        </xsl:call-template>
      </TR>
    </xsl:template>
```

The xsl:call-template element is used to call a template by name. The
xsl:param elements in a template specify the parameters of the template.
The xsl:with-param elements contained in an xsl:call-template element
specify the values of the parameters to pass in to the template it calls.

Because the template is for the room elements, the template with the name
onePeriod has to be modified to this.

```
    <xsl:template name='onePeriod'>
      <xsl:param name='timeSlot'/>
        <xsl:choose>
          <!-- the value for the test attribute must
               be on the same line. But I have to break it up
               to show it here. -->
          <xsl:when
               test='date/meeting/period
                     [from &lt;= $timeSlot and
                     to &gt; $timeSlot]'>
            <TD><img src='black.gif' width='42' height='5'/></TD>
          </xsl:when>
          <xsl:otherwise>
            <TD width='42'> </TD>
          </xsl:otherwise>
        </xsl:choose>
        <xsl:choose>
          <!-- the value for the test attribute must
               be on the same line. But I have to break it up
               to show it here. -->
          <xsl:when
             test='date/meeting/period[from &lt;= $timeSlot + 30 and
                                       to &gt; $timeSlot + 30]'>
            <TD><img src='black.gif' width='42' height='5'/></TD>
          </xsl:when>
```

```
        <xsl:otherwise>
          <TD width='42'> </TD>
        </xsl:otherwise>
      </xsl:choose>
    </xsl:template>
```

Again, the value of an attribute must be on the same line. (We break the values of the `test` attribute of the `xsl:when` elements in this example because the page is not wide enough to show the values; in your XSLT document, you must specify the values on the same line.)

This is not correct yet; we will put in a black bar in a time slot as long as there is a day that the time slot is booked for the room. We can modify the expression to find the `period` elements to this.

```
date[year=$year and month=$month and day=$day]/meeting/period
```

But this is too unwieldy to use in expressions. Instead, you can store the elements of an expression in a variable. The preceding template can be rewritten to this.

```
<xsl:template name='onePeriod'>
  <xsl:param name='timeSlot'/>
  <xsl:variable name='meeting'
      select='date[year=$year and month=$month and day=$day]/meeting'/>
    <xsl:choose>
      <!-- the value for the test attribute must
           be on the same line. But I have to break it up
           to show it here. -->
      <xsl:when
          test='$meeting/period
                [from &lt;= $timeSlot and
                to &gt; $timeSlot]'>
        <TD><img src='black.gif' width='42' height='5'/></TD>
      </xsl:when>
      <xsl:otherwise>
        <TD width='42'> </TD>
      </xsl:otherwise>
    </xsl:choose>
    <xsl:choose>
      <!-- the value for the test attribute must
           be on the same line. But I have to break it up
           to show it here. -->
```

```
        <xsl:when
            test='$meeting/period
                [from &lt;= $timeSlot + 30 and
                to &gt; $timeSlot + 30]'>
        <TD><img src='black.gif' width='42' height='5'/></TD>
        </xsl:when>
        <xsl:otherwise>
          <TD width='42'> </TD>
        </xsl:otherwise>
      </xsl:choose>
    </xsl:template>
```

Let's call this XSLT document *availability.xsl*. We have now finished two XSLT documents.

3.2.10   *Showing Features, Bookings, and Availability*

The third kind of HTML document we want to produce from *bookings.xml* and *rooms.xml* is one that shows the features, availability, and meetings for a meeting room for a particular day. We now know how to show the meetings for all the meeting rooms for a particular day and how to show the availability of all the meeting rooms. Now we'll learn how to show the features of a meeting room. First we'll concentrate on the availability and meetings for a meeting room and then we'll see how to show the features of a meeting room.

Reusing Existing Templates

We will reuse the templates defined in the two previous XSLT documents. We want to reuse the template for the meeting element in *today.xsl* and the template for the room element in *availability.xsl*.

The problem is that there is also a template for room elements in *today.xsl*, but there are a few ways to resolve this problem. The easiest way is to get rid of the template for room elements in *today.xsl* and define a template for the bookings element. That is, originally, we have two templates that look like this.

```
<xsl:template match='room'>
  <xsl:apply-templates/>
</xsl:template>
```

We can change one of the occurrences (in *today.xsl*) to

```
<xsl:template match='bookings'>
  <xsl:apply-templates select='room/date'/>
</xsl:template>
```

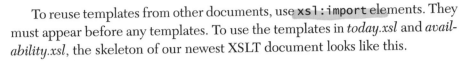

To reuse templates from other documents, use **xsl:import** elements. They must appear before any templates. To use the templates in *today.xsl* and *availability.xsl*, the skeleton of our newest XSLT document looks like this.

```
<?xml version='1.0'?>
<xsl:stylesheet version='1.0'
    xmlns:xsl='http://www.w3.org/1999/XSL/Transform'>

  <xsl:import href='today.xsl'/>
  <xsl:import href='availability.xsl'/>

  <xsl:output method='html' indent='no'/>

  <xsl:param name='year'/>
  <xsl:param name='month'/>
  <xsl:param name='day'/>
  <xsl:param name='room'/>
  .
  .
  .
```

We also defined a parameter for the room name.

The template that matches the document element is rather straightforward.

```
<xsl:template match='/'>
  <HTML>
    <HEAD><TITLE>Today's Meetings</TITLE></HEAD>
    <BODY>
      <H1>Bookings for Room <xsl:value-of select='$room'/> on
        <xsl:value-of select='$month'/> 
          <xsl:value-of select='$day'/>, 
            <xsl:value-of select='$year'/></H1>
      <xsl:apply-templates/>
    </BODY>
  </HTML>
</xsl:template>
```

The template for **bookings** is also quite straightforward.

```
<xsl:template match='bookings'>
  <P>This is today's overall view of the
    meeting room bookings.</P>
  <TABLE cellspacing='0' cellpadding='0'>
    <TR>
      <TD><FONT SIZE='-2'>Room </FONT></TD>
```

```
      <TD><FONT SIZE='-2'>8:00 </FONT></TD>
      <TD><FONT SIZE='-2'>8:30 </FONT></TD>
      <TD><FONT SIZE='-2'>9:00 </FONT></TD>
      <TD><FONT SIZE='-2'>9:30 </FONT></TD>
      <TD><FONT SIZE='-2'>10:00 </FONT></TD>
      <TD><FONT SIZE='-2'>10:30 </FONT></TD>
      <TD><FONT SIZE='-2'>11:00 </FONT></TD>
      <TD><FONT SIZE='-2'>11:30 </FONT></TD>
      <TD><FONT SIZE='-2'>12:00 </FONT></TD>
      <TD><FONT SIZE='-2'>12:30 </FONT></TD>
      <TD><FONT SIZE='-2'>1:00 </FONT></TD>
      <TD><FONT SIZE='-2'>1:30 </FONT></TD>
      <TD><FONT SIZE='-2'>2:00 </FONT></TD>
      <TD><FONT SIZE='-2'>2:30 </FONT></TD>
      <TD><FONT SIZE='-2'>3:00 </FONT></TD>
      <TD><FONT SIZE='-2'>3:30 </FONT></TD>
      <TD><FONT SIZE='-2'>4:00 </FONT></TD>
      <TD><FONT SIZE='-2'>4:30 </FONT></TD>
      <TD><FONT SIZE='-2'>5:00 </FONT></TD>
      <TD><FONT SIZE='-2'>5:30 </FONT></TD>
    </TR>
    <xsl:apply-templates select='room[@name=$room]'/>
  </TABLE>
  <!-- the value of the select of the element below
       must be on one line, but I have to break it up
       to show it here. -->
  <xsl:apply-templates
    select='room[@name=$room]/date[year = $year and
            month = $month and day = $day]/meeting'/>
</xsl:template>
```

The only difference is the additional criterion of `@name=$room`.[7]

Getting Outside Information

Finally, we want to show the features of a meeting room. The template to do
that is simple.

```
<xsl:template match='room' mode='features'>
  <H2>Meeting Room Features</H2>
```

---

7. The `$room` is a reference to the global parameter room.

```
    <P>Capacity: <xsl:value-of select='capacity'/></P>
    <P>Equipment in the room:
      <xsl:for-each select='equipmentList/equipment'>
        <xsl:if test='position() != 1'>
          , 
        </xsl:if>
        <xsl:value-of select='.'/>
      </xsl:for-each>
    </P>
  </xsl:template>
```

In the template, the expression `position() != 1` checks if the position of the context is not 1. The expression . means the current context (the **room** element). The new `xsl:if` element means if the expression in the **test** attribute evaluates to true, then do something; otherwise, do nothing at all.

We specify the **mode attribute** for the template because we don't want to get confused with the other template for **room**. To apply templates with **mode** attributes, simply specify the value of the **mode** attribute in an `xsl:apply-templates` element.

```
<xsl:apply-templates select='room' mode='features'/>
```

However, we do have a problem: The features category of a room is actually in *rooms.xml*, not in *bookings.xml*. XSLT has a function to allow us to access information from outside XML documents: the **document()** function. To apply the template to show the features of a meeting room, simply add the following element to the template for **bookings**.

```
<xsl:template match='bookings'>
  <P>This is today's overall view of the
     meeting room bookings.</P>
  <TABLE cellspacing='0' cellpadding='0'>
    <TR>
      <!-- omitted -->
    </TR>
    <xsl:apply-templates select='room[@name=$room]'/>
  </TABLE>
  <xsl:apply-templates
    select='document("rooms.xml")/rooms/room[@name=$room]'
    mode='features'/>
  <!-- the value of the select must be on the same line.
       It is broken up to show here. -->
```

```
<xsl:apply-templates
  select='room[@name=$room]/date[year = $year and
                                  month = $month and
                                  day = $day]/meeting'/>

</xsl:template>
```

3.3   Summary

If you can write XSLT documents as sophisticated as the three XSLT documents shown in this chapter, you will be able to handle 80 percent of the XSLT documents you will need to write. There are many projects that require only the features explained in this chapter. You have also seen a glimpse of how XSLT projects are handled: First, you have mockups, then you write the XSLT documents in stages. You fulfill the requirements one by one, always making sure that each step of the way you are receiving the expected output. I have tried to avoid formal descriptions of any XSLT features, making the explanations as plain and simple as possible.

3.4   Looking Ahead

Since the remaining 80 percent of XSLT is not as easy to explain with examples, we will examine the fundamental concepts in XSLT starting with the next chapter.

PART II

⟨4⟩

XML Documents as Trees

Now you have a big tree,
and you worry that it is not useful.
Why not plant it on an empty plain,
in the great wilderness.
You can loiter around the tree,
freely laying on the ground under it.
This tree will never be chopped down,
and it will not be harmed.
Why worry that it is useless?

—*Zhuang Zi*

An XML document is a text document, a sequence of characters. The elements, attributes, and entities of an XML document are all represented by characters. Both the data and its structure are represented in the same way.

To make it easier for computer programs to work with the structure and data of an XML document, the document is parsed. The parsed form is then analyzed and stored in an internal format. Computer programs can then process the internal format any way the programmer desires. If the result of the processing is a document, the internal format is converted into the textual form of XML, HTML, or text.

For transformation purposes, it is useful to represent an XML document as a **tree.** From the concrete form of a textual representation of structures in terms of characters (from the level of < characters to the level of start-tags, end-tags, and so on), we can then talk about the abstract form of elements, attributes, and so forth without having to worry about the characters in the textual form.

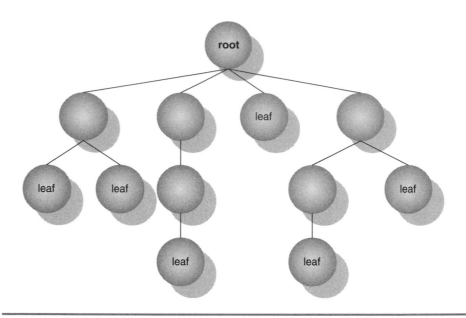

FIGURE

4.1   A tree with the root and leaves

A tree is a simple structure composed of **nodes** and **branches**. Two nodes are connected by one branch. The node at one end is called the **parent**, and the node at the other end is the **child**.

In an XML document tree, nodes represent the elements, attributes, namespace declarations, character data, comments, and so on—in short, markup and character data. The branches show the relationships among the markup and character data. For instance, suppose the document element is `document` and it contains five `chapter` elements. Then the `document` element and its five `chapter` elements are represented by nodes. The `document` element is the parent, and the five `chapter` elements are the child nodes, with five branches connecting the `document` element node to the five `chapter` elements nodes.

There are two rules on how the nodes and branches can be organized. The first rule is that a node can have only one parent, and one node has no parent. This node with no parent is called the **root node** (or simply the **root**) of the tree. The second rule is that every tree must have exactly one root.

A node can have as many child nodes as necessary. If a node has no child nodes, it is called a **leaf node** (or simply a **leaf**). Figure 4.1 shows a tree with the root and the leaves.

FIGURE _____
4.2   A tree with a single node

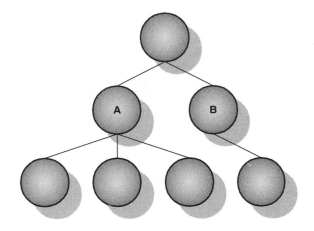

FIGURE _____
4.3   A tree with nodes and branches

Trees can have many different forms. A tree can consist of only one node, as shown in Figure 4.2. This is a perfectly valid tree.[1] Nodes in a tree may have different numbers of children. In Figure 4.3, node A has three children and node B has only one child. Leaves, of course, have no children at all.

4.1   Tree Terminology

Although trees are very simple structures, before we go on, let's define some pertinent terms. You already know what parent nodes and child nodes are, but a tree can have other elements.

_____

1. The minimal HTML document has more than one element. If you see nothing in your output document, then something is probably wrong with your XSLT document.

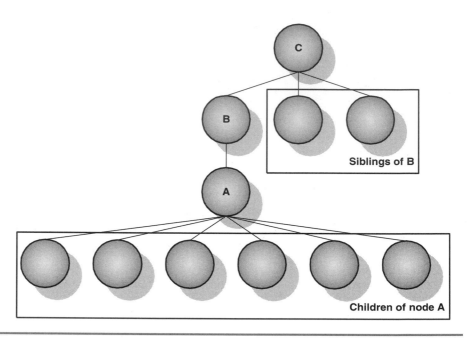

FIGURE
4.4   A tree

DESCENDANTS.   Take the children of a node, the children of the children, and the children of the children of the children, and so on, until there are no more children. (Sooner or later, we will run out of children if we keep going down the tree.) All these nodes are the **descendants** of the node. In Figure 4.4, node A and the children of node A are the descendants of node B.

In a tree diagram, you can easily find the descendants of a node: All the nodes under the node are the descendants of the node. If you cut away everything other than the node and its descendants, you are left with a **subtree** rooted at the node. In an XML document, it is also very easy to find the descendants of an element. Everything contained by the element is a descendant of the element.

ANCESTORS.   The parent of a node, the parent of its parent, and so on all the way up to the root are called the **ancestors** of the node. In Figure 4.4, nodes A, B, and C are the ancestors of the children of node A.

In a tree diagram, all the nodes that are traced from the node in question, in an upward fashion, to the root are the ancestors of the node. This includes the parent of the node.

SIBLINGS. The children of a node are the siblings of each other. The nodes to the left of a node are the **preceding siblings** of the node. The nodes to the right of a node are the **following siblings** of the node. The node with no preceding sibling is the first child of its parent. The node with no following sibling is the last child of its parent.

In Figure 4.4, the siblings of node B are boxed in. All of these siblings are following siblings of Node B. Because node B is the first child of its parent, it has no preceding siblings.

Siblings are just nodes that have the same parent. In terms of the XML document that the tree represents, preceding siblings of a node are elements that occur earlier in the document than the node, and following siblings are elements that occur later in the document.

4.2 Converting an XML Document to a Tree

When an XML document is converted to a tree, all the escapes for the special characters, the CDATA segments, and so on will be changed back to their original content. For instance, `&lt;` becomes < again. In other words, all the characters in the tree represent themselves.

A generic XML document usually has the XML declaration, some processing instructions, the XML document type declaration, some more processing instructions and comments, the document element, then perhaps some comments or processing instructions. Everything is optional except the document element.

The generic XML document tree is shown in Figure 4.5. The document element may contain other elements, comments, and so forth. Figure 4.5 shows the position of the document element in an XML document. The XML document type declaration, if it exists in the XML document, is not visible to XSLT documents. All entity definitions in the XML document type declaration are also not visible.

4.2.1 Converting the Elements Contained in the Document Element

After the document element is identified, there may be some elements in it. For now, ignore the attributes and character data, and consider only the elements in the document. Here is a simple pen-and-paper way to construct a tree from an XML document.

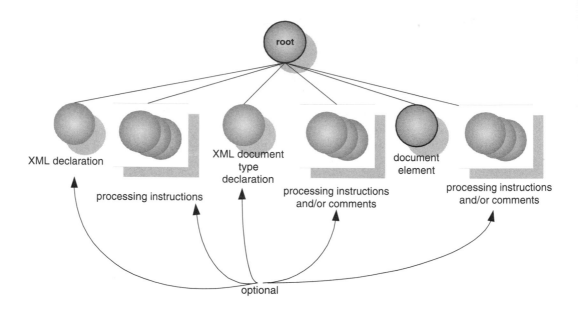

4.5   The tree representing the XML document

1. Start from the beginning of the document. If you find the XML declaration, draw the root of the document. If you do not find the XML declaration, draw the root anyway. Your context is the root of the tree. Since you need to know your context at any point of the conversion process, call this node the current **context node** of your conversion process.

2. Now, scan the XML document to find the next tag. If the tag you find is not an end-tag, start a branch with the context node as the parent node and create a child node at the other end. If there are already other children for the context node, draw the newest child as the rightmost child node of the context node. If the tag begins with <? or <!, keep the context node unchanged. Otherwise, set the newest node to be the new context node.

   If the tag is an end-tag, don't draw anything; just set the parent of the context node as the new context node. For simplicity's sake, an empty element is assumed to have a start-tag and an end-tag (that is, use the `<verified></verified>` form, not the `<verified/>` form).

3. Keep doing this until the end of the document.

4.2.2   *An Example*

Suppose we have the following XML document.

```
<?xml version="1.0"?>
<!-- An example to show how an XML document
     can be converted to a tree -->
<receipt>
  <storename>The Shoe Outline</storename>
  <address>190 Libertarian  Street</address>
  <date>14 October 1999</date>
  <items>
    <item>
      <units>2</units>
      <name>Nighthawk Mountain Boots</name>
      <price>$20.00</price>
      <amount>$40.00</amount>
    </item>
    <item>
      <units>1</units>
      <name>Mountaineer Hiking Shoes</name>
      <price>$15.00</price>
      <amount>$15.00</amount>
    </item>
  </items>
  <taxrate>15</receipt>
```

This is how to convert the XML document into a tree.

1. The first tag is the XML declaration. Draw the root and label the node **root**. Set the context node to be the root node. The tree so far is shown in Figure 4.6, a single-node tree containing only the root node.

2. The next tag is a comment element. Draw a line from the root, the context node. Label this node `<!-- -->`. The actual comment is not important for

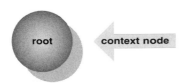

FIGURE
4.6   Tree after the first tag has been inserted

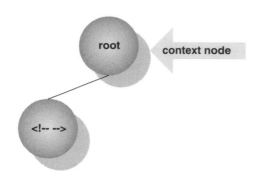

FIGURE

4.7   Tree after the comment node had been inserted

now. Keep the root node as the context node. Figure 4.7 shows the tree after the comment node has been inserted.

3. Next, we have a `<receipt>` tag, the start-tag of an element. We know it is a following sibling of the comment node, so draw a branch from the root to the right of the comment node. Now set the context node to the `receipt` element. Label the node `<receipt>`. Figure 4.8 shows the tree after the `receipt` element in the tree has been inserted.

4. The next tag is `<storename>`, the start-tag of the `storename` element. Draw a line from the context node—the `receipt` node—to create a new child node for it. Then change the context node to the new node. Figure 4.9 shows the tree after the `storename` element has been inserted.

5. Now we have `</storename>`, the end-tag for the `storename` element. Move the context node up to its parent to the `receipt` element. Figure 4.10 shows what the tree looks like after the context node is moved.

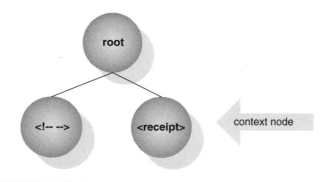

FIGURE

4.8   The tree with the third element

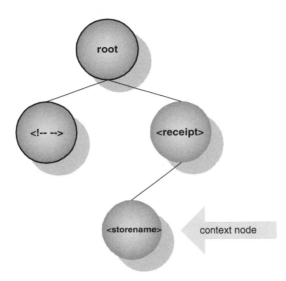

FIGURE
4.9   The tree with the **storename** element

6. The next tag is **<address>**, the start-tag of the **address** element, a sibling of the **storename** element. Draw a line from the context node to the right of the **storename** element. Set the context node to the new node. Figure 4.11 shows the new tree after the new node has been inserted.

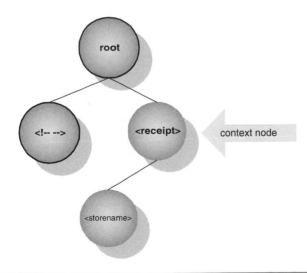

FIGURE
4.10   Finishing up the **storename** element

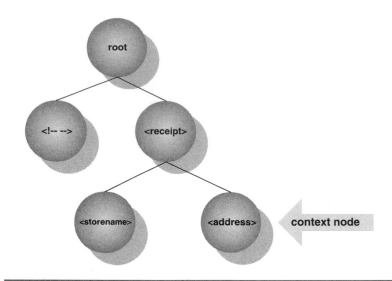

FIGURE
4.11   Inserting the address element

7. Next is `</address>`, the end-tag of the **address** element. Move the context node up to its parent. Figure 4.12 shows the tree after the context node is moved up.

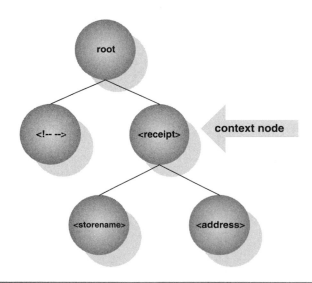

FIGURE
4.12   Moving the context node up after finishing the **address** element

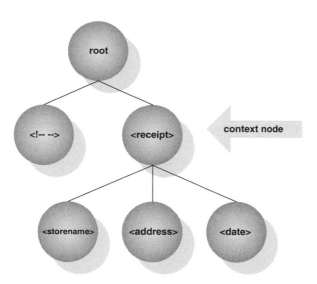

FIGURE 4.13 The tree after the **date** element has been inserted

8. The next tag is **<date>**. This tag and its end-tag are treated as the previous two elements. Figure 4.13 shows the tree after the start-tag and end-tag of the date element are processed.

9. Next is **<items>**. Draw the node and make it the context node. The tree is shown in Figure 4.14.

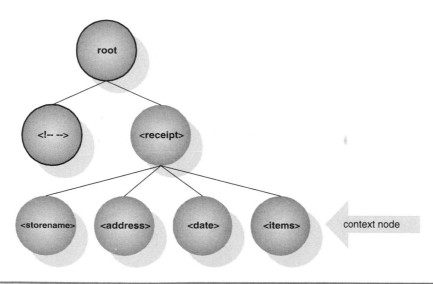

FIGURE 4.14 Inserting the **items** element

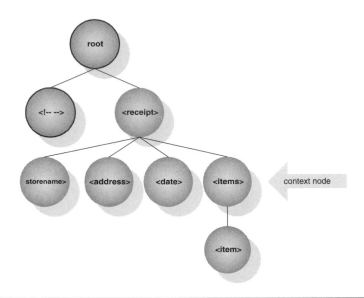

FIGURE

4.15   The tree after inserting all the elements in the XML document

10. We now have `<item>`. Move the context node to this node after drawing the node from the node labeled `<items>`. The result is shown in Figure 4.15.

11. Continue to do this until all the elements have been inserted. Our final tree is shown in Figure 4.16.

4.2.3   *Text Nodes*

An XML document has markups and character data. We have seen how elements and comments are represented in a tree. Character data is also represented in a tree by nodes, just like elements, attributes, and so on. Nodes representing character data are called **text nodes**.

An element may have more than one text node. All of these text nodes are children of the element. In Figure 4.17, one of the nodes in the tree has three text nodes.

Note that whitespaces are significant in XML. Therefore, the XML fragment

```
<book><title>Bookman's Blue</title></book>
```

is not the same as the XML fragment

```
<book>
  <title>Bookman's Blue</title>
</book>
```

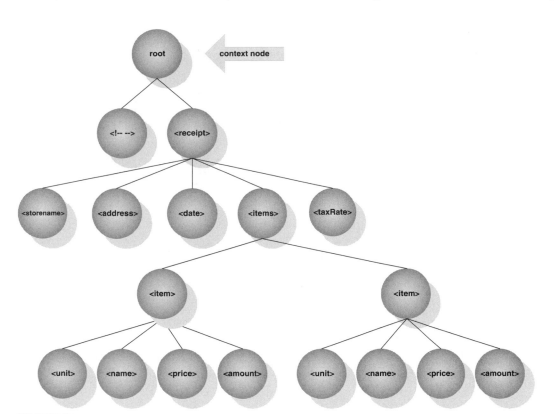

FIGURE 4.16   The tree after all the elements are inserted in the XML document

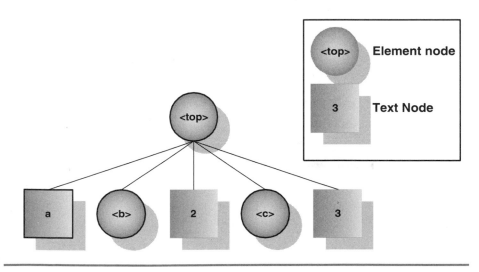

FIGURE 4.17   A node with three text nodes

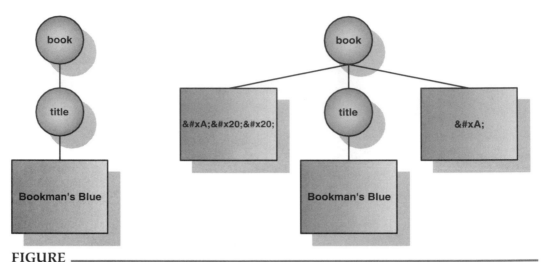

FIGURE
4.18   The trees for the fragments

The difference is that in the second fragment there are whitespaces between the two elements. Figure 4.18 shows the two trees for the fragments. Character references are used for the second tree because only whitespaces are contained in two of the three text nodes. And Figure 4.19 shows the tree with all the text nodes added for the XML document shown in the previous section.

4.2.4   *Attributes*

So far, we have not discussed attributes of elements. Because attributes do not nest, they can be considered as another set of children for the element. (Do not mix the two sets of children together though.) Furthermore, attributes do not have order. For instance, the XML fragment

```
<title isbn="1-56592-132-3"
    year="1999"><author>James Smith</author></title>
```

can be drawn as in Figure 4.20.

In XSLT, every element also carries namespace nodes for all the namespaces that are in effect for the element. Specifically, the namespace prefix xml[2] is in effect for every element node in the document tree. The namespace nodes represent the third set of child nodes for an element.

---

2. The URI is http://www.w3.org/XML/1998/namespace.

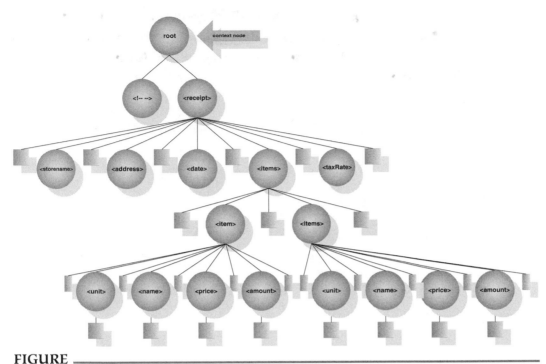

FIGURE
4.19   The tree with all elements and all text nodes inserted

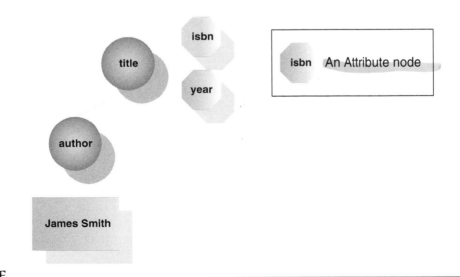

FIGURE
4.20   A node with attributes

In summary, an element has three sets of children. The first set contains all element, comment, processing instruction, and text children; the second set contains all the attributes of the element; and the third set contains all the namespaces that are in effect for the element. The first set can be empty if the element is empty. The second set can be empty if the element does not have any attributes. The third set is never empty; it always contains at least the default xml namespace. Comment, processing instruction, attribute, text, and namespace nodes do not have children.

4.3   Traversing a Tree

Now that we understand the XML document as represented by a tree, let's talk about going from one node to another, with the branches serving as pathways. As we move from one node to another, the nodes are labeled in alphabetical order from the origin to the destination, with a letter indicating the path. For example, in Figure 4.21, to go from node D to node F, we use the path C, B, F.

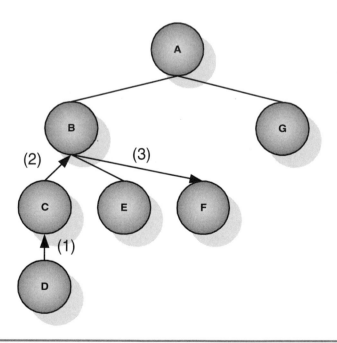

FIGURE
4.21   The path from node D to node F

82

4.3.1   *Enumerating All the Nodes in a Tree*

It is sometimes helpful to list all the nodes in a tree, and there are several ways to do this. One way is called the **depth-first** traversal. If only the names of the elements must be output, for example, the depth-first traversal of a tree would be done like this.

1. Go to the root. Set this as the context node.

2. Output the name of the context node.

3. Go to the leftmost child of the context node that has not been visited, if such a node exists. Set the context node to be that node. Go to step 2.

4. If the context node does not have any children or if all the children of the context node have been visited, set the context node to the parent of the context node. Go to step 3.

5. Do this until the context node is the root and all children of the root have been visited.

4.3.2   *Example*

Using the tree in Figure 4.21, let's traverse the whole tree from the root step by step. The numbers in parentheses before each step in the traversal are from the procedure in Section 4.3.1.

1. (1) Set the context node to the root of the document.

2. (2) Output the name of the node: A.

3. (3) The leftmost unvisited child of node A is node B. Set the context node to B. Go to procedure step 2.

4. (2) Output the name of the node: B.

5. (3) The leftmost unvisited child of node B is node C. Set the context node to C. Go to procedure step 2.

6. (2) Output the name of the node: C.

7. (3) The leftmost unvisited child of node C is node D. Set the context node to D. Go to procedure step 2.

8. (2) Output the name of the node: D.

9. (3) There is no unvisited child for node D. Go to procedure step 4.

10. (4) The parent of node D is node C. Set the context node to C. Go to procedure step 3.

11. (3) There is no unvisited child for node D. Go to procedure step 4.

12. (4) The parent of node C is node B. Set the context node to B. Go to procedure 3.

13. (3) The leftmost unvisited child of node B is node E. Set the context node to node E. Go to procedure step 2.

14. (2) Output the name of the node: E.

15. (3) There is no unvisited child for node E. Go to procedure step 4.

16. (4) The parent of node E is node B. Set the context node to node B. Go to procedure step 3.

17. (3) The leftmost unvisited child of node B is F. Set the context node to F. Go to procedure step 2.

18. (2) Output the name of the node: F.

19. (3) There is no unvisited child for node F. Go to procedure step 4.

20. (4) The parent of node F is node B. Set the context node to B. Go to procedure step 3.

21. (3) There is no unvisited node for node B. Go to procedure step 4.

22. (4) The parent of node B is node A. Set the context node to node A. Go to procedure step 3.

23. (3) The leftmost unvisited child of node A is node G. Set the context node to node G. Go to procedure step 2.

24. (2) Output the name of the node: G.

25. (3) There is no unvisited child for node G. Go to procedure step 4.

26. (4) The parent of node G is node A. Set the context node to node A. Go to procedure step 3.

27. (3) There is no unvisited child for node A. Go to procedure step 4.

28. (4) There is no parent for node A. The whole tree has been traversed. Stop.

The depth-first traversal of a tree is quite similar to the way we read an XML document: We read from the top to the bottom, matching the begin-tag and end-tag as we go, going deeper inside an element and coming up from an element all the time. The depth-first traversal is just a more formal way of specifying how this is done.

4.4 Document Order

We call the order of the nodes representing the elements, comments, and processing instructions when we perform a depth-first traversal the **document order** of the nodes. This is an intuitive concept. It is the same order you use when you read an XML document from the beginning to the end, from top to bottom.

The attributes of an element are not ordered among themselves. They occur later than the element they appear in but earlier than the children of the element.

The namespace declarations in effect for an element are also not ordered among themselves. They occur later than the element they appear in and before the attributes of the element and the children of the element.

Two more terms must be introduced to discuss document orders of nodes.

1. preceding The preceding nodes of a node are the elements that precede the node in the document order of the XML document.

2. following The following nodes of a node are the elements that follow the node in the document order of the XML document.

For the tree in Figure 4.22, the preceding nodes of node E are nodes A, B, C, and D. The following nodes of the node E are nodes F and G.

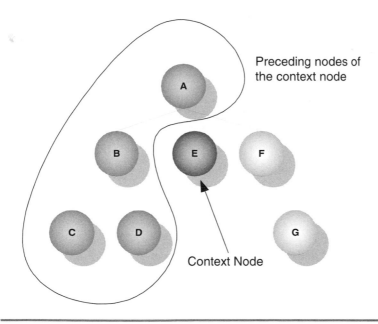

FIGURE 4.22 The preceding nodes of a node

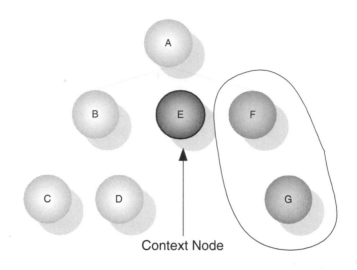

FIGURE

4.23   The following nodes of a node

4.5   Distinctness of Nodes in a Tree

Two nodes in the same tree are different if their preceding nodes have different document orders. The contents of the nodes are not used to differentiate them. In other words, two nodes are distinct if they are in different parts of the same tree.

4.6   Summary

This chapter may not be terribly exciting, but it is one of the most important chapters in this book. XML documents can be represented as trees with nodes and branches. A tree has a root, which is simply the node in a tree that does not have a parent. The other nodes must have exactly one parent, although they may have as many children as needed. Nodes with no child nodes are the leaves.

An XML document can be converted to a tree in a systematic way. Elements contained in other elements are the descendants of the containing element. When you apply this relationship in a nested manner, you get the tree representation of an XML document. The document order of the nodes in the tree is the order in which they appear in the XML document. The document order of all the nodes in a tree can be obtained by performing a depth-first traversal of the tree.

4.7   Looking Ahead

Now that you are familiar with the terminology of the tree representation of XML documents, you are ready to look at a very important aspect of XSLT: how to navigate in a tree. In other words, given a node in a tree, how to navigate from this node to any other node or nodes in the tree. In XSLT, the notation used to navigate in a tree is called XPath (the XML Path Language).

⟨ 5 ⟩

Paths

> Paths are created by people walking;
> names are created by people calling.
>
> —*Zhuang Zi*

When we use XSLT to transform XML documents, we have one or more source trees (from the input XML documents), one instruction tree (from the XSLT document), and one result tree.

The source trees represent XML documents. There is one initial source tree, which is the one we specify to the XSLT processor before the start of the transformation process. Additional source trees may be specified during the transformation.

The instruction tree represents the XSLT document, holding all the instructions for the transformation. It tells the XSLT processor how to transform the source trees and how to produce the result tree.

Using the instructions in the instruction tree, the XSLT processor constructs the result tree from the source trees and the instruction tree. Other information is calculated by the processor, using the instructions in the instruction tree. Not all information in the result tree comes from the source trees.

Regardless of the source of the information in the result tree, we need a way to specify where that information is. The notation used in XSLT to specify a piece of information in the source trees is called **XPath**, the **XML Path Language**, which is the topic of this chapter. In Chapter 3, we saw XPath expressions used in the `select`, `test`, and `match` attributes of the elements `xsl:template`, `xsl:apply-templates`, `xsl:if`, and so on.

5.1   Paths and Expressions

We expect a programming language to be able to handle basic arithmetic operations. Since XML documents are text documents, we expect string operations for convenience, and XPath has these operations.

But XML document processing has one important requirement that other programming languages do not have: the manipulation of the components in a tree—nodes and branches. Of course, for other programming languages, other operations and constructs that can be used to handle trees are specified. But these programming languages do not treat trees as one of the basic data structures. In XSLT, the tree is the basic data structure. XPath allows you to select nodes in a tree according to a pattern based on the location of the nodes in the tree, the names of the nodes, and nodes contained by the nodes.

For both the ordinary arithmetic and string expressions, as well as expressions for nodes and branches, the XPath notation specifies expressions. An expression produces one of four types of values: a number, a string, a Boolean value, or a set of nodes.

5.1.1   *Numbers*

A number in XPath can be a positive (`-84`) or negative (`323`) whole number. The number can be a decimal. If the number is between 0 and 1, then the zero in front of the decimal point is optional (`.5`, `-.5`). The number can also be a whole number followed by a decimal point (`10.`).

5.1.2   *Strings*

A string is a sequence of characters enclosed in quotes. As long as both opening and closing quotes are the same, single or double quotes can be used. A string can also have embedded quote characters as long as they are escaped or are different quote characters from the enclosing quotes. Some examples of strings are: `'a string'`, `"another string"`, `'quotes "inside" a string'`, and `'escaped quote&quot;'`, where `&quot;` is the entity reference to the `'` character.

5.1.3   *Boolean Values*

A Boolean value can be either `true` or `false`. However, you cannot specify a literal Boolean value in XPath. You obtain a Boolean value only as the value of an expression.

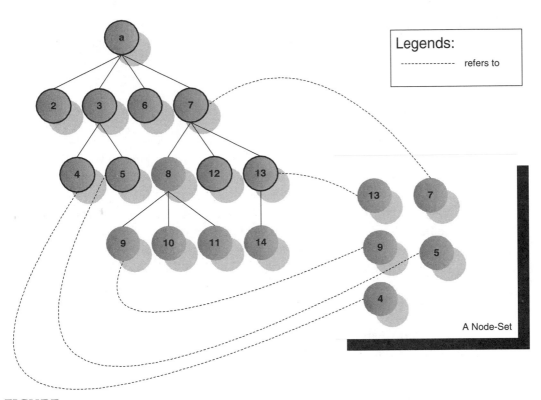

FIGURE
5.1   An XML tree and a node-set containing nodes from the tree

5.1.4   *Node-Sets*

An XPath expression can result in a set of nodes in the source trees called a node-set.[1] As for Boolean values, you cannot specify literal values for node-sets. You obtain node-sets as the results of expressions. A node-set can be empty or have only one node. (Of course, there can be more than one node in a node-set.) There cannot be more than one copy of the same node in a node-set. All duplicates (nodes that are not distinct—see Section 4.5 for the definition of *distinctness*) are removed when you combine two node-sets. Nodes in a node-set can be placed in order as they are referenced, but the nodes themselves do not have a specific order in the node-set.

In Figure 5.1, an XML document is shown on the left. On the right is a node-set containing some of the nodes in the document. Every node in a node-set

---

1. Or nodesets, depending on where you look. I will use node-sets.

refers to a node in an XML document. However, it is not cut off from the XML document. It still has a parent, which is simply the parent of its corresponding node in the XML tree. Anything that can be said about a node in an XML document can be said about a node in a node-set.

5.2   Location Paths

There are two ways to produce a node-set: by referring to a set of nodes in the source trees or by combining or performing other operations on existing node-sets.

When creating node-sets, an XPath expression, called a **location path,** is used. We have seen location paths in Chapter 3 during the discussion on values of the `match` attribute of the templates. Location paths are also used in many of the values of the `select` attribute of the `xsl:value-of` elements.

A location path can be broken up into steps. For example, we saw the following location path in Chapter 3.

```
room[\@name=$room]/date[year = $year and month = $month and day
    = $day]/meeting
```

There are three steps in the location path, separated by the / character. Here is a simpler example, also with three steps.

```
room/date/meeting
```

Let's examine the difference between these two location paths.

5.2.1   *Context*

Location paths are used to refer to nodes in a tree. Because we don't always want to refer to nodes from the root, we have to know the starting point of a location path. The starting point is called the **context node** in a location path.

Besides the context node, we need other information. We call all the elements of information the **context** of the location path. There are six members in a context.

1. The context node
2. The position of the context node in the context, called the **context position**
3. The size of the context, called the **context size**
4. The set of variables that are in scope
5. The functions available
6. The namespaces in effect

A context is created by the XSLT processor before an XPath expression is evaluated. The context also changes from one step to the next step. So the sequence for evaluating a path is (1) the context is received from the XSLT processor, (2) it is used to evaluate the first step, (3) the result of the step is turned into a context for the second step, and (4) the process continues until no more steps remain. The final result is the value of the whole location path.

When you are trying to understand or specify an XPath expression, always keep the context in mind. The value of an XPath expression depends on the context at the time the XPath expression is evaluated.

5.2.2 A Step

A step in a location path can be further broken down into three parts: an **axis**, a **node test**, and **predicates**. The generic step looks like this.

axis::*node-test*[*predicate*]

The axis is separated from the node test by ::. Each predicate is enclosed between brackets ([]).

5.2.3 The Axis

The axis of a step specifies the relationship between the context node and the nodes to select. You can choose one out of 13 axes for a step; however, only four of the axes are frequently used.

We will use as an example the XML tree and the context node shown in Figure 5.2. The context node will be node 6.

1. child   The child axis selects all the children of the context node and is the most used axis. Figure 5.3 shows the node-set containing all the nodes in the child axis of the context node. More than half of the steps in all the location paths will be specified using the child axis. Therefore, you can omit the child axis. *A step without an explicit axis is assumed to have the child axis.*

Here is an example of a location path that uses only the child axis.

```
child::rooms/child::room
```

This location path is almost always written as

```
rooms/room
```

2. attribute   The attribute axis selects the attributes of the context node. Figure 5.4 shows the nodes in the axis. The XPath specification does not specify an order of the attributes nodes.

The attribute axis is probably the second most used axis. It has the abbreviation @. When this abbreviation is used, the delimiter :: is omitted—for example,

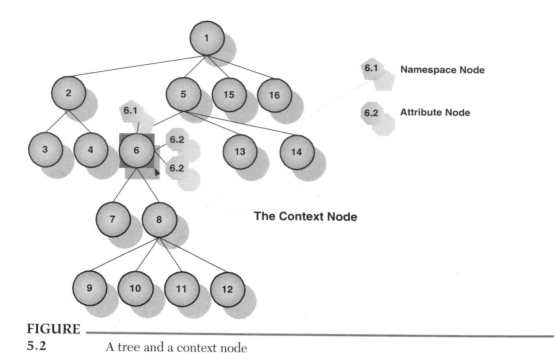

FIGURE

5.2   A tree and a context node

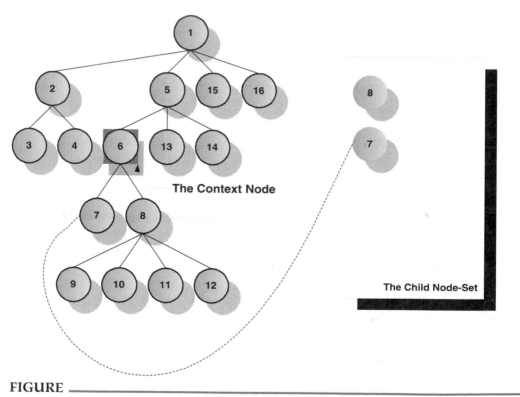

FIGURE

5.3   The node-set containing the nodes in the child axis of the context node

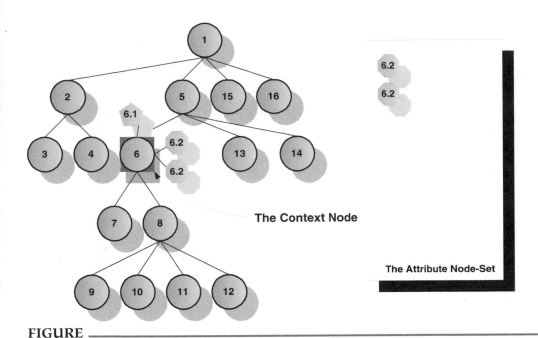

The Context Node

The Attribute Node-Set

FIGURE
5.4
The node-set containing the nodes in the attribute axis of the context node

`@name`, not `@::name`. Here is a location path with an attribute axis that you have seen before.

`room/@name`

You can also write it this way.

`room/attribute::name`

Usually, however, it's written in the abbreviated form.

3. self The self axis selects the context node itself. Figure 5.5 shows the node-set in the self axis. The self axis is frequently used as the value of the `select` attribute of the `xsl:value-of` when the string value of the context node is needed, and it is used frequently in other ways. One special location form, however, predominates when we use the self axis: `.`. This is an abbreviation of the location path

`self::node()`

We will talk about the node test `node()` in Section 5.2.4. It means "any node."

4. parent The parent axis selects only the parent of the context node. Figure 5.6 shows the parent of the context node as the only node in the node-set selected by the axis.

95

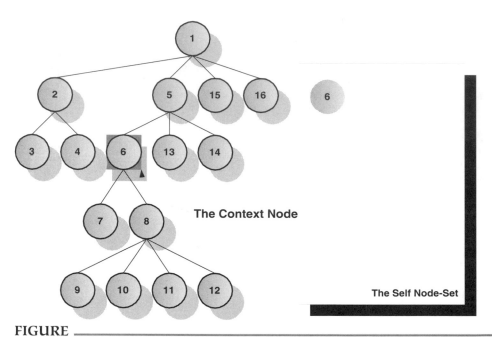

FIGURE
5.5   The node-set containing the nodes in the self axis of the context node

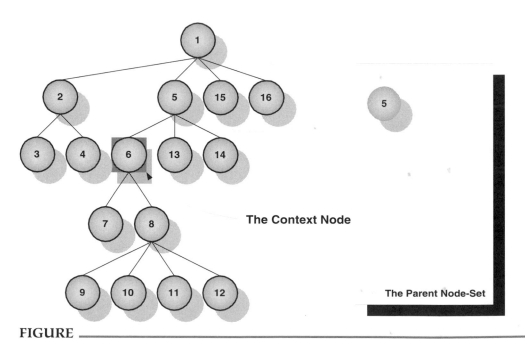

FIGURE
5.6   The node-set containing the nodes in the parent axis of the context node

In Chapter 3, we used the parent axis a few times. For example,

```
<H4>Room: <xsl:value-of select='../../@name'/></H4>
```

where

```
../../@name
```

is just an abbreviated version of

```
parent::node()/parent::node()/attribute::name
```

5. descendant   The descendant axis selects all the nodes that are descendants of the context node. Figure 5.7 shows the node-set in the descendant axis. Here is an example of a location path using the descendant axis.

```
descendant::node()
```

This will select all nodes contained in the current context node.

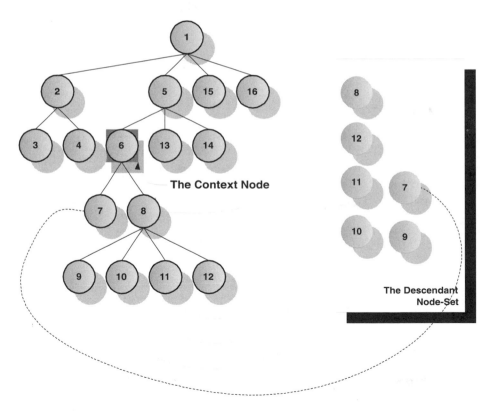

The Context Node

The Descendant Node-Set

FIGURE 5.7   The node-set containing the nodes in the descendant axis of the context node

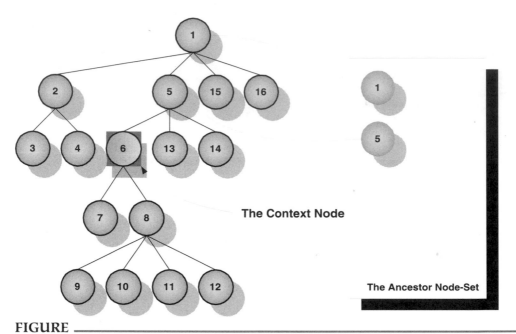

FIGURE
5.8   The node-set containing the nodes in the ancestor axis of the context node

6. ancestor   The ancestor axis selects all the nodes that are the ancestors of the context node. The node-set in the ancestor axis is shown in Figure 5.8. This axis is not used very often, probably because we feel more comfortable finding nodes by starting from the root and going to the current context node than going up from the current context node to the root.

7. preceding-sibling   The preceding-sibling axis selects all the nodes that are the preceding siblings of the context node. Figure 5.9 shows the node-set in the preceding-sibling axis for the context node.

The preceding-sibling axis can be used to find the previous node that is similar to the current context node. For instance, if you know the current context node is a `meeting` element and you want to find the previous `meeting` elements, you specify

```
preceding-sibling::meeting
```

8. following-sibling   The following-sibling axis selects all the nodes that are the following siblings of the context node. Figure 5.10 shows the node-set in the following-sibling axis.

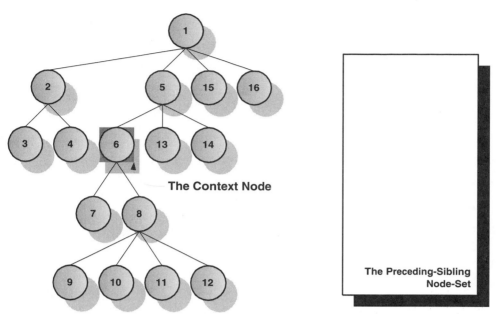

FIGURE
5.9   The node-set containing the nodes in the preceding-sibling axis of the context node

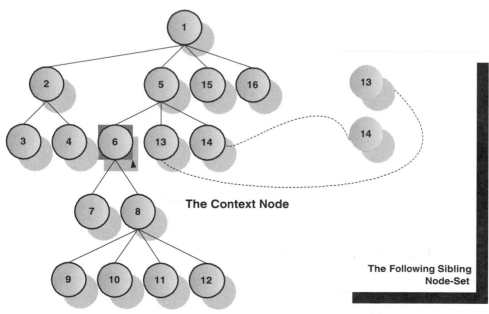

FIGURE
5.10   The node-set containing the nodes in the following-sibling axis of the context node

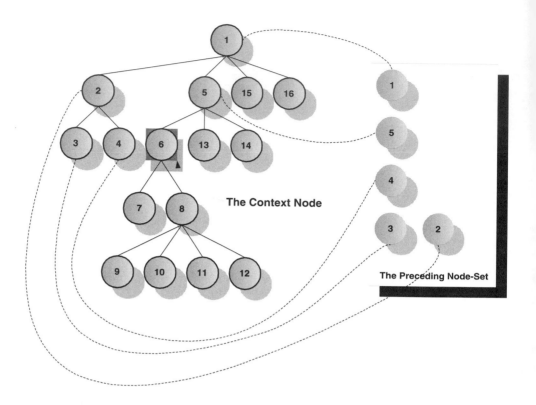

FIGURE
5.11   The node-set containing the nodes in the preceding axis of the context node

The following-sibling axis can be used in the same way as the preceding-sibling axis: to find the next occurrences of your current context node. Therefore, the next `meeting` element is

```
following-sibling::meeting
```

9. preceding The preceding axis selects all the nodes that precede the context node in the document order. Figure 5.11 shows all the nodes preceding the context node.

You may not find this axis terribly useful, but it might come in handy if you need to cross-reference some elements in an XML document. The preceding-

sibling axis may be too restrictive in that situation. For example, say you have
the following XML document fragment.

```
<book>
  <author>John Smith</author>
  <title>The Adventure of A Strange Character</title>
</book>
<book>
  <author>Brad Smith</author>
  <title>Omnibus? Is that a word?</title>
</book>
<book>
  <author>John Smith</author>
  <title>From the Head, not from the Heart: How to Survive in
  the business world</title>
</book>
```

If your context node is the `author` element of the third `book` element, and you
want to find the authors of the previous books, you can specify

```
preceding::author
```

and the result will be all the `author` elements before the current context node.

    10. following The following axis selects all the nodes that follow the con-
text node in the document order. Figure 5.12 shows all the nodes following
the context node. The following axis is seldom used. Usually you won't want to
match for what is only after the current context node.

    11. descendant-or-self The descendant-or-self axis selects all the nodes
that are descendants of the context node and the context node itself. Figure 5.13
shows the node-set in the descendant-or-self axis. The node-set is the same as
that in the descendant axis with the addition of the context node itself.

    You will probably find yourself using the descendant-or-self axis often be-
cause it is so convenient. For instance, when you want to find a `meeting` element, you can figure out what the current context node is and specify a location
path to match that element, but after a few unsuccessful attempts, you will
probably end up using

```
.//meeting
```

which is an abbreviated form of

```
self::node()/descendant-or-self::node()/child::meeting
```

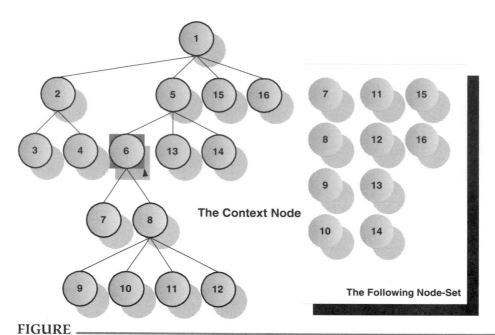

FIGURE
5.12   The node-set containing the nodes in the following axis of the context node

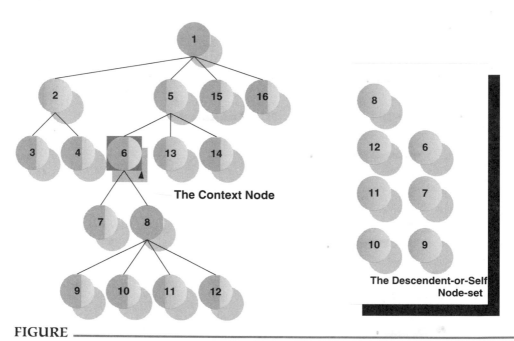

FIGURE
5.13   The node-set containing the nodes in the descendant-or-self axis of the context node

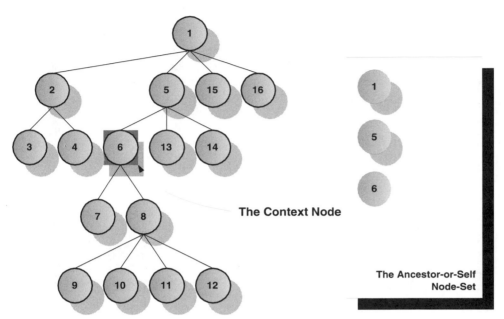

The Context Node

**The Ancestor-or-Self
Node-Set**

**FIGURE
5.14** The node-set containing the nodes in the ancestor-or-self axis of the context node

It will match all meeting elements that are descendants (and you always know the current context node is not a meeting element) of the current context node.

This will work most of the time. However, the location path is not very specific, and as a consequence, you usually have to do additional checking before you can nail down the element you are trying to match.

12. ancestor-or-self The ancestor-or-self axis selects all the ancestors of the context node and the context node itself. Figure 5.14 shows the node-set in this axis.

13. namespace The namespace axis selects the namespace attributes of the context node. This axis is seldom used when transforming XML documents to HTML documents. Figure 5.15 shows the node-set in the namespace axis of the context node.

Some axes select nodes that precede the context node in the document order, and some axes select nodes that follow the context node in the document order. Some axes select the context node itself in addition to nodes preceding or following the context node.

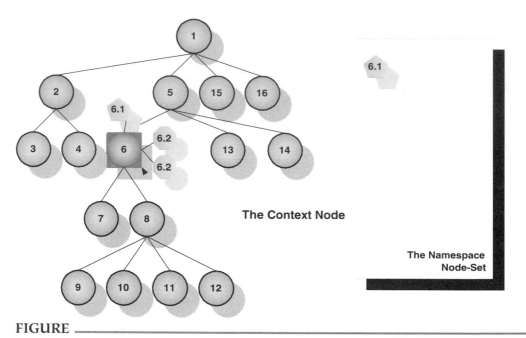

FIGURE
5.15   The node-set containing the nodes in the namespace axis of the context node

A **reverse** axis selects nodes preceding the context node and perhaps the context node as well. The other axes are **forward axes**. So, reverse axes include the ancestor, ancestor-or-self, preceding, and preceding-sibling axes.

Whether the axis is a reverse or a forward axis is critical when the position of the nodes is of primary importance. For instance, if you have the location path

```
preceding-sibling::meeting[position() = 1]
```

do you assume the `meeting` element is the first `meeting` child element of the parent of the current context node? Or could it be the most immediate previous `meeting` element of the current context node (see Figure 5.16)? The answer is the latter, because the `preceding-sibling` is a reverse axis, and counting is done from the current context node to the root of the document in reverse document order.

An axis also has a **principal node type.** The attribute axis has the attribute as its principal node type, the namespace axis has the namespace as its principal node type, and all the other axes have the element as their principal node type. The principal node type of an axis is used to differentiate the type of nodes in

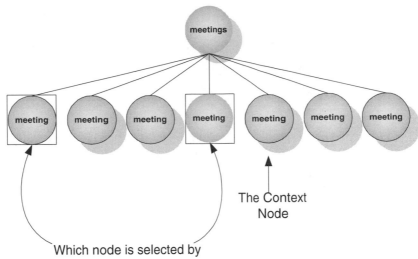

Which node is selected by
preceding-sibling::meeting[position()= 1]?

FIGURE

5.16   Importance of forward or reverse axis

the second part of a step: node-set. The second part of a step is the **node test** part.

5.2.4   *Node Tests*

In the node test, you can specify a name, a pattern for names, or a node type (a comment, a processing instruction, a text node, or any type of node) to filter out the nodes in which you have no interest.

Name Tests

Name tests are probably used more than 80 percent of the time in location paths. When a name test is used, the name of a node of the principal node type of the axis is specified. If there is no explicit axis, the child axis is used. Because there are only three kinds of principal node types—element, attribute, and namespace—name tests can be used only for these node types.

You can specify a literal name. For instance, if you want to select only the attribute with the name `location`, then use the step

```
@location
```

You can also specify * to match all the nodes of the principal node type. The namespace prefix can be used with *. For example, if you wanted to select the nodes on the child axis (principal node type is element) that have the namespace prefix book, you would specify

```
book:*
```

Remember, however, that the prefix is only an alias to a namespace URI. So the URI of the nodes will be compared with the URI of the book prefix. If an element node on the child axis has a namespace URI identical to the book prefix URI, the node is selected whether the prefix of the element matches book or not.

Let us look at one example. Suppose we have an XML document that looks like this.

```
<?xml version='1.0'?>
<books>
  <buku:book xmlns:buku='http://www.wireoptional.com/ontology'>
    A Malay book.
  </buku:book>
  <book:book xmlns:book='http://www.wireoptional.com/ontology'>
    An English book.
  </book:book>
</books>
```

To enumerate all the elements in the namespace with the URI

```
http://www.wireoptional.com/ontology
```

we can have the following XSLT document.

```
<xsl:stylesheet version='1.0'
    xmlns:xsl='http://www.w3.org/1999/XSL/Transform'>
  <xsl:output method='html'/>
  <xsl:template
    match='/' xmlns:book='http://www.wireoptional.com/ontology'>
    <HTML>
      <HEAD>
        <TITLE>Selecting nodes with different
               prefixes but the same namespace</TITLE>
      </HEAD>
      <BODY>
        <xsl:for-each select='books/book:*'>
```

```
        <H3><xsl:value-of select='name()'/></H3>
      </xsl:for-each>
    </BODY>
  </HTML>
 </xsl:template>
</xsl:stylesheet>
```

The result looks like this (if you use xt).

```
<HTML xmlns:book="http://www.wireoptional.com/ontology">
<HEAD>
<TITLE>Selecting nodes with different
              prefixes but the same namespace</TITLE>
</HEAD>
<BODY>
<H3>buku:book</H3>
<H3>book:book</H3>
</BODY>
</HTML>
```

Testing the Node Type

The other kind of node test selects only nodes of a certain type. You can select only the comments, only the text nodes, or only the processing instructions from the nodes on the axis of a context node.

To select only the comments, use the node test comment(). For instance, child::comment() selects only the children of the context node that are comments.

There are two ways to select processing instructions. You can select any processing instructions, or you can select only those processing instructions with a certain target. To select all processing instructions that are descendants of the context node, you can use descendant::processing-instruction(). To select only the processing instructions with the target java, you can use descendant::processing-instruction('java').

To select only the text nodes among the nodes on an axis of the context node, the node test text() can be used. For instance, to select all the text nodes that are following siblings of the context node, you can use following-sibling::text().

Sometimes it doesn't matter what type of node is selected by the axis. In that case, the node test node() can be used.

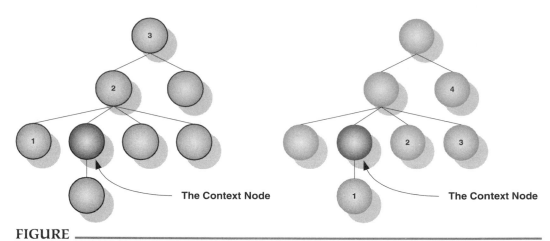

FIGURE
5.17   Proximity positions of nodes in the preceding and following axes of the context
node

Positions of Nodes in a Node-Set

We need to look at one more concept before we can talk about how to evaluate
a step. The nodes in a node-set do not have a fixed order. However, we can
impose an order to the nodes in a node-set according to the axis. If the axis is a
forward axis, the nodes are put in document order. If the axis is a reverse axis,
the nodes are put in reverse document order. Once the nodes are in order, the
position of the node in that order is called its **proximity position.** Figure 5.17
shows how the proximity positions of the nodes are computed on the nodes on
the preceding and the following axes of the context node.

Now that we know how the axis and the node-test portions of a step are
specified, we can go on to evaluation of the two parts.

5.2.5   *Evaluating the Axis and Node Test*

Before a location path is evaluated, the XSLT processor constructs a context.
As we already know, the context contains a context node, the context size, the
context position of the context node, the variables in scopes, the functions
available for the evaluation, and the namespaces in effect. This context will
be the basis for the evaluation of the location path. Here is how a step with no
predicates is evaluated:

1. Take the context node, examine the axis of the step, and find all the nodes
   in the axis of the context node and put them in a node-set.

2. Examine the node test of the step. If it is a name test, then remove all the nodes in the node-set that do not match the name specified. If the node test is a node-type test, then remove all the nodes in the node-set that are not the node type specified. The result is a node-set.

3. Compute the proximity positions of all the nodes in the node-set according to the axis of the step. If you want to remove more nodes in a step according to some criteria that cannot be specified using an axis and a node test, you must use one or more predicates to specify the criteria.

5.2.6   *Predicates*

Each step in a location path can have predicates that specify additional conditions. (Some steps have no predicates.) These conditions are applied to the nodes selected by the node test from the nodes in the axis. If there is no predicate in a step, then the nodes selected by the node test will be put into a node-set. This node-set is the result node-set for the step.

Let's say we have predicates. This is the procedure, starting with the first predicate.

1. Create a context for each of the nodes in the node-set that results from evaluating the axis and the node test part of the step. The node is now the new context node. The number of nodes in the node-set is the new context size. The proximity position of the node in the node-set is the new context position.

2. Use each of these contexts to evaluate the predicate. Convert the result to a Boolean value. If the Boolean value is true, the node is kept. If the value is false, the node is discarded.

3. Collect all the nodes that are kept. This is the new context. Recompute the proximity positions of the nodes.

4. Follow the same context-creation process again to obtain a new set of contexts. For each of the contexts, evaluate the second predicate.

5. Continue this process until all predicates have been evaluated. The final set of nodes is the final node-set of the step.

If a predicate only has a number—say, 10—then the predicate is assumed to be an abbreviation of `[position() = 10]`. The function `position()` simply returns the context position of the context node.

Let's look at some examples. In Chapter 3, the first location path that has a predicate is

```
date[year=$year and month=$month and day=$day]
```

This location path has only one step, the implicit axis of the step is the child axis, and the node test is a name test for the `date` element (because the principal node type of the child axis is the element). Before we evaluate the predicate, we know that the axis and the node test evaluates to the `date` child elements of the initial context node.

Then for each of the nodes in the node-set, we create a context. Suppose the source XML document is *bookings.xml*, provided in Chapter 3. Let's assume that the initial context node is the `<room name='Red'>` element. After the node test, we have (details of the meetings omitted)

```
<date>
  <year>2000</year>
  <month>June</month>
  <day>23</day>
  <meeting> ... </meeting>
  <meeting> ... </meeting>
</date>
<date>
  <year>2000</year>
  <month>July</month>
  <day>10</day>
  <meeting> ... </meeting>
</date>
```

The proximity position of the first node is 1, and the proximity position of the second node is 2.

In Chapter 3, we used the date June 23, 2000. Therefore, we can assume the value of the variable `year` to be `2000`, the value of the variable `month` to be `June`, and the value of the variable `day` to be `23`.

We will create two contexts. The first has the first `date` element as the context node, its context position is 1, its context size is 2, and its set of visible variables includes these three variables (`year`, `month`, and `day`). The other elements of the context are not needed here. The second context has the second `date` element as the context node, its context position is 2, its context size is 2, and its set of visible variables is the same as for the first context.

Now, evaluate the predicate using the first context. The predicate checks if the value of the location path `year` is the same as `$year`, the value of the location path `month` is the same as `$month`, and the value of the location `day` is the same as `$day`.

Notice how you are allowed to use location paths inside a predicate. To evaluate the predicate, we need to find out the values of three location paths: `year`, `month`, and `day`. Using the first context we constructed, the value of `year` is

```
<year>2000</year>
```

which is a node-set with only the above node. The value of `month` is

```
<month>June</month>
```

which, again, is a node-set with only the above node. Finally, the value of `day` is

```
<day>23</day>
```

which is also a node-set with only the above node.

We already know how to evaluate these single-step location paths with no predicate. We can break down the expression in the predicate to `year=$year`, `month=$month`, and `day=$day`. (We'll discuss how to compare a node-set to a string later; for now, we only need to know that all these expressions compare the values of the text nodes to the value of the variables.) Since all of them match, the predicate evaluates to the Boolean value true. The context node for the first context will stay.

We now repeat the steps with the second context. The three location paths evaluate to

```
<year>2000</year>
```

for `year`,

```
<month>July</month>
```

for `month`, and

```
<day>10</day>
```

for `day`. Comparing their text nodes with the values of the variables, we find one match. The text nodes of the location paths `month` and `day` do not match the values of the variables `month` and `day`, respectively. The context node of the second context is removed. Keeping only the first `date`, the result node-set of the location path

```
date[year=$year and month=$month and day=$day]
```

is then a node-set that contains only the first `date` element. If there are additional predicates, we simply repeat the constructions of the contexts.

5.2.7   *Summary of Evaluating One Step*

Let's just summarize what we have learned about the evaluation of a step in a location path. A step has three parts: the axis, the node test, and the optional list of predicates. The axis selects only nodes that are related—in terms of locations in the XML document—to the context node in a certain way. The node test chooses nodes with a certain name or nodes of a certain type. The predicates are used to specify criteria that are more complicated.

The evaluation of a step in a location path is always based on the context node in question. Finding the nodes in the axis and matching the node test use only the context node at the beginning. The result is a node-set with the proximity positions of the nodes computed. To evaluate the predicates, the nodes selected by the axis and the node test become context nodes in new contexts. Each of the new contexts is used to evaluate the first predicate. Only those nodes whose contexts evaluate the predicate to true will stay. If there is a second predicate, the nodes that stay after evaluation of the first predicate will go through the same process. The process is repeated until all the predicates of the step have been evaluated. The final set of nodes are put into a node-set to become the result node-set of the step. These are only for one step of a location path, but a location path can have multiple steps.

5.3   Combining Steps

A location path can have one or more steps. If there is more than one step, then two consecutive steps are combined using either `/` or `//`. The location path is then processed.

1. Determine the initial context for the location path. This is done by the XSLT processor.

2. Evaluate the first step, using the context given by the XSLT processor.

3. If there is a next step, construct a new context for each of the nodes in the result node-set of the previous step. The node is the new context node. The number of nodes in the node-set is the new context size. The proximity position of the context node in the node-set is the new context position. Evaluate the second step for each of the new context nodes.

4. Combine the result node-sets of a step to form one node-set. If you do not combine them, the proximity positions of the nodes will be incorrect.

5. Repeat this process until all steps have been processed.

6. Put all the result node-sets into one node-set. Remove duplicates. This is the result node-set of the whole location path.

Why do we combine the result node-sets in each step to form one big node-set? Suppose you have the following XML document.

```
<node1><number>1</number>
  <node2><number>1</number>
    <node3><number>1</number></node3>
    <node3><number>2</number></node3>
    <node3><number>3</number></node3>
    <node3><number>4</number></node3>
    <node3><number>5</number></node3>
  </node2>
  <node2><number>2</number>
    <node3><number>1</number></node3>
    <node3><number>2</number></node3>
    <node3><number>3</number></node3>
    <node3><number>4</number></node3>
    <node3><number>5</number></node3>
  </node2>
  <node2><number>3</number>
    <node3><number>1</number></node3>
    <node3><number>2</number></node3>
    <node3><number>3</number></node3>
    <node3><number>4</number></node3>
    <node3><number>5</number></node3>
  </node2>
  <node2><number>4</number>
    <node3><number>1</number></node3>
    <node3><number>2</number></node3>
    <node3><number>3</number></node3>
    <node3><number>4</number></node3>
    <node3><number>5</number></node3>
  </node2>
</node1>
```

And suppose you have the following simple XSLT document.

```
<xsl:stylesheet version='1.0'
  xmlns:xsl='http://www.w3.org/1999/XSL/Transform'>

  <xsl:output method='html'/>

  <xsl:template match='/'>
    <HTML>
      <HEAD><TITLE>Multiple Steps</TITLE></HEAD>
      <BODY>
        <xsl:apply-templates select='node1/node2/node3'/>
      </BODY>
    </HTML>
  </xsl:template>

  <xsl:template match='node3'>
    <P>Position is: <xsl:value-of select='position()'/></P>
  </xsl:template>
</xsl:stylesheet>
```

This is the result.

```
<HTML>
<HEAD>
<TITLE>Multiple Steps</TITLE>
</HEAD>
<BODY>
<P>Position is: 1</P>
<P>Position is: 2</P>
<P>Position is: 3</P>
<P>Position is: 4</P>
<P>Position is: 5</P>
<P>Position is: 6</P>
<P>Position is: 7</P>
<P>Position is: 8</P>
<P>Position is: 9</P>
<P>Position is: 10</P>
<P>Position is: 11</P>
<P>Position is: 12</P>
```

```
<P>Position is: 13</P>
<P>Position is: 14</P>
<P>Position is: 15</P>
<P>Position is: 16</P>
<P>Position is: 17</P>
<P>Position is: 18</P>
<P>Position is: 19</P>
<P>Position is: 20</P>
</BODY>
</HTML>
```

Notice how all the nodes selected are combined. This is different from the output from the following XSLT document.

```
<xsl:stylesheet version='1.0'
  xmlns:xsl='http://www.w3.org/1999/XSL/Transform'>

  <xsl:output method='html'/>

  <xsl:template match='/'>
    <HTML>
      <HEAD><TITLE>Multiple Steps</TITLE></HEAD>
      <BODY>
        <xsl:apply-templates select='node1'/>
      </BODY>
    </HTML>
  </xsl:template>

  <xsl:template match='node1'>
    <xsl:apply-templates select='node2'/>
  </xsl:template>

  <xsl:template match='node2'>
    <xsl:apply-templates select='node3'/>
  </xsl:template>

  <xsl:template match='node3'>
    <P>Position is: <xsl:value-of select='position()'/></P>
  </xsl:template>
</xsl:stylesheet>
```

This XSLT document simulates the output that would be produced. The output looks like this.

```
<HTML>
<HEAD>
<TITLE>Multiple Steps</TITLE>
</HEAD>
<BODY>
<P>Position is: 1</P>
<P>Position is: 2</P>
<P>Position is: 3</P>
<P>Position is: 4</P>
<P>Position is: 5</P>
<P>Position is: 1</P>
<P>Position is: 2</P>
<P>Position is: 3</P>
<P>Position is: 4</P>
<P>Position is: 5</P>
<P>Position is: 1</P>
<P>Position is: 2</P>
<P>Position is: 3</P>
<P>Position is: 4</P>
<P>Position is: 5</P>
<P>Position is: 1</P>
<P>Position is: 2</P>
<P>Position is: 3</P>
<P>Position is: 4</P>
<P>Position is: 5</P>
</BODY>
</HTML>
```

We will use an example from Chapter 3 again. One of the first location paths we have in that chapter is

```
bookings/lastUpdated/@date
```

The context node is the root of the XML document in *bookings.xml*. Of course, this location path is easy: The first step selects one node, the document element. The second step selects one node again, as there is only one `lastUpdated` element in the `bookings` element. And finally, the last step selects the `date` attribute of the `lastUpdated` element, again only one node. The result node-

set for the whole location path has only one node, the `date` attribute of the `lastUpdated` element.

The second location path from Chapter 3 is

```
rooms/room
```

and the context node is the root of the XML document in *rooms.xml*. The first step selects the document element. This time the second step selects all the `room` element child nodes of the document element. The result node-set contains all the `room` elements.

Finally, let's look at the location path

```
date/meeting/period[from &lt;= $timeSlot and to &gt; $timeSlot]
```

The initial context node is a `room` element. The first step selects all the `date` elements. For each of the `date` elements, select its `meeting` child elements. Then for each of the `meeting` elements, select only the elements that satisfy the predicate

```
from &lt;= $timeSlot and to &gt; $timeSlot
```

5.3.1 *Initial Context*

When you specify a location path, you can use the context node given by the XSLT processor or you can start from the root of the source tree of the context node. Simply prefix your location path with the `/` character. Such a location path is called an **absolute location path**. For an absolute location step, the initial context contains only the root of the source tree.

You can also select the root of a different source tree by using the `document()` function. For instance, if you want to use the root of the source tree representing the XML document *a.xml*, specify `document('a.xml')`. Selecting the document element of the document is simply `document('a.xml')/*`, if you do not care about the name of the document element.

You can also select a node using its ID with the `id()` function. Of course, you can only use this function if a node in the source tree has the ID specified in the function.[2] For instance, `id('NODE1')/descendant::second` selects the descendants of the node with the ID `NODE1` that have the name `second`.

---

2. In an XML document type declaration, you can define an attribute of an element to be of type `ID`. The value of an attribute with this type is the ID checked by the `id()` function.

You can also select all the nodes that have a certain key. The function `key()` is used for this purpose. (See Section C.1.17 for more details on how to use this function.)

You can select the descendants of the root and the root itself as the initial context. This is done by using `//` as the prefix of a location path. For instance, `//text()` selects all the text nodes in the source tree. This location path is an abbreviated form of `/descendant-or-self::node()/text()`. The character `//` is also used in place of `/` to separate consecutive steps to mean `descendant-or-self::node()`.

You can also use an expression as the initial step. The expression must return a location path. It can have predicates that are used the same way as predicates in other steps. The following is a location path with the first step as an expression.

```
(//second | //third)/fourth
```

This location path means: For all the descendants of the roots that have the name `second` or the name `third`, choose their children with the name `fourth`.

You can try this by using the following XML document

```
<first>
  <second>
    <fourth/>
  </second>
  <third>
    <fourth/>
  </third>
</first>
```

and this template

```
<xsl:template match='/'>
  <xsl:for-each select='(//second | //third)/fourth'>
    <xsl:message><xsl:value-of select='name(..)'/></xsl:message>
  </xsl:for-each>
</xsl:template>
```

Abbreviated Axis and Node Test Pairs

There are some abbreviations that are convenient for specifying location paths. The step `self::node()` can be replaced by `..` Notice that no predicate is allowed when this abbreviation is used. For example, `.[2]` is not allowed.

You have seen that the step `descendant-or-self::node()` can be shortened to `//` between two steps. No predicates are allowed when this abbreviation is used. Also, two consecutive `//`s are not allowed.

5.3.2   *Designing a Location Path*

When you design an XSLT document, it is usually apparent what the result node-set of a location path should look like. The challenge is in developing a good location path that produces the node-set you want.

First, write down a location path that will give you the desired node-set. You can test the location path by using a test XML document. Once you are satisfied that it indeed produces the node-set you want, you can then consider the efficiency of the location path.

Make sure you select the minimum number of nodes in each of the steps. You want to use the most restrictive axis possible, which, in combination with the most restrictive node test, should give you a very good location path.

Avoid predicates. Predicates are expensive[3] because each node of the node-set selected by the axis and node test will be used as the context node for the predicates. Predicates with embedded location paths are especially expensive.

Of the three parts of a step in a location path, the cheapest is the node test. Specify it as simply as possible. Some axes are less expensive than others, particularly `self`, `following-sibling`, `preceding-sibling`, `parent`, `ancestor`, `child` and `ancestor-or-self`.

Of course, if the context node has a lot of siblings, the two axes that select the siblings of the context node become more expensive. But in general, selecting the siblings and the ancestors of the context node is usually cheaper than selecting the descendants of the context node.

In most cases, the most expensive axes are the `preceding` and the `following`. Of course, if the context node is very close to the beginning of the document, then the `preceding` axis will be inexpensive. A context node close to the end of the document means the `following` axis is even cheaper. The most expensive location paths are those that start with `//`, because they select all the nodes in the source tree.

Now we are ready to talk about data types and their operations.

---

3. I define "expensive" as the amount of processing required by the XSLT processor. No matter how efficient the processor, processing XPath expressions with predicates will take up more time than processing XPath expressions without predicates.

5.4   Data Types and Operations

Remember that there are four data types in XPath: numbers, strings, Booleans, and node-sets. Operations in XPath include or, and, = , !=, <, <=, >, and >=. The operators = and != are called **comparison operations**. The operators <, >, <=, and >= are called **relational operations**. All of them are left-associative—that is,

    1 < 2 < 3

means

    (1 < 2) < 3

In addition, arithmetic operations +, -, *, div, mod, and the unary negation - operation are defined for numbers.

5.4.1   *Strings*

Only the comparison operations take strings as operands. All the other operations convert the string operands to whatever data type is native to the operation before the operation is carried out.

Comparison and Relational Operations

It is easy to determine if two strings are equal: If they have identical UCS character sequences, they are equal.

All characters are significant, including white spaces. For instance, ab␣c and abc are different, as are abc␣ and abc␣␣.

A string in a relational operation is first converted to a number, which is then used for the operation. For example, the result of 123 < 99 is the expected false.

5.4.2   *Numbers*

XPath provides operations for numbers: addition, subtraction, multiplication, division, and remainder.

Addition and Subtraction

The operator used to represent addition is +. Subtraction is represented by -, but because - is a valid character in XML names, always surround the subtraction operator with whitespace. For example, abc␣-␣def means evaluating the location paths abc and def. When they are converted into numbers and sub-tracted, the result is a number. On the other hand, abc-def means evaluating the location path abc-def (abc-def is a valid name for elements). The result is a node-set.

Multiplication, Division, and Remainder

The operator used to represent multiplication is *, and that for division is the word div. It is possible for division to yield an answer that cannot be represented by a number—for example, 1 div 0 is positive infinity.

The operator used to represent remainder is the word mod. Again, it is possible that the remainder may yield an answer that is not a proper number. The sign of the remainder can be quite confusing.

> A positive number mod a positive number yields a positive number: 501 mod 2 is 1.

> A positive number mod a negative number yields a positive number: 501 mod -2 is 1.

> A negative number mod a positive number yields a negative number: -501 mod 2 is -1.

> A negative number mod a negative number yields a negative number: -501 mod -2 is -1.

Converting to String

A number can have the following values.

1. NaN, not a number
2. Positive zero
3. Negative zero
4. Positive infinity
5. Negative infinity
6. One of the normal numbers: e.g., 1, 0.2, 30, etc.

A normal number is represented by its decimal number, with negative numbers preceded by a minus sign. For NaN, the string NaN is used. For both the positive and negative zeroes, 0 is used. For positive infinity, the string Infinity is used. For negative infinity, the string -Infinity is used.

You can explicitly convert a number to a string by using the `string()` function. For instance, `string(123)` is 123. You usually use an `xsl:value-of` element to evaluate an expression like

```
<xsl:value-of select='string(123)'/>
```

Of course, you can use it wherever an expression is allowed.

Converting a String to a Number

To convert a string to a number, the leading and trailing white spaces, if there are any, are first removed from the string. Then, if the resulting string has a minus sign, the number is a negative number. The format of the string must adhere to the format of a number as explained in Section 5.1.1. If there is a non-digit character or the format is not valid, the NaN value is used. You can explicitly convert a string to a number by using the `number()` function—for example, `number(45)` is 45.

Comparison and Relational Operations

Comparing two numbers is straightforward in most cases, but there are certain rules for unusual cases.

> If one of the numbers has the NaN value, then all the relational operators return `false`. The equality operator also returns `false`. However, the inequality operator (`!=`) returns `true`. This brings out the interesting fact that NaN `!=` NaN is true.

> Negative infinity is smaller than every other number; but it is equal to another negative infinity.

> Positive infinity is greater than every other number; but it is equal to another positive infinity.

> Positive zero and negative zero are equal to each other.

> Other numbers follow the normal rules.

If one of the operands of a comparison or a relational operation is a number and the other is a string, then the string is first converted to a number before the comparison or relational operation takes place.

5.4.3   *Booleans*

There are two operators that apply to Boolean values only: **and** and **or**. Both operators take two Boolean values. For the **and** operator, if both Boolean values are `true`, the result is also true. Otherwise, the result is false. For the **or**

First Value	Second Value	Result of and	Result of or
true	true	true	true
true	false	false	true
false	true	false	true
false	false	false	false

TABLE 5.1   The result of applying and and or

operator, the result is false only if both values are false. Table 5.1 illustrates the result of using the two operators on all possible Boolean values. For example,

```
$val > 5 and $val < 300
```

returns `true` if the numeric value of the `val` variable is greater than 5 and smaller than 300.

Because you cannot specify a literal Boolean value, you must use the functions `true()` and `false()` if you need explicit Boolean values. Of course, you can also use any expression to produce the Boolean value you want. For instance, 1 = 1 produces the Boolean value true, and 1 = 0 produces the Boolean value false.

Converting a String into a Boolean Value

If a string has at least one character, then the string, when converted to a Boolean value, is considered to have the value `true`. If the string is empty, then it is converted to `false`.

Converting a Number into a Boolean Value

A number is converted to `true` if the number is not positive zero, negative zero, or NaN. Otherwise, the number is converted to `false`. According to this rule, converting the string `false` to Boolean produces the Boolean value true. You can convert a string to a Boolean value by using the function `boolean()`. For instance, `boolean('null')` produces the Boolean value true.

Converting a Boolean Value into a Number

The true value is converted to the number 1. The false value is converted to the number 0. The function `number()` can be used to convert a Boolean value to a number. The expression `number(boolean('network'))` is the number 1.

Converting a Boolean into a String

The false value is converted to the string `false`. The truth value is converted to the string `true`.

Comparison and Relational Operations

The true value is equal to itself and not equal to the false value. The false value is equal to itself and not equal to the true value.

When using a relational operator, Boolean values are first converted to numbers. Table 5.2 lists all the possibilities.

If one of the operands of a comparison operation is a Boolean value and the other a number, then the number is first converted to a Boolean before they are compared. If the operation is a relational operation, then the Boolean value is first converted to a number before the relational operation is carried out. For example, `true() = 123` is true: 123 is converted to Boolean first, yielding the Boolean value true. And `true() < -2` is `false`: `true()` is converted to a number first, yielding the number 1, and 1 is greater than -2.

If one of the operands of a comparison operation is a Boolean value and the other a string, then the string is first converted to a Boolean value before the operation is carried out. If the operation is a relational operation, then both the Boolean and the string are converted to numbers before they are compared. For example, `true() = ''` is `false`: `''` is converted to Boolean first, yielding false. And `true() < '23'` is true: `true()` is converted to a number first, yielding 1, and then `'23'` is converted to a number, yielding 23, and 1 is less than 23.

5.4.4   *Node-Sets*

The operation that takes two node-sets is the union operation: `|`. It takes two node-sets and combines all the nodes in the node-sets together after removing duplicate nodes.

Converting Other Data Types into Node-Sets

It is not allowed to convert a number, a string or a Boolean to a node-set.

Converting into a String

Converting a node-set into a string is based on converting a node into a string, and it depends on the type of node. Any node can be converted into a string.

First Operand	Operator	Second Operand	Result
true	=	true	true
true	!=	true	false
true	<	true	false
true	<=	true	true
true	>	true	false
true	>=	true	true
true	=	false	false
true	!=	false	true
true	<	false	false
true	<=	false	false
true	>	false	true
true	>=	false	true
false	=	true	false
false	!=	true	true
false	<	true	true
false	<=	true	true
false	>	true	false
false	>=	true	false
false	=	false	true
false	!=	false	false
false	<	false	false
false	<=	false	true
false	>	false	false
false	>=	false	true

TABLE 5.2   The comparison of two Boolean values

THE ROOT NODE.   Converting the root node into a string is equivalent to removing all markups from the XML document. The character data of the document is the string value of the root.

ELEMENT NODE.   To convert an element node into a string, remove all the markups contained by the element. Suppose the following is the XML document.

```
<story> <writer email="prautins@jmedium.com">Peter Rautins</writer>
<dateline>(posted May 23, 3:15 pm)</dateline>
<leadin>Dan Hughes quit as coach of the Edmonston
Farmers on Monday after
refusing an offer to return for another season
at the same salary he
earned in 1998-2000.</leadin></story>
```

Its string value is

```
Peter Rautins
(posted May 23, 3:15 pm)
Dan Hughes quit as coach of the Edmonston
Farmers on Monday after
refusing an offer to return for another season
at the same salary he
earned in 1998-2000.
```

ATTRIBUTE. The string value of an attribute is the normalized value of the attribute value. Normalization of attribute values is already half done when an XML document is converted into an XML tree, as all the entity references are replaced. This is the remainder of the normalization process.

1. Consecutive linefeed, carriage return, space, and tab characters are replaced by a space character ␣. The sequence 
 is replaced by one single .

2. If the XML parser is a validating parser (a kind of parser for XML documents that checks if an XML document is valid or not) and the attribute type is character data, then this is the end of the normalization process. If the type is not character data, then the leading and trailing whitespaces are stripped from the attribute value.

3. If the XML parser used by the XSLT processor is not a validating one, then this is also the end of the normalization process.

The string value of an element node does not include the string values of its attributes. Suppose an element looks like this.

```
<top name='identification'/>
```

The string value of the attribute name is identification.

NAMESPACE.   To find the string value of a namespace prefix, get the namespace URI of the prefix. If the URI is a relative URI, the absolute URI must be computed first. The absolute URI is the string value of the namespace prefix.

PROCESSING INSTRUCTION.   The string value of a processing instruction starts from the first non-whitespace character after the target of the processing instruction to the last non-whitespace character leading to the ending ?>. For instance, if the processing instruction is like this

```
<?java class='java.io.*'?>
```

then the target is java and the string value of the processing instruction is class='java.io.*'.

COMMENT.   To find the string value of a comment, strip out the opening <!-- and the closing -->. The result is the string value of the comment. For instance, if the comment node is

```
<!-- This is a comment -->
```

then the string value of the node is This␣is␣a␣comment.

TEXT NODE.   The character data of a text node is its string value.

Converting a Node-Set into a String

The string value of a node-set is the string value of the first node in the document order. It is possible to have a node-set containing nodes from two different documents—for example, when the document() function is used, you would have document('a.xml')/* | document('b.xml')/*. The relative order of the two roots is up to the XSLT processor.

Converting a Node-Set to a Number

To convert a node-set to a number, first convert the node-set to a string and then convert the string to a number. Figure 5.18 shows this process.

Converting a Node-Set to a Boolean Value

To convert a node-set to a Boolean value, first determine if the node-set is empty. If the node-set is empty, then it is converted to false; otherwise, it is converted to true.

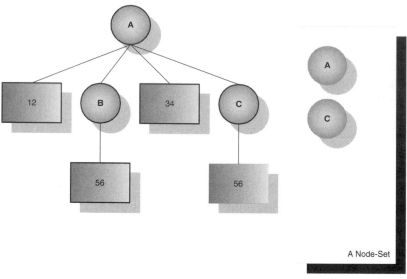

A Node-Set

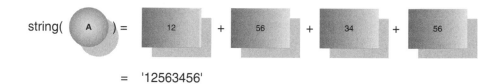

= '12563456'

number('12563456') = 12563456

FIGURE

5.18   Converting a node-set to a number

Comparing and Other Relational Operations

To compare a node-set and a string, convert all the nodes in the node-set to strings. If at least one of the strings compares to the string returning **true**, then the comparison of the node-set and the string is also true. Otherwise, the comparison of the node-set and the string returns **false**.

Using the node-set in Figure 5.18, suppose you are comparing the string that is 56 and the operator that is =. The result is **true** because node C in the node-set has the string value of 56. Node A has the string value of 12563456, which, of course, is not equal to 56.

To compare a node-set and a number, convert all the nodes to strings and then convert all the strings to numbers. If at least one number matches the number returning **true**, then the comparison also returns **true**. Otherwise, the comparison of the node-set and the number returns **false**.

To compare a node-set and a Boolean value, convert the node-set to a Boolean value first. Compare the two Boolean values. If the result is true, then the comparison is true. Otherwise, the result is false.

To compare two node-sets, convert each node in both node-sets into a string. If there is at least one node in the first node-set that compares to one node in the second node-set and returns true, the comparison returns true; otherwise, the result is false.

Figure 5.19 shows two node-sets. These two node-sets are not equal, because none of the nodes in the first node-set has a string value equal to the string value of any node in the second node-set. If the operator is <, then the first node-set is less than the second node-set. If the operator is >, then the first node-set is greater than the second node-set. This may sound contradictory, but there is a node (node c) in the first node-set whose value, after being converted to a string and then to a number, is less than a node (node B) in the second node-set after it too has been converted to a string and then a number. Also, after conversion, node A in the first node-set is greater than node B in the second node-set. Table 5.3 lists all the conversions necessary to compare two operands.

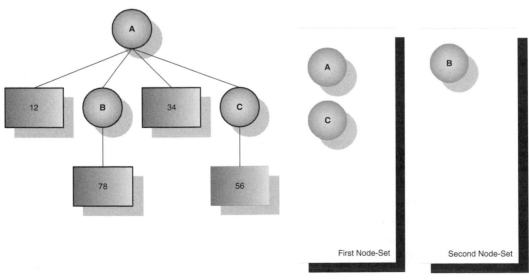

FIGURE 5.19   Two node-sets

One Operand Is	Operator	The Other Operand Is	Convert First Operand to	Convert Second Operand to
String	= or !=	String	No conversion	No conversion
String	<, <=, >, or >=	String	Number	Number
String	= or !=	Number	Number	No conversion
String	<, <=, >, or >=	Number	Number	No conversion
String	= or !=	Boolean	Boolean	No conversion
String	<, <=, >, or >=	Boolean	Number	Number
String	= or !=	Node-set	No conversion	Convert each node in the node-set to string and compare to first operand
String	<, <=, >, or >=	Node-set	No conversion	Convert each node in the node-set to string and compare to first operand
Number	= or !=	Number	No conversion	No conversion
Number	<, <=, >, or >=	Number	No conversion	No conversion
Number	= or !=	Boolean	Boolean	No conversion
Number	<, <=, >, or >=	Boolean	No conversion	Number
Number	= or !=	Node-set	No conversion	Convert each node in the node-set to string and then to number and compare to first operand
Number	<, <=, >, or >=	Node-set	No conversion	Convert each node in the node-set to string and then to number and compare to first operand
Boolean	= or !=	Boolean	No conversion	No conversion
Boolean	<, <=, >, or >=	Boolean	Number	Number
Boolean	= or !=	Node-set	No conversion	Boolean
Boolean	<, <=, >, or >=	Node-set	No conversion	Boolean
Node-set	= or !=	Node-set	No conversion	No conversion
Node-set	<, <=, >, or >=	Node-set	No conversion	No conversion

TABLE 5.3   The conversion table for different operands for comparison

Priority (Highest to Lowest)	Operators
1	- (negation)
2	*, div, mod
3	+, -
4	<, <=, >, >=
5	=, !=
6	and
7	or
8	|

TABLE
5.4   The priorities of the operators in XPath

5.4.5   *Operator Priorities*

The priority of the operators in XPath is like that in many other programming languages. Table 5.4 shows the priorities, from the highest to the lowest.

5.5   Names of Nodes

This is a good time to explain the different names used in XML. Every element, attribute, namespace, and processing-instruction node has a prefix. Comment nodes, text nodes, and the root node, on the other hand, do not have names.

5.5.1   *Expanded Names*

Although expanded names have been associated with only element nodes and attributes so far, XPath assigns expanded names to other types of nodes as well.

The Root Node

The root node of a document has no expanded name.

Elements and Attributes

The expanded name of an element node is the combination of the local-name and the URI associated with the namespace of the local-name. If the namespace is not present, then the URI is the one declared as the URI for the default namespace. If the default namespace does not have a namespace declaration, then the URI is null.

It is the same for attributes—for example,

```
<kk:x xmlns:kk='http://www.jmedium.com'/>
```

has the local-name x and the URI http://www.jmedium.com. The expanded name consists of x and http://www.jmedium.com.

Suppose the XML document looks like this.

```
<x xmlns='http://www.jmedium.com/default'>
  <y/>
</x>
```

Then the expanded name for the x element is the combination of local-name x and URI http://www.jmedium.com/default. The expanded name for the y element is local-name y and URI http://www.jmedium.com/default.

Namespace Nodes

For a namespace node, the local-name is the namespace name. The URI is empty—for example, in

```
<x xmlns:abc='http://www.jmedium.com'/>
```

the namespace node xmlns:abc has the local-name abc and no URI. Be careful to separate the expanded name of the node and the association of a URI with a namespace.

Processing Instructions

The target of the processing instruction is the local-name, and the URI is empty. For example,

```
<?java class='java.io'?>
```

has the local-name java and a null URI.

Comment Nodes

Comment nodes do not have expanded names (and they don't have local names either).

Text Nodes

Text nodes do not have expanded names or local names.

5.5.2   *Some Oddities*

The conversion rules in XPath can produce some strange results. To prevent conversion mishaps, study the conversion rules carefully. If you are in doubt, check the rules again to ensure that you do not have the wrong steps.

Here are some odd results you may see.

> The expression `boolean('false')` evaluates to the Boolean value true.

> The expression `number(boolean('0'))` results in the number 1.

> The expression `string(boolean('false'))` results in the string `'true'`.

5.6   Examples of XPath Expressions

Let's look at a few examples of XPath expressions. Some are samples, and some are from a real project.

This location path selects `chapter` elements whose `name` attribute is `'introduction'` and whose parent is a `book` element and the document element of the document.

```
/book/chapter[@name = 'introduction']
```

This location path selects all the `chapter` elements in the document only if there is a `book` element in the document with a `chapter` child element whose `name` attribute is `'introduction'`.

```
//chapter[//book/chapter[@name = 'introduction']]
```

The result of this XPath expression is the number 1.

```
1
```

This location path selects the `box` child nodes of the context node whose `name` attribute has the value `'analyst_column'`.

```
box[@name='analyst_column']
```

This location path returns true if the context node has exactly one `story` descendant. The XPath function `count` returns the number of nodes in a node-set.

```
count(.//story) = 1
```

This location path returns the `headline` elements in `article` elements in the first `story` element of the document. The predicate of the `story` step

[1] is a short form for the expression [position() = 1]. The XPath function position returns the context position of the context node.

```
//story[1]/article/headline
```

This location path returns all but the first story element in the context node's subtree.

```
.//story[position() > 1]
```

This XPath expression finds out if the value of the variable $page_year is divisible by 400. If it is not, it checks whether it is divisible by 4 but not divisible by 100.

```
($page_year mod 400 = 0) or (($page_year mod 4 = 0)
and ($page_year mod 100 != 0))
```

This XPath expression converts the value of the variable $temp_firstDay to a number, finds the remainder of that number after dividing it by 7, and adds one to the remainder. The XPath function number converts its argument to a number.

```
1 + number($temp_firstDay) mod 7
```

This XPath expression returns true or false, depending on whether the value of the variable cal_type is the string 'large' or not.

```
$cal_type='large'
```

This XPath expression returns false if the value of the variable $month is not the number 2. Otherwise, it returns true if the variable leap holds the Boolean true. Otherwise, it returns false.

```
$month= 2 and $leap
```

This XPath expression returns true if the position of the context node is an odd number but the context node is not the last node in the context. The function last returns the number of nodes in the context, and the function position returns the position of the context node in the context.

```
(position() mod 2 = 1) and not(position()=last())
```

This XPath expression selects the parent of the context node. It then selects the download child node of the parent of the context node whose position is the same as the value of the variable '$i' plus one.

```
../download[position()=$i + 1]
```

This XPath expression returns true if the context node is not the last node in the context.

```
not(position()=last())
```

This XPath expression finds the number of story nodes in the XML tree whose parent is a lineup element.

```
count(//lineup/story)
```

This XPath expression is left to the reader.

```
../../..//golf-tournament[@name=$current_tournament]/event-
    state/@state='recent'
```

This XPath expression has a step with a predicate that contains a location path with another predicate. The purpose of the expression is to find the label of the title of the conference standings with the team whose alias is stored in the variable team.

```
//hockey-nhl-conference-standings[.//team-name[@alias=$team]]
/title/@label
```

This XPath expression finds all the ontology nodes of the XML tree whose name attribute has the value of 'month'. It then returns the numeric value of the node-set, which contains the values of the value attribute of these nodes.

```
number(//ontology[@name='month']/@value)
```

5.7 Summary

XPath expressions are used for different purposes. They are used for numeric, string, relational, and Boolean operations. Most computations that can be done in other programming languages can be done using XPath expressions as well.

The more important purpose of XPath expressions is the specification of nodes in an XML tree. They are used in two ways: to specify the actual nodes in the XML tree to be handled and to specify what characteristics a node must possess before some processing should be applied to the node. In Chapter 3, we saw that an element like xsl:value-of uses XPath expressions in the first way in its select attribute. An xsl:template element, on the other, uses XPath expressions for its match attribute.

There are two basic kinds of XPath expressions: those that result in a node-set and those that do not. Obviously, the expressions that result in a node-set (the location paths) are much more interesting than the other kind.[4] For expressions that return a node-set, the concept of the context and a context node is most important.

5.7.1   *Context Node*

The context node, a node in an XML tree, is provided by the XSLT processor in the beginning of an XPath expression. The processor also provides the context position of the context node, the size of the context, and other items an XPath expression needs.

Each step of a location path uses the context node (and its position in the context, the size of the context, and so forth) to compute the resulting node-set. For the first step of an XPath expression, there is only one context node, but the result node-set of a step can contain more than one node. Each of the nodes in the resulting node-set becomes a context node for the next step. In effect, for a node in the result node-set, the next step is evaluated using it as the context node. Therefore, the next step is evaluated in parallel, with each distinct thread of execution using one of the nodes in the result node-set of the last step. At the end of the last step of a location path, all the resulting node-sets are combined to form the final node-set, the result node-set of the whole location path.

5.8   Looking Ahead

Now we know how to perform operations, how to select any node in a tree, and how to determine how many and which nodes to select. We are now ready to discuss transformation in XSLT.

---

4. Be aware that expressions that do not return a node-set may contain subexpressions that do.

⟨ 6 ⟩

Transformation

Once, I dreamt I was a butterfly.
Flying around I felt like a butterfly;
feeling happy by myself,
I did not feel like a human.
When I woke up,
verily, I felt like a human.
I do not know whether I dreamt I was a butterfly,
or a butterfly dreams it is a human.
A butterfly and a human are different.
And this is called transformation of materials.

—*Zhuang Zi*

How do we perform transformation? Chapter 3 introduced templates that specify patterns to match nodes in the source trees. In this chapter, we will look at the process in greater detail.

We now know that to start the process the XSLT processor always seeks out the template that matches the root of a source tree. Although it is just an ordinary template, we will give it a name here for convenience: the **root template**. Keep in mind, however, that this name is not used anywhere else.

6.1 Visualizing Transformation

A visual description makes it easier to grasp the concept of transformations performed in XSLT. Once you understand what is involved in the process, you can consult the XSLT specification for information about the processing model.

We will examine the internal operations of an XSLT processor and perform some of its functions. Once you are familiar with transformations, you will be able to write XSLT documents that produce the desired results.

We will use the following simple XML document as the source document. Obviously, it is oversimplified and of little use, but a more complicated document would have more detail than we want to deal with right now. If you can handle this simple document, you can handle bigger and more realistic ones, too.

```
<?xml version='1.0'?>
<warehouse>
  <item>
    <name>orange</name>
    <country>US</country>
  </item>
  <item>
    <name>ice wine</name>
    <country>Canada</country>
  </item>
</warehouse>
```

The source tree is depicted in Figure 6.1.

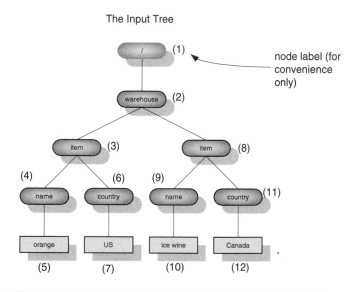

FIGURE

6.1   The source tree

6.1.1   *The Simplest Transformation*

In Chapter 5, we saw that the XSLT processor uses the instructions in the instruction tree to transform the source trees into the result tree.

The first step in the transformation is the creation of the root of the result tree. The XSLT processor also designates the root of the source tree as the **current node** for the root of the result tree, and puts this node into the **current node list** for the root of the result tree. We can imagine that each node in the result tree has its own current node and current node list, as well as the position of the current node in the current node list.

The processor then finds the template that matches the root of the source tree. (We will look at exactly how this is done later.) Let's say there is a template that matches the root. The processor copies everything in the template to the result tree. We'll use the simplest template possible.

```
<xsl:template match='/'/>
```

This template is empty, so it will match the root of an XML tree and then stop the transformation at that point.

Figure 6.2 shows the result after the root of the result tree has been initialized and after the content of the root template has been copied to the result

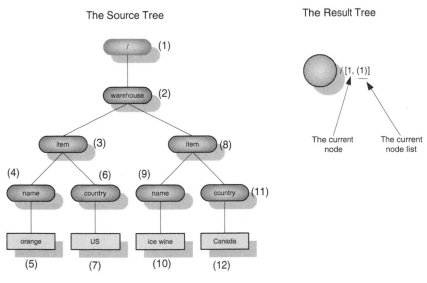

FIGURE 6.2   The input tree

tree. Since the root template does not contain anything, nothing is copied to the result tree.

We then traverse the result tree to find the first XSLT element. In our example, the result tree does not contain anything at all, so we stop the process.

At the end of the transformation, the result tree is converted to the textual presentation of XML again. Because the result tree is empty, the result document is empty as well.

6.2 Literal Result Elements

An empty root template is not very useful. So let's look at a more complicated example. Suppose the root template looks like this.

```
<xsl:template match='/'>
  <warehouse>
    <country>US<item><name>orange</name></item></country>
    <country>Canada<item><name>ice wine</name></item></country>
  </warehouse>
</xsl:template>
```

The initial step is the same: The root of the result tree is constructed with the root of the main source tree as its current node and the only member of its current node list.

After we find the root template, its content is copied to the result tree. This time we actually have something to copy. Figure 6.3 shows the result of copying the content of the root template to the result tree. You can see that every node has a current node and a current node list associated with it.

We can now traverse the result tree. Again, we find no XSLT elements at all. So we will translate the result tree back to the textual form of an XML document.

```
<warehouse><country>US<item><name>orange</name></item>
</country><country>Canada<item><name>ice wine</name>
</item></country></warehouse>
```

The whole document is one long line of elements. (It was necessary to break it into three lines to fit on the page.)

The Source Tree

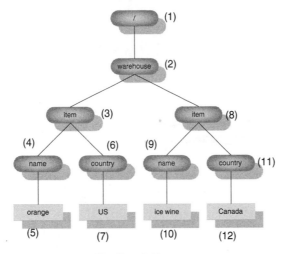

The Result Tree

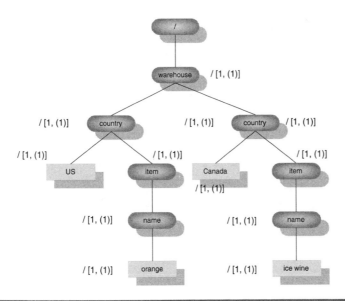

FIGURE

6.3   After copying a nonempty root template

6.3 A Simple Template with an `xsl:apply-templates` Element

Let's look at an XSLT document that allows us to illustrate the importance of the current node and the current node list. Suppose we have the following two templates.

```
<xsl:template match='/'>
  <xsl:apply-templates/>
</xsl:template>

<xsl:template match='warehouse'>
  <storage>
     Nothing in the storage.
  </storage>
</xsl:template>
```

The initialization of the result tree is the same. We find the root template and copy its content to the result tree. Figure 6.4 shows the result tree after this step is done.

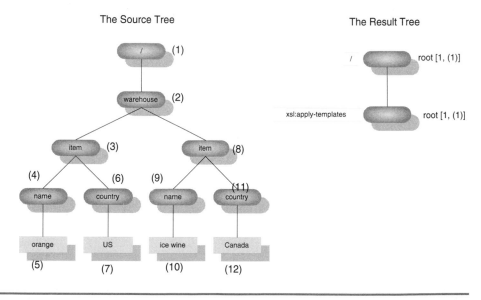

FIGURE 6.4 The result tree after the root template is copied over

We now traverse the result tree. This time we find an XSLT element: `xsl:apply-templates`. In Chapter 3, we saw that an `xsl:apply-templates` with no **select** attribute applies templates to all the child nodes of the current node. The current node is the node used as the focus. If we are matching the child nodes of the current node, we are using the current node as the context node, assuming that we have a **select** attribute that looks like this for the `xsl:apply-templates` element.

```
select='node()'
```

Actually, we also use the current node list as the context, the position of the current node in the current node list as the context position, and the size of the current node list as the context size before the XPath expression is evaluated.

In this case, the only child of the root of the source tree is the document element **warehouse**. We find a template that matches this node, which is the one with **warehouse** as the value of its **match** attribute.

Copy the content of this template to the result tree, replacing the original `xsl:apply-templates`. The **warehouse** element becomes the current node. The nodes matched by the XPath **node()** becomes the current node list, and because only one node is matched, the current node list contains only the **warehouse** element. Figure 6.5 shows the result tree after the copying with the current node and current node list for all the nodes. After the copying, we

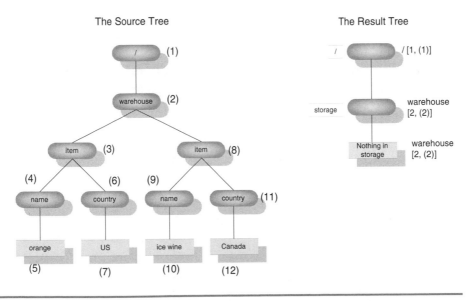

FIGURE 6.5   The result tree after the template matching **warehouse** is copied over

go back to the result tree and see whether there are more XSLT elements. For our simple example, there are none, so the transformation is finished. The final step is to convert the tree back to a textual form.

6.4   Nested `xsl:apply-templates` Elements

What if the template matching `warehouse` in Figure 6.5 also has an `xsl:apply-templates` element? Suppose we have the following templates instead.

```
<xsl:template match='/'>
  <xsl:apply-templates/>
</xsl:template>

<xsl:template match='warehouse'>
  <storage>
    <xsl:apply-templates select='item/country'/>
  </storage>
</xsl:template>

<xsl:template match='country'>
  <xsl:copy-of select='.'/>
</xsl:template>
```

The result tree looks like Figure 6.4 after the root template has been copied to the result tree; nothing is different.

Traversing the result tree, we find the `xsl:apply-templates` and copy the content of the template matching `warehouse` to the result tree. This time the result tree looks different (see Figure 6.6).

As we do every time we finish copying a template to the result tree, we traverse the result tree to find XSLT elements. Of course, we will find the `xsl:apply-templates` element in the tree.

The same procedure applies if you want to use the current node as the context node, the current node list as the context, the size of the current list as the context size, and the position of the current node in the current node list as the context position. The XPath expression this time is `item/country`. The result of the expression is a node-set containing the two `country` nodes.

To make it a little easier to understand what happens next, let's insert an intermediate step here. We'll insert the two nodes to the result tree. Instead of a solid outline, we'll use a dotted outline for the nodes, as shown in Figure 6.7.

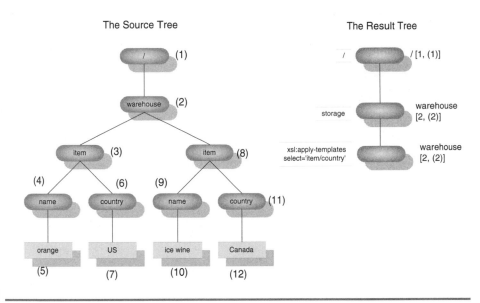

FIGURE

6.6   The result tree after the template matching warehouse is copied over

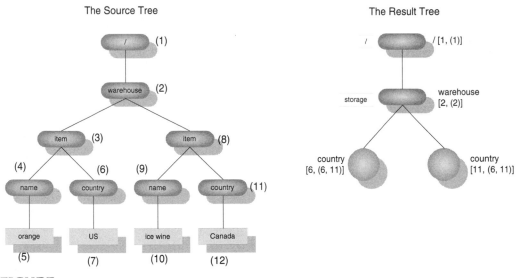

FIGURE

6.7   The result tree after inserting the two country nodes

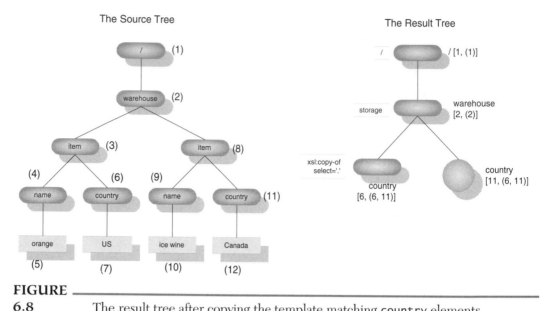

FIGURE 6.8   The result tree after copying the template matching **country** elements

The current node of the first **country** node is the first node in the node-set produced by the XPath expression in the **select** attribute, and its current node list contains both nodes of the node-set. For the second node, the current node is the second node in the node-set. Its current node list is the same as that for the first node.

Now we have to find the template that matches the first node—the one with **country** as its **match** attribute value. To do this, copy the content of the template to the result tree. The result can be seen in Figure 6.8. Do the same for the second node in the node-set returned by the XPath expression. The result is shown in Figure 6.9.

Why do we have to do it twice? We want to handle one node at a time because there might be another template like the following in the document.

```
<xsl:template match='country[1]'>
  <first-country>
    <xsl:copy-of select='.'/>
  </first-country>
</xsl:template>
```

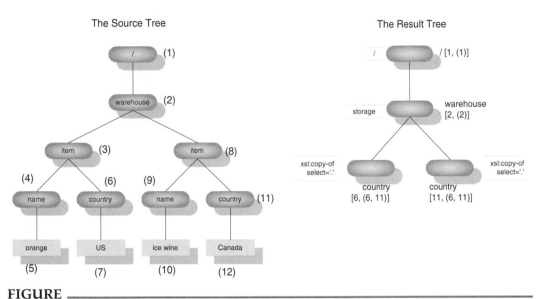

FIGURE 6.9 The result tree after copying the template matching **country** elements the second time

This template will have been copied to the result tree for the first node, but it will not be copied to the result tree for the second node.

Now we'll traverse the result tree. There are two XSLT elements this time, which we will deal with one at a time in the document order. The first XSLT element is `xsl:copy-of,` with . as the value of the **select** attribute. Before evaluating the XPath expression, let's set the current node as the context node, the position of the current node in the current node list as the context node, and the size of the current node list as the context size. Then we evaluate the XPath expression .. The result is a node-set containing only the current node. The `xsl:copy-of` means "to copy to the result tree the entire subtrees rooted at each of the nodes in the node-set produced by evaluating the XPath expression of the **select** attribute." Now copy the subtree rooted at node number 6 to the result tree. (The same applies to the second XSLT element in the result tree, except that the subtree to be copied is the one rooted at node number 11.) The result of the copying is shown in Figure 6.10. Traversing the result tree this time, we find no more XSLT elements. We can stop the process.

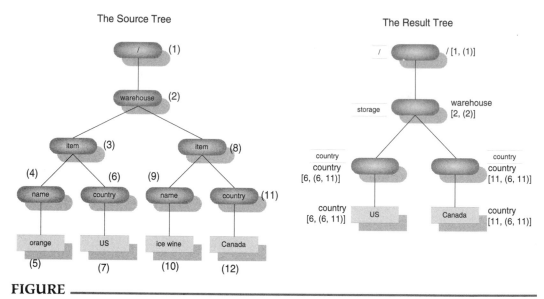

FIGURE 6.10 The result tree after copying the subtrees from the source tree

Now we have seen the copying of information from the instruction tree (when we use the `xsl:apply-templates` element) and from the source tree (when we use the `xsl:copy-of` element).

6.5 Patterns

So far, we have assumed that the XPath expressions are the same everywhere. This need not be true. Some elements allow a subset of XPath expressions, called **patterns**.

Only the `match` attribute of the `xsl:template` element and `xsl:key` elements and the `from` and `count` attributes of the `xsl:number` element can have patterns. A pattern allows only two axes: child and attribute. It also allows the special operator `//` to be used. The `|` operator is allowed in a pattern at the top level. For instance, `a | b` is a valid pattern. The efficient transformation of source trees to the result tree is made possible by the combination of the patterns, the priorities of templates, and the matching procedure.

6.6 Matching Template

But how do we find the matching template when we encounter an `xsl:apply-templates` element in traversing the result tree? Let's use the templates we already have to answer this.

```
<xsl:template match='/'>
  <xsl:apply-templates/>
</xsl:template>

<xsl:template match='warehouse'>
  <storage>
    <xsl:apply-templates select='item/country'/>
  </storage>
</xsl:template>

<xsl:template match='country'>
  <xsl:copy-of select='.'/>
</xsl:template>

<xsl:template match='country[1]'>
  <first-country>
    <xsl:copy-of select='.'/>
  </first-country>
</xsl:template>
```

After we have the two `country` nodes as the result of the expression `item/country`, we want to find the template matching each of them in turn. Using the first node, which is the current node, we do the following.

1. Collect all the XPath expressions (the patterns) in the `match` attribute of all the templates in the XSLT document. Call this the template pattern list[1] for short.

2. Use the parent of the current node as the context node, set the context position and context size to 1, and evaluate each of the expressions in the template pattern list. Keep only the templates that have expressions that evaluate to a node-set containing the current node.

---

1. Again, this term is used only for our purposes here.

3. Use the parent of the parent of the current node as the context node, set the context position and context size to 1, and evaluate each of the expressions in the template pattern list again. Again, keep only the templates that have expressions that evaluate to a node-set containing the current node.

4. Repeat until the root is reached.

If only one template is kept in the process, then that template is used. Otherwise, you must compute the priorities of the templates remaining and find the template with the highest priority. We will do this later on, but let's look at our example first.

6.6.1 *Matching the First Node*

Let's process the first node—node number 6 in the source tree—as the current node. Our template pattern list has these expressions.

```
/
warehouse
country
country[1]
```

The parent of the current node is an `item` element. Using this node as the context node in a context all by itself, evaluate the expressions one by one:

/ The result node-set contains the root itself, definitely not containing the current node.

warehouse The result node-set is empty, since the `item` element has no warehouse children.

country The result node-set contains node 6 and node 11. We will keep this template.

country[1] The result node-set contains node 6 only. We will keep this template also.

Now, let's use the parent of the parent of the current node—a warehouse element—as the context node in a context all by itself.

/ The result node-set contains the root itself, definitely not containing the current node.

warehouse The result node-set is empty.

country The result node-set is empty.

country[1] The result node-set is empty.

No templates are kept from this iteration.

We can keep doing this until the root is reached. At the end of the process, we find two templates that match the current node. Section 6.7 deals with how to find the right template.

6.6.2 *The Second Node*

The second node in the node-set is processed in the same way. The only difference is that when its parent is used as the context node, only one template is kept. Because there is only one template matching this node, that template can be used for the node.

6.7 Template Priority

If there are two templates matching the current node, which template should you use? The answer is the template with the highest priority, which usually has the most specific matches. But how do we find out the priorities of templates?

For each `xsl:template` element, there is an optional `priority` attribute to which a value can be assigned. The value is a positive or negative floating-point number. The smaller the number, the lower the priority of the template. However, an explicit priority is seldom assigned to a template.[2] Instead, the default priority of a template is used.

Suppose we have found all the templates that match the current node. Compute the default priority of each of the templates this way.

1. Break all the matching templates with the | operator. Each of the alternatives is treated as a separate template, and all alternatives that do not match are eliminated. For instance, suppose one of the matching templates looks like this.

   ```
   <xsl:template match='//top|node()'>
     <top/>
   </xsl:template>
   ```

   Say the node to be matched is a **top** element. After the template is broken into two templates, the following two templates are obtained.

   ```
   <xsl:template match='//top'>
     <top/>
   </xsl:template>
   ```

---

2. In fact, it is usually wrong to assign your own priorities.

```
<xsl:template match='node()'>
  <top/>
</xsl:template>
```

In this case, both will be kept. If the node to be matched is a `bottom` element, however, the template that matches `top` will be eliminated, leaving only the template that matches `node()`.

2. Now compute the default priorities for all the remaining templates. If it has the child or attribute axis, and no predicates, then the default priorities are as follows.

> If the node test is the name of a node or is `processing-instruction` (`'literal'`), then the default priority is 0. Examples include `story`, `date`, `processing-instruction('java')`, `book:title`.

> If the node test has a namespace and the name of the node is `*`, then the default priority is -0.25. An example is the pattern `book:*`.

> Otherwise, the default priority is -0.5. Examples include `comment()`, `processing-instruction()`, `node()`, '`*`'.

All other patterns have the default priority of 0.5. After the priorities of the templates have been computed, the template with the highest priority is selected.

There cannot be more than one template with the same highest priority for a node that is being matched. The XSLT processor can choose to signal the error and to select the template defined last in the XSLT document.

Examples

Here are some examples of comparing the priorities of templates.

> The pattern `country` (priority 0) has a lower priority than `country[1]` (priority 0.5). However, `story[true()]` (0.5) and `story[1]` (0.5) have the same priority, even though `true()` does not add anything to the pattern.

It is also possible to have a pattern that looks like `story[position() != 1]` for all the `story` elements other than the first. This pattern and the pattern `story[1]` do not have a conflict because the nodes they match are mutually exclusive.

> A more specific pattern has a higher priority. The patterns `basketball/story` (0.5) and `baseball/story` (0.5) have higher priorities than `story` (0).

Although you are allowed to specify absolute paths as patterns, resist the temptation. Templates with absolute patterns are tied to exactly one class of document and are seldom reused. They are also not very flexible.

6.7.1   *Template Matching Revisited*

Let's complete our example from the section on matching templates. We will pick up from the point where two templates were found to match the first `country` node. The values of the `match` attribute for the two templates are `country` and `country[1]`. From the calculation for default priority, we now know `country[1]` (priority 0.5) has a higher priority than `country` (priority 0). Therefore, the template with `country[1]` is applied.

6.8   Current Node and Current Node List Versus Context Node and Context

It has been a long journey, but we are finally at the point where we can tie together all the major concepts in XSLT and XPath. We can now talk about specifics, such as how to get the initial context node for an XPath expression, how the result node-set of some XSLT elements is converted into a current node list, and so forth.

The beginning of the story is when the root of the result tree is first constructed. The XSLT processor constructs the current node list for this node to contain only the root of the main source tree. Its current node is, of course, the only node in the current node list: the root of the main source tree.

The matching root template is then copied to the result tree. From there the process goes like this.

> If an `xsl:apply-templates` or an `xsl:for-each` element is encountered, evaluate the location path specified in its `select` attribute (or the default `select` value if it is an `xsl:apply-templates` and no explicit `select` is given in the element).
>
> The context node is constructed using the current node. The context is constructed using the current node list. The context position is simply the position of the current node in the current node list. The context size is simply the size of the current node list.
>
> The result node-set of this location path replaces the current node list of the `xsl:apply-templates` element. The ordering of the nodes in the

new current node list is done using the proximity positions of the result node-set.

> If there are xsl:sort elements inside the xsl:apply-templates element or the xsl:for-each, reorder the nodes in the current node list according to the xsl:sort elements.

> If it is the xsl:apply-templates element, each node in the current node set is used to find the template that matches it. The contents of the template are copied to the result tree.

> If it is the xsl:for-each element, the contents of the for-each element are copied for each node of the current node list.

> All the new nodes in the result tree are given the current node and current node list of the node they replace.

6.9   Another Look at XSLT Documents

The document element of an XSLT document is xsl:stylesheet. It has a synonym, xsl:transform, but we will use only xsl:stylesheet.

There are three kinds of XSLT elements: (1) a **top-level element**, which can only be child elements of the xsl:stylesheet element, (2) an **instruction**, which can only be inside an xsl:template element, and (3) both.

The xsl:import elements must be the first elements in an XSLT document. The only mandatory attribute for an xsl:stylesheet element is the version attribute. Right now, the value of the attribute must be 1.0. You must declare the XSLT namespace for the document as well.

6.9.1   *Non-XSLT Elements*

You can also have non-XSLT elements as the children of xsl:stylesheet. They can serve as annotations of the stylesheet, but they are ignored by the processor. Here is an example.

```
<?xml version='1.0'?>
<xsl:stylesheet version='1.0'
    xmlns:xsl='http://www/w3/org/1999/XSL/Transform'>

<comment class='general'>This is an example of
showing how non-XSLT
elements can be included in an XSLT document for annotation
purposes.</comment>
```

```
<!-- This is a comment node in the XSLT document,
not to be confused with a comment element. -->

<comment class='topLevel'>The next element is the
<element>xsl-output</element> element.
</comment>

<xsl:output method='html'/>

<comment class='template'>The next element is a
<element>template</element> element.</comment>

<xsl:template match='/'>
   <html><body><h1>Something</h1></body></html>
</xsl:template>

</xsl:stylesheet>
```

The `comment` and the `element` elements in the XSLT document are not XSLT elements.[3] They annotate the XSLT document. The XML comment with a `<!--` prefix has a different role.

6.9.2   *More About the* `xsl:template` *Element*

This is the syntax of an `xsl:template` element.

```
<xsl:template
  match = pattern
  name = name
  priority = number
  mode = mode-name>
  <!-- Children: (xsl:param(0 or more), body of the template) -->
</xsl:template>
```

There are no mandatory attributes for the `xsl:template` element as long as you have a `match` attribute or a `name` attribute.

You can declare parameters for a template. Each declaration is an `xsl:param` element. The declaration must precede the body of the template. The body of a template contains a mix of instructions and literal result elements.

---

3. Their namespace is the null URI. Therefore, they are different from the `comment` and `element` in the XSLT namespace.

Templates with the `name` attributes are called **named templates**. They are copied by name to the result tree and usually are meant for some specific tasks. Some are used to perform calculations, and some are used to output elements that are static in order to avoid having the same elements in the XSLT document over and over again.

The optional `priority` attribute of a template is used by the developer to decide which template has higher priority if more than one template matches a node in the input tree. We saw examples of templates with the `mode` attribute in Chapter 3.

6.9.3   *More About the* `xsl:apply-templates` *Element*

This is the syntax of the `xsl:apply-templates` element.

```
<!-- Instruction Element -->
<xsl:apply-templates
  select = node-set-expression
  mode = qname>
  <!-- Content: (xsl:sort | xsl:with-param)(0 or more) -->
</xsl:apply-templates>
```

An `xsl:apply-templates` element, like the `xsl:for-each` element, can contain an `xsl:sort` element so that the nodes in the node-set selected can be sorted in a certain way. (There will be more about `xsl:sort` in Chapter 7.) You can supply parameters to the matched template with an `xsl:apply-templates` by using one or more `xsl:with-param` elements inside the `xsl:apply-templates` element.

6.9.4   *Default Templates*

When matching templates, it is possible that no matching template will be found. XSLT defines four sets of **default templates** to ensure that if no templates are found among the templates defined in an XSLT document, one of the default templates can be used. The first default template matches all elements and the root. The template looks like this.

```
<xsl:template match="*|/">
  <xsl:apply-templates/>
</xsl:template>
```

It just continues the transformation process by reapplying templates for the child elements (not attributes or namespaces) of the current node.

The second default template is really a combination of many templates. They are almost identical to the previous default template except that they have the `mode` attribute. Each of them matches one of the modes defined in the XSLT document.

The third default template matches the text nodes and the attributes of the elements. The default behavior is to send the values of these nodes to the output. The default template is as follows.

```
<xsl:template match="text()|@*">
  <xsl:value-of select="."/>
</xsl:template>
```

This default behavior, however, may not be desirable. To prevent the default template from being invoked erroneously, declare a template that matches text nodes and attribute values.

The last default template matches the processing instructions and comments. Its default behavior is to ignore them, which is usually what you want.

```
<xsl:template match="processing-instruction()|comment()">
</xsl:template>
```

From Section 6.5, we know that we cannot specify a location path that will match a namespace node (because the only allowed axes are the child and attribute axes). The default template for namespace nodes is the only one capable of matching namespace nodes. For instance, if you have the following `xsl:apply-templates`

```
<xsl:apply-templates select='namespace::*'/>
```

you will see nothing in the output because you cannot specify your own template to match the namespace nodes of an element, and the default template does nothing.[4]

6.9.5 *More About the* `call-template` *Element*

An `xsl:call-template` element is very similar to an `xsl:apply-templates` element. Both copy elements from the XSLT document to the result tree. However, `xsl:call-template` does not change the current node and the current node list, but it associates the same ones for all the nodes inside the template copied to the result tree.

---

4. This means you have to use `xsl:for-each` elements to enumerate or examine namespace nodes.

6.9.6   *Parameters*

Each `xsl:template` element can have `xsl:param` elements to declare its parameters, which are used to pass in information.

The actual values of the parameters are assigned using `xsl:with-param` elements. For example, if the template looks like this

```
<xsl:template match='top'>
  <xsl:param name='name'/>
  <xsl:value-of select='$name'/>
</xsl:template>
```

then the corresponding `xsl:apply-templates` element can look like this.

```
<xsl:apply-templates>
  <xsl:with-param name='name' select='123'/>
</xsl:apply-templates>
```

In this example, the value `123` is assigned to the parameter called `name`.

Parameters are matched by names. If the name of a parameter cannot be found in the templates used, it is assumed to be empty. The ordering of the `xsl:with-param` elements inside an `xsl:apply-templates` element or an `xsl:call-template` element is not important.

6.9.7   *Copying*

There are two XSLT elements for copying nodes from the source documents to the result tree. They are the `xsl:copy-of` element and the `xsl:copy` element. An `xsl:copy-of` element has a `select` attribute. The element evaluates the value of the `select` attribute as an XPath expression and then copies the nodes and their contents in the result node-set of the expression to the result tree. An `xsl:copy` replaces itself with the current node.

Suppose we have a `story` element that is already in HTML (albeit in well-formed XML format) in the source tree. We just want to copy the whole story to the result tree.

```
<?xml version='1.0'?>
<news>
  <byline>John Smith</byline>
  <date>October 28, 1999</date>
  <headline>Company Heads Meet</headline>
  <story>The CEO of <b>100</b> companies meet in
downtown Toronto today to discuss the feasibility of
```

```
forming an association to fight proposed legislation on the
regulation of waste paper.</story>
</news>
```

This is the XSLT template that copies everything in the story element in the source document.

```
<xsl:template match='story'>
  <xsl:copy-of select='.'/>
</xsl:template>
```

If you just want to copy the current node (not the current element or what it contains) to the result tree, use the `xsl:copy` element. For instance, suppose you want to process only one kind of element in the source tree and copy the rest to the result tree. You can specify the following templates to handle the `target` element

```
<xsl:template match='/'>
  <xsl:apply-templates/>
</xsl:template>

<xsl:template match='*|@*'>
  <xsl:copy>
    <xsl:apply-templates select='@*|node()'/>
  </xsl:copy>
</xsl:template>

<xsl:template match='target'>
  <!-- whatever you want to do for the element -->
</xsl:template>
```

If you want to remove all the `target` elements and their descendants, simply specify an empty template for that element. Or you can eliminate only the `target` elements but not their descendants by using the following template.

```
<xsl:template match='target'>
  <xsl:apply-templates/>
</xsl:template>
```

6.10   Summary

Transformation in XSLT can be summarized as follows.

1. Set the root of the main XML source tree as the only node in the current node-set for the root of the result tree.

2. Find the best template for each of the nodes in the current node-set.

3. Copy the body of the templates selected to the result tree.

4. Traverse the result tree in depth-first fashion and repeat the same procedure to the elements in the result tree until no element in the result tree has the XSL namespace.

6.10.1 *The Current Node*

Like a context node for a location path, each node in the result tree has a current node. The current node and the current node list are assigned by `apply-templates` and `xsl:for-each` elements. The `select` attribute of these elements sets the new current node-set, the size of the current node-set, and the order of nodes in the node-set.

The current node of a node becomes the initial context node when an XPath expression is encountered in that node. This is how the XSLT processor provides the initial context node to an XPath expression. The current node-set becomes the context, the size of the current node-set becomes the context size, and the position of the current node in the current node-set becomes the context position of the context node.

6.11 Looking Ahead

The next chapter will build on what we learned in this chapter and explain other constructs in XSLT that are necessary in the transformation process. Most of these elements can be considered as the control elements in XSLT. That is, they do not copy nodes to the result tree but only manipulate nodes that are already in the result tree.

〈 7 〉

Control

Life and death are important
but he is not transformed by them.
Even if the Heaven collapses and the Earth sinks,
he is not destroyed by them.
He can identify reality;
he is not confused by hallucination;
and he cannot be transformed with materials.
He controls the transformation of everything,
and preserves the real and fundamental Way.

—*Zhuang Zi*

Some elements, such as `xsl:copy-of` and `xsl:copy`, copy part of the source tree to the result tree; others, such as `xsl:apply-templates` and `xsl:call-template`, copy part of the instruction tree to the result tree. In this chapter we examine the elements you need to create a result tree that is exactly the way you want it to be. These elements do not copy elements from the source tree or from the instruction tree. They manipulate the elements that have already been copied to the result tree.

7.1   The `xsl:if` Element

If you have an `xsl:if` element, the XPath expression in its **test** attribute is evaluated and converted to a Boolean value. If the Boolean value is true, then the content of the `xsl:if` element replaces the `xsl:if` element. If the Boolean value is false, the whole `xsl:if` element is removed from the result tree.

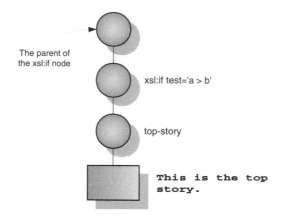

The parent of
the xsl:if node

xsl:if test='a > b'

top-story

This is the top
story.

The result tree containing an `xsl:if` element

Suppose we have the following `xsl:if` element.

```
<xsl:if test='a > b'>
  <top-story>
    This is the top story.
  </top-story>
</xsl:if>
```

Figure 7.1 shows the nodes in the element. If the value of **a** is not greater than the value of **b**, then the `xsl:if` element will be removed. Otherwise, the outcome is this.

```
<top-story>
  This is the top story.
</top-story>
```

The two outcomes are shown in Figure 7.2.

7.1.1   *The* xsl:choose *Element*

If you need to choose among some alternatives to stay in the result tree, you can use the `xsl:choose` element. An `xsl:choose` always has at least one `xsl:when` child node. This is the skeleton of the element.

```
<xsl:choose>
  <xsl:when test='expr1'>something</xsl:when>
  <xsl:when test='expr2'>something else</xsl:when>
  <xsl:otherwise>The fallback plan</xsl:otherwise>
</xsl:choose>
```

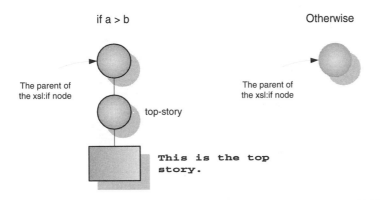

FIGURE
7.2   The two possible outcomes of the `xsl:if` element

An `xsl:choose` works by evaluating the XPath expressions in the `test` attributes of its `xsl:when` children. Each of them is evaluated from the first `xsl:when` to the last one. Whenever an XPath expression is evaluated to true, the evaluation process stops. The content of the `xsl:when` element remains in the result tree, and the other `xsl:when` elements are simply removed. If the `xsl:choose` element has an `xsl:otherwise` element, that is removed, too.

If no expression evaluates to true, then the content of the `xsl:otherwise` remains. If there is no `xsl:otherwise` element in the `xsl:choose` element, then the whole `xsl:choose` element is removed. This situation is shown in Figure 7.3. The three possible outcomes are shown in Figure 7.4. If both `expr1`

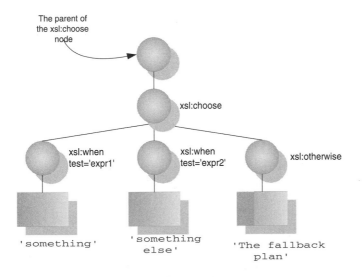

FIGURE
7.3   The result tree containing an `xsl:choose` element

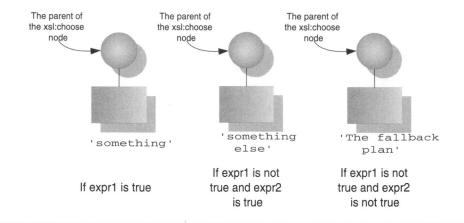

The parent of the xsl:choose node

The parent of the xsl:choose node

The parent of the xsl:choose node

'something'

'something else'

'The fallback plan'

If expr1 is true

If expr1 is not true and expr2 is true

If expr1 is not true and expr2 is not true

FIGURE

7.4   The result tree containing an `xsl:choose` element

and `expr2` evaluate to false and the `xsl:otherwise` element is missing, then the original `xsl:choose` element will be removed from the result tree.

7.2   The `for-each` Element

Both the `xsl:if` element and the `xsl:choose` element prune the result tree, but the `xsl:for-each` element expands the result tree. The `xsl:for-each` element, like the `xsl:apply-templates` element, has a `select` attribute that selects some nodes from the source trees. In the beginning, it behaves very similarly to the `xsl:apply-templates`, but it differs on the matching part. An `xsl:apply-templates` element finds the matching template for each of the nodes in the node-set returned by the XPath. It then copies the content of the template to the result tree. For an `xsl:for-each`, the content of the `xsl:for-each` is copied for each of the nodes in the node-set. The association of the current node and current node list is then done the same way as in an `xsl:apply-templates`. Therefore, the `xsl:for-each` element is really an `xsl:apply-templates` element without template matching.

Suppose we have this XML document.

```
<?xml version='1.0'?>
 <items>
   <item>Shoes</item>
   <item>Shirts</item>
   <item>Dog food</item>
 </items>
```

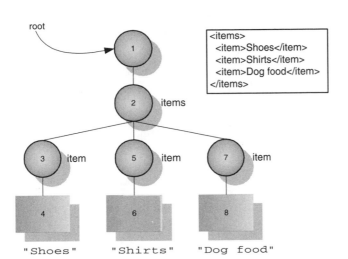

```
<items>
  <item>Shoes</item>
  <item>Shirts</item>
  <item>Dog food</item>
</items>
```

FIGURE 7.5 The input tree for `for-each` example

The tree representing this document is shown in Figure 7.5. Here is a simple XSLT document to show each item in an H1 element in HTML.

```xml
<?xml version='1.0'?>
<xsl:stylesheet version='1.0'
    xmlns:xsl='http://www.w3.org/1999/XSL/Transform'>
  <xsl:output method='html'/>

  <xsl:template match='/'>
    <html>
      <body>
        <xsl:for-each select='items/item'>
          <h1><xsl:value-of select='.'/></h1>
        </xsl:for-each>
      </body>
    </html>
  </xsl:template>
</xsl:stylesheet>
```

After copying the root template to the result tree, the result tree looks like Figure 7.6. The XPath expression of the xsl:for-each selects all the item elements in the source document. Figure 7.7 shows the result tree after the nodes from the result node-set are inserted. Now all we have to do is to evaluate

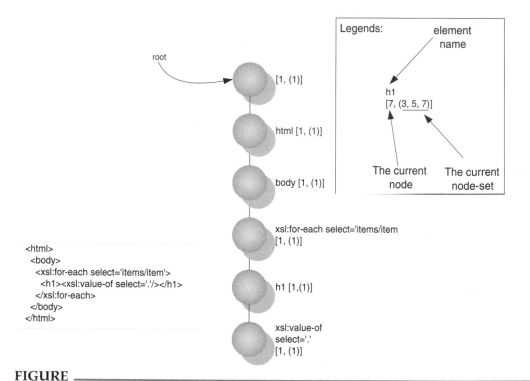

```
<html>
  <body>
    <xsl:for-each select='items/item'>
      <h1><xsl:value-of select='.'/></h1>
    </xsl:for-each>
  </body>
</html>
```

FIGURE 7.6   The result tree containing an xsl:for-each element

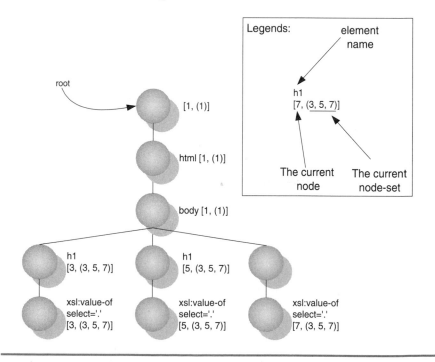

FIGURE 7.7   The result tree after the XPath expression has been evaluated and nodes inserted

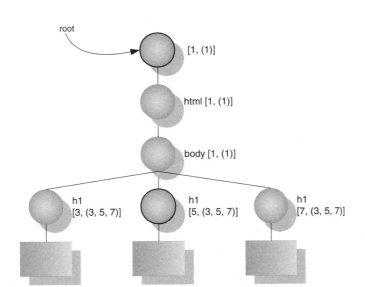

FIGURE
7.8
The result tree after the `xsl:value-of` elements have been processed

the `xsl:value-of` elements in the result tree. The final result tree is shown in Figure 7.8.

The `xsl:for-each` element is needed in addition to the `apply-templates` element because the content of an `xsl:for-each` is already in the result tree. The element may replicate more copies of the content in the result tree, but no copying is performed from the XSLT document.

7.3   Looping with Named Templates

If you find yourself in a situation where you have to do something several times, you can use a named template.

1. Determine the initial condition to start the looping.
2. Determine the terminating condition.
3. Determine what each iteration should do.
4. Following the instructions for the iteration, the template should include an element that computes the value of the condition for the next iteration. It should also call itself recursively for the next iteration.

5. Design a named template to perform an iteration in the loop, with the termination condition as the test expression of an `xsl:if` element in the template.

6. In the template that requires the loop, call the named template with the initial condition.

Let's look at a simple example to illustrate the point. Suppose you want to output the `<top/>` element five times. This is the named template performing the iterations.

```
<xsl:template name='do5'>
  <xsl:param name='times'/>
  <xsl:if test='$times > 0'>
    <top/>
    <!-- To prepare for the next iteration -->
    <xsl:call-template name='do5'>
      <xsl:with-param name='times' select='$times - 1'/>
    </xsl:call-template>
  </xsl:if>
</xsl:template>
```

To call the named template, insert the following element in a template, which will insert the top element five times.

```
<xsl:call-template name='do5'>
  <xsl:with-param name='times' select='5'/>
</xsl:call-template>
```

The terminating and initial conditions can be a lot more complicated than in this element, but the structure of the named template is the same for any kind of looping construct.

Figures 7.9 to 7.16 show this sample element. Again, we will skip the initial steps and go straight to the point where the result tree contains the `xsl:call-template` node, as shown in Figure 7.9. Replace the `xsl:call-template` node in the result tree with the body of the template named `do5`, and set up the state so that the parameter named `times` has the value 5 (the result of evaluating the XPath expression in the `xsl:with-param` element). The result tree is shown in Figure 7.10. Since the current node and the current node list are not relevant to this procedure, they are not shown for the nodes.[1] The state of the processor,

---

1. Recall that named templates do not change the current node and the current node list at all.

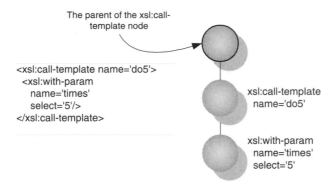

The parent of the xsl:call-template node

```
<xsl:call-template name='do5'>
  <xsl:with-param
    name='times'
    select='5'/>
</xsl:call-template>
```

xsl:call-template
name='do5'

xsl:with-param
name='times'
select='5'

FIGURE

7.9 The result tree with the `xsl:call-template` element

however, is very important for this example, and it is the reason we show the value of the variable named **times** in the figure.

Next evaluate the XPath expression in the **test** attribute of the **xsl:if** node. The expression evaluates to **true** (because the **times** variable has the value 5 and the expression tests whether the variable has a value greater than 0). The content of the **xsl:if** remains in the result tree. The result tree is shown

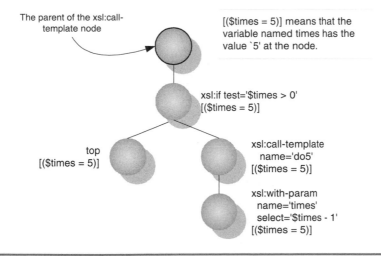

The parent of the xsl:call-template node

[($times = 5)] means that the variable named times has the value `5' at the node.

xsl:if test='$times > 0'
[($times = 5)]

top
[($times = 5)]

xsl:call-template
name='do5'
[($times = 5)]

xsl:with-param
name='times'
select='$times - 1'
[($times = 5)]

FIGURE

7.10 The result tree with the `xsl:call-template` node replaced by the body of the template

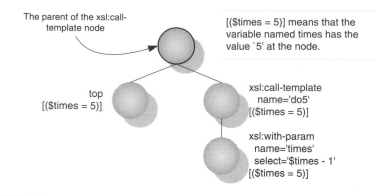

The parent of the xsl:call-template node

[($times = 5)] means that the variable named times has the value `5' at the node.

top
[($times = 5)]

xsl:call-template
name='do5'
[($times = 5)]

xsl:with-param
name='times'
select='$times - 1'
[($times = 5)]

FIGURE

7.11   The result tree after evaluating the `xsl:if` node

in Figure 7.11. The next node with the XSLT namespace is the `xsl:call-template` node. Copy the body of the template to the result tree. The value of the variable named `times` is updated to the value of evaluating `$times - 1`. The result is 4. The result tree we have now is in Figure 7.12.

The next step is to evaluate the `xsl:if` node. Again, the result is `true`. The body of the node stays in the result tree, which is shown in Figure 7.13. This process is continued until the value of the variable named `times` has the value 0. The result tree in Figure 7.14 shows this.

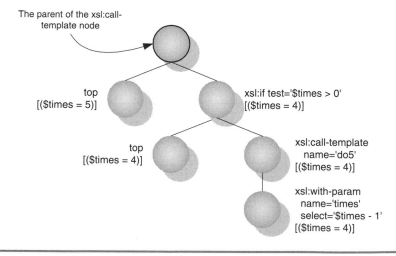

The parent of the xsl:call-template node

top
[($times = 5)]

xsl:if test='$times > 0'
[($times = 4)]

top
[($times = 4)]

xsl:call-template
name='do5'
[($times = 4)]

xsl:with-param
name='times'
select='$times - 1'
[($times = 4)]

FIGURE

7.12   The result tree after inserting the body of the template again

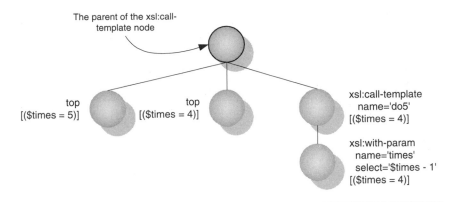

FIGURE
7.13   The result tree after evaluating the `xsl:if` node

After the body of the template is copied to the result tree, we have the result tree in Figure 7.15. The XPath expression in the `xsl:if` node evaluates to `false`. The whole `xsl:if` node is removed from the result tree. The result tree now is shown in Figure 7.16. Because this part of the result tree does not have any nodes with the XSLT namespace left, there will not be any processing for this part of the result tree.

The example shows an `xsl:call-template` element that stops after five `top` elements in the result tree have been inserted. If the terminating condition is not set up properly, it may keep inserting more and more `top` elements until

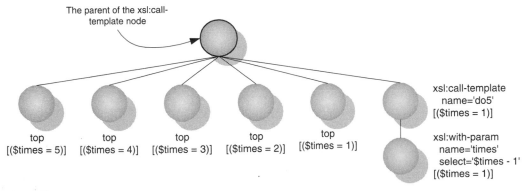

FIGURE
7.14   The result tree when the value of `times` is 0

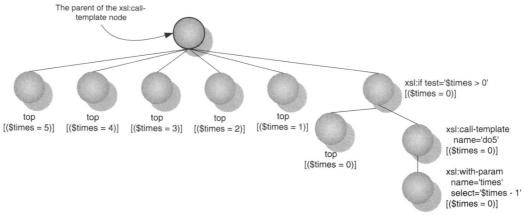

The parent of the xsl:call-template node

top
[($times = 5)]

top
[($times = 4)]

top
[($times = 3)]

top
[($times = 2)]

top
[($times = 1)]

top
[($times = 0)]

xsl:if test='$times > 0'
[($times = 0)]

xsl:call-template
name='do5'
[($times = 0)]

xsl:with-param
name='times'
select='$times - 1'
[($times = 0)]

FIGURE

7.15   The result tree after copying the body of the template

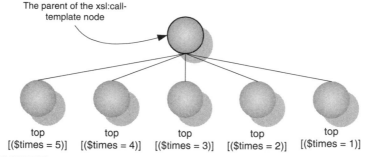

The parent of the xsl:call-template node

top
[($times = 5)]

top
[($times = 4)]

top
[($times = 3)]

top
[($times = 2)]

top
[($times = 1)]

FIGURE

7.16   The result tree after evaluating the `xsl:if` node when the value of the `times` variable is 0

the XSLT processor cannot handle the number of nodes in the result tree and crashes.[2]

7.3.1   *Checking the Condition Last*

Do this if you want to check the condition after the iteration is done.

1. The body of the iteration executes copy.

2. Update the condition.

---

2. When the processor crashes due to this problem, the error message you see will probably say something like "the stack has overflowed." You may want to check your `xsl:call-template` elements when that happens.

3. If the condition is still true, go back to step 1.

Here is an example of a loop checking the condition last.

```
<?xml version='1.0'?>
<xsl:stylesheet
 xmlns:xsl='http://www.w3.org/1999/XSL/Transform'
 version='1.0'>

<xsl:output method='html'/>

<xsl:template match='/'>
  <xsl:variable name='var' select='-20'/>
  <xsl:call-template name='repeat'>
    <xsl:with-param name='var' select='$var'>
  </xsl:call-template>
</xsl:template>

<xsl:template name='while'>
   <xsl:param name='var'/>
   <!-- do something here -->
   <xsl:if test="$var < 0">
      <!-- do something here -->
      <xsl:call-template name='repeat'>
        <xsl:with-param name='var' select='$var + 1'/>
      </xsl:call-template>
   </xsl:if>
</xsl:template>

</xsl:stylesheet>
```

At least one iteration is always carried out.

7.4   Sorting

XSLT provides a sorting element that can be used to sort elements according to
a pattern. For instance, suppose you want to sort a list of companies according
to their names. Say the source document looks like this.

```
<?xml version='1.0'?>
<companies>
  <company>
    <name>The ABC and co.</name>
  </company>
```

```
<company>
  <name>Selecting Incorporated</name>
</company>
<company>
  <name>Clean Your Shirt Drycleaning</name>
</company>
<company>
  <name>Snakes Import and Export</name>
</company>
<company>
  <name>Science and Pseudo-Science Hobbies</name>
</company>
</companies>
```

This XSLT document outputs a sorted list.

```
<?xml version='1.0'?>
<xsl:stylesheet
 version='1.0'
 xmlns:xsl='http://www.w3.org/1999/XSL/Transform'>
  <xsl:output method='xml' indent='yes'
    omit-xml-declaration='no'/>
  <xsl:template match='/'>
    <companies>
    <xsl:for-each select='companies/company'>
      <xsl:sort select='name'/>
      <company>
        <name><xsl:value-of select='name'/></name>
      </company>
    </xsl:for-each>
    </companies>
  </xsl:template>
</xsl:stylesheet>
```

First, the xsl:for-each element selects a node-set in the principal axis of the XPath expression in the source document. The xsl:sort element then sorts these nodes (changing their positions in the current node list) by specifying the criterion to change the positions. The result is a different current node list containing the same set of nodes as before.[3] Additional xsl:sort elements

---

3. Unlike a node-set, the current node list does have an ordering of the nodes in it.

can be specified as well. Note that all the `xsl:sort` elements are handled at the same time to produce the sorting order intended. After the sorting, the `for-each` (or the `xsl:apply-templates`) element is handled as usual.

7.4.1 *Sorting Data Types*

Sorting can be performed according to the sorting keys being considered as numbers or as strings, using the `data-type` attribute. The value of this attribute can be the string `text` or `number`. The default value for the `data-type` attribute is `text`. The value must be chosen carefully because the result may be quite different from what is expected. For example, suppose the source document has the following elements.

```
<value>1234</value>
<value>456</value>
```

Using this `xsl:sort` element

```
<xsl:sort select='value'/>
```

to sort the two elements produces

```
<value>1234</value>
<value>456</value>
```

even though 456 is obviously less than 1234. The elements are sorted this way because the two elements are compared as strings. The first character of 1234— 1—is smaller than the first character of 456—4. If the `xsl:sort` is changed to sort the elements as numbers, like this,

```
<xsl:sort select='value' data-type='number'/>
```

then the output would be the expected one, like this.

```
<value>456</value>
<value>1234</value>
```

Of course, the comparison of text nodes in this way is different from the comparison of two strings. Always remember that unless you want the text nodes to be considered as numbers, they will be considered as text, in alphabetical order.

7.4.2   *Ascending or Descending*

When performing sorting, the attribute `order` can be used to sort the elements in ascending or descending order. The meaning of the attribute is obvious. The allowed values are `ascending` and `descending`. The default order is ascending.

7.4.3   *Cases*

It is also possible to instruct the XSLT processor to consider uppercase to be less than lowercase or the other way round. The attribute to do this is `case-order`. The values of the attribute can be `upper-first` or `lower-first`. The default is language dependent.

Not all languages have the notion of uppercase and lowercase. The whole internationalization issue should be considered carefully before it becomes an XSLT issue.

7.4.4   *Language-Dependent Sorting*

There is a `lang` attribute in the `xsl:sort` element. The values allowed are the language designations allowed in XML. The language attribute decides how sorting should be performed according to what is involved. For example, sorting of characters in Chinese does not make a lot of sense unless it is for a dictionary. And the traditional way of sorting them in a dictionary is quite arbitrary in some details, although the basic principles are widely accepted and used.

7.4.5   *Multilevel Sorting*

It is possible to sort in more than one level—for example, sort both the `last-name` attribute and the `firstname` attribute after sorting the `lastname` attribute. So after sorting the `lastname` attribute, if there are two or more elements with the same value for their `lastname` attribute, you can sort these elements by their `firstname` attribute values.

```
<?xml version='1.0'?>
<xsl:stylesheet
 xmlns:xsl='http://www.w3.org/1999/XSL/Transform'
 version='1.0'
xmlns:kk='http://www.jmedium.com'>

<xsl:template match='/'>
  <persons>
  <xsl:for-each select='persons/person'>
```

```
      <xsl:sort select='@lastname'/>
       <xsl:sort select='@firstname'/>
         <person><xsl:attribute name='lastname'>
           <xsl:value-of select='@lastname'/>
           </xsl:attribute>
           <xsl:attribute name='firstname'>
           <xsl:value-of select='@firstname'/>
           </xsl:attribute><xsl:value-of select='.'/>
         </person>
    </xsl:for-each>
    </persons>
  </xsl:template>

</xsl:stylesheet>
```

Given this input XML file

```
<?xml version='1.0'?>
<persons>
   <person firstname='John' lastname='Doe'>3</person>
   <person firstname='Chuck' lastname='Morris'>3</person>
   <person firstname='Semi' lastname='More'>3</person>
   <person firstname='Bruce' lastname='Willy'>3</person>
   <person firstname='Neil' lastname='Campbell'>3</person>
   <person firstname='Eliza' lastname='Doe'>3</person>
   <person firstname='Demi' lastname='More'>3</person>
</persons>
```

the output looks like this.

```
<?xml version="1.0" encoding="utf-8"?>
<persons xmlns:kk="http://www.jmedium.com">
 <person lastname="Campbell" firstname="Neil">3</person>
 <person lastname="Doe" firstname="Eliza">3</person>
 <person lastname="Doe" firstname="John">3</person>
 <person lastname="More" firstname="Demi">3</person>
 <person lastname="More" firstname="Semi">3</person>
 <person lastname="Morris" firstname="Chuck">3</person>
 <person lastname="Willy" firstname="Bruce">3</person>
</persons>
```

7.5   Sending Messages to the Console

It is possible to copy string values from the result tree to the console using the
xsl:message element. This element is for logging purposes only (including
debugging the XSLT document). For instance, to write to the console when
the root template is executed by the XSLT processor, you can use this simple
xsl:message element.

```
<xsl:template match='/'>
  <xsl:message>Inside the root template of the XSLT
  document</xsl:message>
</xsl:template>
```

If this message is not found in the log file or on the console after the XSLT
document has been executed, then it is most likely because the XSLT processor
used a different root template than this one.

This element has an optional **terminate** attribute. If this attribute is present
and its value is **'yes'**, the XSLT processor is stopped immediately when this
element is encountered in the traversal of the result tree. What the result tree
looks like when this happens is not specified in the XSLT specification.

7.6   Parameters Outside the XSLT Document

Sometimes it is necessary to pass information from the outside to an XSLT
document. There are a few ways to do this.

7.6.1   *Using Top-Level Parameters*

The first way is to use the XSLT xsl:param element at the top level as a child
of the xsl:stylesheet element. The setting of the parameters is processor-
dependent. The declaration of a top-level parameter is identical to the declaration of an xsl:param inside a template. For instance, to declare a parameter
named **date**, do this

```
<xsl:param name='date'/>
```

for a child of the xsl:stylesheet element. When the XSLT document is
executed, the value of the parameter is magically set by the XSLT processor.

If you use XT, this is the command line used to assign the value of the **date**
parameter.

```
% xt data.xml date.xsl date="19991103"
```

This is assuming the date is November 3, 1999. The XSLT document `date.xsl` may look like this.

```
<?xml version='1.0'?>
<xsl:stylesheet
 xmlns:xsl='http://www.w3.org/1999/XSL/Transform'
 version='1.0'>
<xsl:output method='html'/>
<xsl:param name='date'/>

<xsl:template match='/'>
  <xsl:message><xsl:value-of select='$date'/></xsl:message>
</xsl:template>

</xsl:stylesheet>
```

This is the output from XT.

```
file:/e:/KYeeFung/Private/Book/tex/19991103/date.xml:1: 19991103
```

Using the SAXON XSLT processor, the mechanism is the same but the output looks like this.

```
19991103
```

This is due to the difference in the way the XSLT processors handle the `xsl:message` element.

7.7 Summary

This chapter explains the XSLT elements that do not copy portions of an input tree or the instruction tree to the result tree. In other languages, these are called the control constructs. They include the `xsl:if` element, the `xsl:for-each` element, and the `xsl:choose` element.

You have also seen how the `xsl:call-template` element can be used to emulate looping in XSLT. The `xsl:sort` element is the only XSLT element that modifies the ordering of nodes in the current node list.

7.8 Looking Ahead

We will see more XSLT elements in the next chapter, including elements used to specify the output method, to include the document type definition in the output, variables, and to construct comments, processing elements, and so forth in the result tree.

⟨8⟩

Constructing the Result Tree

> Dividing is creating.
> Creating is destroying.
> Any thing has no creation or destruction,
> both are really the same.
> Only the wise understands this oneness.
>
> —*Zhuang Zi*

We have seen elements that copy parts of the source trees and instruction tree to the result tree and elements that manipulate elements that are already in the result tree. Now we will discuss elements that determine what the result tree will look like.

8.1   The `xsl:output` Element for HTML

If you want to output HTML properly, you need an `xsl:output` element with its `method` attribute set to `html`. This is important because HTML is not XML, and its elements must be handled in the HTML way.

This is the minimum that you need to do.

```
<xsl:output method='html'/>
```

According to the XSLT specification, an XSLT processor is not required to follow what is requested in the `output` element, although it should do so. If you want to make sure your HTML documents are output properly, use an XSLT processor that takes the hint.

The `version` and the `indent` attributes are the two interesting attributes for transformations to HTML. The version of HTML used is defaulted to 4.0. If this is not the right one, set the right version yourself. The `indent` attribute is defaulted to `yes`. Because all browsers do not handle whitespaces the same way,[1] it is a good idea to set the `indent` attribute to `no` for HTML output.

8.1.1   *Elements with No End-Tags*

Some elements in HTML do not have end-tags. In your XSLT document, you must specify end-tags for these elements. When these elements are converted to their textual form, the end-tags will be stripped away by the processor. For example, if you have this

```
<xsl:template match='/'>
  <HTML>
  <BODY>
    <BR/>
  </BODY>
  </HTML>
</xsl:template>
```

then the HTML output looks like this.

```
<HTML>
<BODY>
  <BR>
</BODY>
</HTML>
```

You are not allowed to write the preceding template as this.

```
<xsl:template match='/'>
  <HTML>
  <BODY>
    <BR>
  </BODY>
  </HTML>
</xsl:template>
```

---

1. How whitespaces should be handled is quite clear in the HTML specification, but the fact remains that different versions of Web browsers do not handle them exactly the same way. This is, of course, one of the annoying things about browsers.

The XSLT document will be rejected by the XML parser because the XML is not well formed (the BR element does not have an end-tag).

The other HTML 4.0 elements that the XSLT processor should output without an end-tag are AREA, BASE, BASEFONT, COL, FRAME, HT, IMG, INPUT, ISINDEX, LINK, META, and PARAM.[2]

8.1.2   *Boolean Values*

The XSLT processor must also be able to handle Boolean attribute values. In HTML, if the value of a Boolean attribute is `true`, the value of the attribute is omitted. If the value is `false`, the attribute is absent. For instance, if the SELECTED attribute of the OPTION element is present, then the HTML output should look like this.

```
<OPTION SELECTED>
```

However, in a template in an XSLT document, this element must be written this way.

```
<xsl:template match='/'>
  <OPTION SELECTED='SELECTED'/>
</xsl:template>
```

The output is the proper

```
<OPTION SELECTED>
```

8.1.3   *Processing Instructions*

Processing instructions in XML always end with ?>. However, in HTML, processing instructions end with >. The HTML developer does not have to be concerned with this issue because processing instructions should always be created using `xsl:processing-instruction`. The XSLT processor will be responsible for writing a valid HTML processing instruction to the output when the element `xsl:processing-instruction` is used. Here is a simple example of an HTML processing instruction.

```
<?font family=ariel size=10pt style=bold>
```

---

2. The elements with optional end-tags are output with end-tags. These elements include the familiar P element.

There are other forms of processing instructions in HTML, but this one is probably the most common form.[3]

8.1.4   *Document Type Declarations*

When the `method` attribute of the `xsl:output` is set to `html` and one of the attributes `doctype-public` and `doctype-system` is set, the doctype declaration for the output HTML document is generated. There are four combinations for the doctype declaration in the output HTML document.

1. Both `doctype-system` and `doctype-public` are absent. In this case, no document type declaration will be written to the output.

2. Only the `doctype-public` attribute is present. In this case, the doctype declaration has the public identifier. For example, if the `xsl:output` looks like this

   ```
   <xsl:output method='html'
           doctype-public="-//W3C//DTD HTML 4.0//EN"/>
   ```

   then the doctype declaration in the output document is this.

   ```
   <!DOCTYPE html PUBLIC "-//W3C//DTD HTML 4.0//EN">
   ```

3. Only the `doctype-system` attribute is present. In this case, the document type declaration contains the system URI. Suppose the `xsl:output` element looks like this.

   ```
   <xsl:output method='html'
      doctype-system="http://www.w3.org/TR/REC-html40/strict.dtd"/>
   ```

   The doctype declaration in the output document looks like this.

   ```
   <!DOCTYPE html SYSTEM
           "http://www.w3.org/TR/REC-html40/strict.dtd">
   ```

4. Both the `doctype-system` and `doctype-public` attributes are present. In this case, both identifiers will be written to the output. If the `xsl:output` element looks like this.

   ```
   <xsl:output method='html'
   doctype-public="-//W3C//DTD HTML 4.0//EN"
   doctype-system="http://www.w3.org/TR/REC-html40/strict.dtd"/>
   ```

---

3. See Section B.3.6 in the HTML 4.01 specification for more examples of HTML processing instructions.

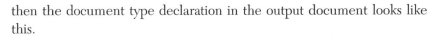

then the document type declaration in the output document looks like this.

```
<!DOCTYPE html PUBLIC
 "-//W3C//DTD HTML 4.0//EN"
 "http://www.w3.org/TR/REC-html40/strict.dtd">
```

Do not include a literal <!DOCTYPE element anywhere in an XSLT document because the XSLT processor won't like it.

8.2   Including Literal Result Elements

If you want a template to insert an HTML element in the result tree, simply include the element in the template. An HTML element in a template is a literal result element. Of course, you can include character data in a template, too. Make sure the elements nest properly. A template such as the following will not be allowed by the XML parser.

```
<xsl:template match='/'>
  <top>
</xsl:template>
```

The end-tag of the **top** element is missing. Even if the end-tag is in another template, it is still not acceptable.

```
<xsl:template match='/'>
  <top>
  <xsl:choose>
    <xsl:when test='$a=2'>
      </top>
    </xsl:when>
    <xsl:otherwise>
      something here before </top>
    </xsl:otherwise>
  </xsl:choose>
</xsl:template>
```

One of the correct ways to write this template is

```
<xsl:template match='/'>
  <xsl:choose>
    <xsl:when test='$a=2'>
      <top>
      </top>
```

```
      </xsl:when>
      <xsl:otherwise>
        <top>something here before </top>
      </xsl:otherwise>
    </xsl:choose>
  </xsl:template>
```

Then the nesting is proper.

8.2.1   *Attribute-Value Templates*

In many cases, the value of an attribute of a literal result element is the value of an `xsl:value-of` element. You can use shorthand for an `xsl:value-of` element. The shorthand uses a pair of braces to enclose an XPath expression. When the attribute is output, the XPath expression is evaluated, and its string value replaces the braces and the XPath expression enclosed in it. This is called an **attribute-value template.** For example, suppose you have this.

```
<link><source>http://www.w3.org</source>
<label>The W3C</label></link>
```

And you want to transform it into this.

```
<a href='http://www.w3.org'>The W3C</a>
```

You can have a template like this.

```
<xsl:template match='link'>
  <a href='{source/text()}'><xsl:value-of
      select='label/text()'/></a>
</xsl:template>
```

More than one attribute-value template can be used in the same attribute. For instance, the attribute-value template {`element`}/{`/top`} is a valid one. However, attribute-value templates do not nest. Therefore, {`element/{/top}}` does not do what you think it should.

You can use attribute-value templates for literal result elements and some XSLT elements only. If you use an attribute-value template in a literal result element, the output should be fine. But if you use an attribute-value template in an XSLT element, first check the syntax of the element to make sure it is allowed. For example, if you look at the syntax of the `xsl:element` element in Section C.1.11, you see that both its `name` and `namespace` attributes are specified with braces ({ and }) surrounding their data types. This means that you can specify attribute-value templates for these attributes.

8.2.2 *Context Node for an Attribute-Value Template*

Many attribute-value templates are specified for attributes for literal result elements. Where do the initial context node of these XPath expressions come from? In Chapter 6, we saw that every node in the result tree has a current node and a current node list. The context for an attribute-value template is constructed from the current node and current node list of the element in which it appears.

For example, suppose you have this.

```
<A HREF='{link/@ref}'><xsl:value-of select='link/@name'/></A>
```

You already know how an `xsl:value-of` element works. But how about the attribute-value template `link/@ref`? It is handled just like an XPath expression in the `select` attribute of an `xsl:value-of` element. The initial context node is the current node of the `A` element, the context position is the position of the current node in its current node list, and the context size is the number of nodes in the current node list.

8.3 Constructing Elements

Sometimes, you want to contruct elements using information from the source tree. Say we have this document

```
<link>
  <caption>The W3C Consortium</caption>
  <location>http://www.w3.org</location>
</link>
```

that we want to transform into the `<a>` element in HTML.

```
<a href='http://www.w3.org'>The W3C Consortium</a>
```

This is the XSLT template to create the element.

```
<a>
  <xsl:attribute name='href'><xsl:value-of
      select='location'/></xsl:attribute>
  <xsl:value-of select='caption'/>
</a>
```

We assume here that the name of the element is known. Suppose there are two possibilities, `image` or `link`, in the source document. Then we can use an `xsl:choose` element.

```
<xsl:variable name='image' select='img'/>
<xsl:variable name='link' select='a'/>

<xsl:choose>
  <xsl:when test='name()="image"'>
    <xsl:element name='{$image}'>
      <xsl:attribute name='src'><xsl:value-of
        select='location'/></xsl:attribute>
      <xsl:value-of select='caption'/>
    </xsl:element>
  </xsl:when>
  <xsl:otherwise>
    <xsl:element name='{$link}'>
      <xsl:attribute name='href'><xsl:value-of
          select='location'/></xsl:attribute>
      <xsl:value-of select='caption'/>
    </xsl:element>
  </xsl:otherwise>
</xsl:choose>
```

The `xsl:element` element can also be used to construct elements whose names are not known when the XSLT document is written. For instance, if the source document looks like this

```
<?xml version='1.0'?>
<new-element>
  <element>top</element>
  <text>The text for the top element.</text>
</new-element>
```

and if the desired output is

```
<top>The text for the top element.</top>
```

then this is the way to construct the output (assuming the current node is the `new-element` node).

```
<xsl:element name='{element}'>
  <xsl:value-of select='text'/>
</xsl:element>
```

8.3.1   *The* `xsl:attribute-set` *Element*

Often the same set of attributes is used over and over again in various areas of the same Web page. For instance, the FONT element may be used in all table elements on a Web page. Having the font attributes over and over in different places in the XSLT document can be difficult to maintain. To change some of the values of the attributes, all the places that have the FONT elements must be identified.

An `xsl:attribute-set` element can be used to group related attributes. For example, for the FONT element, the `xsl:attribute-set` element would look like this.

```
<xsl:attribute-set name='font'>
  <xsl:attribute
      name='COLOR'>#336699</xsl:attribute>
  <xsl:attribute
      name='FACE'>verdana,geneva,arial,ms sans serif</xsl:attribute>
</xsl:attribute-set>
```

To use the attribute-set, use the `xsl:use-attribute-sets` attribute in the element that should include the set of attributes.

```
<FONT xsl:use-attribute-sets='font'>Something here</FONT>
```

An `xsl:attribute-set` element can also use the `xsl:use-attribute-sets` attribute to build on a set of attributes.

8.4   Inserting Comments

If it is necessary to insert comments to the output, the `xsl:comment` element must be used. Do not place literal comments in a template, since they will be stripped before output anyway. For instance, in this template, the comments will be stripped before the template is copied to the result tree.

```
<xsl:template match='/'>
  <!-- comment 1 -->
  <top/>
  <!-- comment 2 -->
</xsl:template>
```

To insert the comments to the result tree, use this template instead.

```
<xsl:template match='/'>
  <xsl:comment> comment 1 </xsl:comment>
  <top/>
```

```
<xsl:comment> comment 2 </xsl:comment>
</xsl:template>
```

The result tree will look like this.

```
␣␣<!--␣comment␣1␣-->
␣␣<top/>
␣␣<!--␣comment␣2␣-->
```

8.5   Inserting Processing Instructions

As with the output of comments, inserting processing instructions in the result tree requires a special XSLT element. The element is `xsl:processing-
instruction`. Here is an example.

```
<xsl:processing-instruction
    name='java'>class='java.io.*'</xsl:processing-instruction>
```

The output looks like this.

```
<?java class='java.io.*'?>
```

For HTML output, it will look like this.

```
<?java class='java.io.*'>
```

The `name` attribute of the `xsl:processing-instruction` element specifies
the target of the processing instruction to be generated. The content of the element is the value of the processing instruction. Care must be take to ensure that
only text nodes are sent to the output in the processing instruction. Otherwise,
it is an error.

8.6   The `xsl:text` Element

There are situations where a text node must be generated. For instance, in
HTML documents, there may be JavaScript fragments. As JavaScript has a very
different syntactic structure than HTML, you can use the `xsl:text` element
to output JavaScript fragments. For example, suppose you want to output the
following.

```
function numString(num) {
  if (num < 10)
    sNum = "0" + String(num);
  else
```

```
      sNum = String(num);
   return sNum;
}
```

Usually, the character < is replaced by the entity < in the output. However, for HTML documents, the JavaScript fragments should have the character < written as is. To do that, use the xsl:text. Set the disable-output-escaping attribute to yes, and the character will be written out to the output as is. This is the xsl:text to output the preceding code fragment.

```
<xsl:text disable-output-escaping='yes'>
function numString(num) {
   if (num &lt; 10)
     sNum = "0" + String(num);
   else
     sNum = String(num);
   return sNum;
}
</xsl:text>
```

If you put the fragment in a SCRIPT element, then the escape will not be performed by default.

8.7   The xsl:value-of Element

The xsl:value-of element is used to evaluate an XPath expression and convert it to a string. For example, to insert the value of 1 + 10 as a string, you would do this.

```
<xsl:value-of select='1 + 10'/>
```

The value of the select attribute can be arbitrarily complex, of course. However, the result is always converted to its string value. See Section 5.4 for information about how conversion to string is done for the four data types.

8.8   Variables

In XSLT, a variable is given a value using an xsl:variable element. If you want to assign the value 123 to a variable called var, it would look like this.

```
<xsl:variable name="var" select="123"/>
```

The variable var now has the numeric value 123.

If you want to obtain the value of a variable, use the $ prefix. This is how you would get the value of the variable var.

```
<xsl:value-of select="$var"/>
```

You cannot change the value of a variable. You can only refer to its value after the variable has been assigned a value using an xsl:variable element. Suppose we have this template.

```
<xsl:template name="example">
  <xsl:variable name='var' select='123'/>
  <block name='A'>
    <xsl:variable name='var' select='456'/>
  </block>
  <xsl:value-of select='$var'/>
</xsl:template>
```

Because there is an attempt to change the value of the variable var inside the block element, this template is not correct.

8.8.1   Global Variables

A global variable is a variable assigned a value in an xsl:variable element that is a child of the xsl:stylesheet element. For instance, the variable global is a global variable and the variable local is not a global variable (because it is not a child of the xsl:stylesheet element).

```
<?xml version='1.0'?>
<xsl:stylesheet version='1.0'
      xmlns:xsl=http://'www.w3.org/1999/XSL/Transform'>
  <xsl:variable name='global' select='123'/>
  <xsl:template match='/'>
    <xsl:variable name='local' select='456'/>
  </xsl:template>
</xsl:stylesheet>
```

8.8.2   Visibility of Variables

The scope (or the visibility) of a variable in XSLT is the set of nodes that are the descendants of the variable element and its following siblings and their descendants. Suppose there is a template like this.

```
<xsl:template match='abc'>
  <sbcdg><!-- something here --></sbcdg>
  <xsl:variable name='var' select='0'/>
  <sibling-one>
    <sibling-two/>
  </sibling-one>
  <sibling-three/>
</xsl:template>
```

Then the scope of the variable named var is the set of nodes that include
<sibling-one> and its descendants, <sibling-two> and its descendants, and
<sibling-three>.

Figure 8.1 shows some examples of declaring a variable improperly.

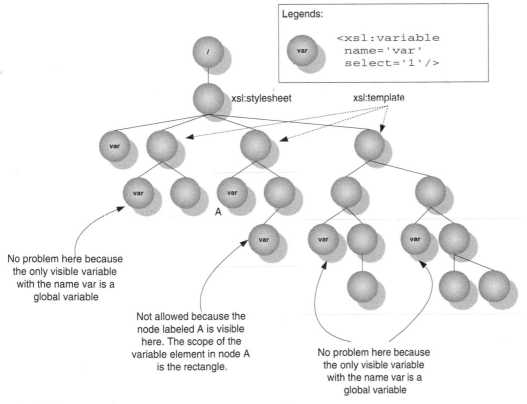

FIGURE
8.1   Visibilities of variables

8.9   Result Tree Fragments

XSLT adds a fifth data type to the data types allowed by XPath: result tree fragments. The operations allowed on result tree fragments are the same operations as those allowed on strings. The difference is that when `xsl:copy-of` is used to copy the value of a variable holding a result tree fragment, the whole result tree fragment is copied to the result tree. Here is an example.

```
<xsl:variable name="var"><top>text in top</top></xsl:variable>
```

The variable `var` actually holds the XML fragment.

```
<top>text in top</top>
```

When the XSLT element

```
<xsl:copy-of select='$var'/>
```

is encountered in the result tree, the whole fragment is copied to the result tree, replacing the `xsl:copy-of` element in the result tree.

If you use anything other than an `xsl:copy-of` element, the result tree fragment is treated as a string. The value of the string is simply the string value of the result tree fragment. For example, if you have the following

```
<xsl:variable name='rsf'><writing-tool>
  <name>pen</name>
  <kind>all-point</kind></writing-tool>
</xsl:variable>
<xsl:value-of select='$rsf/name'/>
```

do not expect the result to be `pen`. Instead, you will get an error. The problem is that result tree fragments are not node-sets, and the result of each step of a location path must be a node-set. Because the value of `$rsf` is actually a string, `$rsf/name` does not make sense. Since the result of the first step is a string, the second step cannot be executed.

8.10   Whitespace-Only Text Nodes

In XSLT, a text node will never be removed under any circumstances unless it contains nothing but whitespace characters (a space, a tab, a linefeed, or a carriage return). Even if there are only whitespaces in a text node, it may or may not be removed, depending on which tree the text node is in.

8.10.1   *XSLT Document*

If whitespace-only text node is in the XSLT document, the text node is removed unless it is in an `xsl:text` element.

8.10.2   *Source Document*

If whitespace-only text node is in a source tree, then it depends on whether you want it preserved or stripped. The source document may also specify whether whitespace-only text nodes should be preserved or not.

Preserving or Stripping Space

You can use two top-level elements in XSLT to specify two groups of elements in the source trees, elements that should preserve their whitespace-only text nodes, and elements that should remove their whitespace-only text nodes. For an element that preserves its whitespace-only text nodes, all text nodes are preserved, whether they contain only whitespaces or not. For an element that strips its whitespace-only text nodes, all its text nodes with only whitespace characters will be stripped.

Use the `xsl:preserve-space` element to specify the elements that preserve their whitespace-only text nodes. Use the `xsl:strip-space` element to specify the elements that strip their whitespace-only text nodes.

Initially, before any `xsl:strip-space` or `xsl:preserve-space` elements are encountered, all elements are assumed to preserve their whitespace-only text nodes. To specify that the elements `story` and `summary` should have their whitespace-only text nodes removed, an `xsl:strip-space` element can be specified as follows with a space-separated list of elements.

```
<xsl:strip-space elements='story summary'/>
```

Although XSLT documents included by other XSLT documents can have their own `xsl:strip-space` and `xsl:preserve-space` elements, in most cases it is probably a good idea to have these elements only in XSLT documents that will not be imported by other XSLT documents. If you want to specify all elements, use * as the value.

8.10.3   *The* `xml:space` *Attribute*

Suppose you do not specify an element in both the `xsl:strip-space` and the `xsl:preserve-space` elements. The default says that the whitespace-only text nodes for the element should be preserved. However, this default can be overridden by an `xml:space` attribute in the source document.

> For each of the ancestors of the text node, starting from its parent to the root in order, check if there is an xml:space attribute in the element.

> If there is such an attribute and the value of the attribute is preserve, then the text node is not removed.

> If there is such an attribute and the value of the attribute is default, then the text node is removed. If it is in the XSLT document; otherwise, it is preserved.

> Only the first occurrence of the attribute will be considered in the order from the parent of the text node to the root.

If there is no xml:space attribute found, then depending on whether the text node is in the source document or in the XSLT document, it will be handled differently.

You can also specify the xml:space attribute in your XSLT documents. Be careful not to specify it in HTML elements: The attribute itself is not stripped. So if you specify it in an HTML element, the attribute will go to the result tree. For example, suppose you have the following template.

```
<xsl:template match='/'>
  <HTML xml:space='preserve'>
    <HEAD>
      <TITLE>Do not Strip Space</TITLE>
    </HEAD>
    <BODY>
      <H1>A newline right here:
      </H1>
    </BODY>
  </HTML>
</xsl:template>
```

The result looks like this

```
<HTML xml:space="preserve">
    <HEAD>
      <TITLE>Do not Strip Space</TITLE>
    </HEAD>
    <BODY>
      <H1>A newline right here:
      </H1>
    </BODY>
  </HTML>
```

even if you specify that indentation is not to be used. Furthermore, the
xml:space attribute stays with the HTML element. The xml:space will be in
your output.

If you want to preserve the whitespace-only text nodes in the template,
use the following template instead with the xml:space attribute moved to the
template, not the HTML element.

```
<?xml version='1.0'?>
<xsl:stylesheet version='1.0'
    xmlns:xsl='http://www.w3.org/1999/XSL/Transform'>

  <xsl:output method='html' indent='no'/>

<xsl:template match='/' xml:space='preserve'>
  <HTML>
    <HEAD>
      <TITLE>Do not Strip Space</TITLE>
    </HEAD>
    <BODY>
      <H1>A newline right here:
      </H1>
    </BODY>
  </HTML>
</xsl:template>

</xsl:stylesheet>
```

The result looks like this.

```
␣␣<HTML>
␣␣␣␣<HEAD>
␣␣␣␣␣␣<TITLE>Do not Strip Space</TITLE>
␣␣␣␣</HEAD>
␣␣␣␣<BODY>
␣␣␣␣␣␣<H1>A newline right here:
␣␣␣␣␣␣</H1>
␣␣␣␣</BODY>
␣␣</HTML>
```

The difference between this output and the output when xml:space is an
attribute of HTML is the whitespaces before and after the HTML element. In
the previous example, the whitespaces before and after the HTML are removed

(because the default action for text nodes with only whitespaces in an XSLT document is removal).

8.11   Summary

You have now seen all the elements that you can use to create the result tree from input trees and the instruction tree. In this chapter, you saw the elements that you can use to construct elements, attributes, processing instructions, comments, and document type declaration. You have also seen how to declare a variable and get the value of an XPath expression.

8.12   Looking Ahead

If we put all the templates for a project in the same file, isn't it difficult to reuse templates that might be helpful for other projects? The next chapter shows you how to include other XSLT documents in a document.

$\langle\,9\,\rangle$

Combining Templates

It is always a good practice to group related templates together. It makes it easier to maintain the group. And, anyway, if you are using XSLT in a project, you seldom generate only one HTML document with one XML source document. When you generate multiple HTML outputs from one XML document, you will frequently use the same templates in different XSLT documents.

We saw an example of this in Chapter 3, and we learned that the XSLT elements `xsl:include` and `xsl:import` are used to combine XSLT documents. The XSLT processor handles these elements before the transformation begins, so you have to know what XSLT documents you want to include or import when you design an XSLT document.

9.1   The `xsl:include` Element

An `xsl:include` element includes all the elements from another XSLT document. The element's `href` attribute specifies the document to be included. The elements in the included document are effectively inserted in the including document at the point of the `xsl:include` element. The included elements will replace the `xsl:include` element itself.

199

Here is an example of the xsl:include element in use. The templates in the document referred to by the URI http://www.jmedium.com/templates are included in the current XSLT document.

```
<?xml version='1.0'?>
<xsl:stylesheet
 xmlns:xsl='http://www.w3.org/1999/XSL/Transform'
 version='1.0'>
  <xsl:output method='html'/>
  <xsl:include href='http://www.jmedium.com/templates'/>
</xsl:sylesheet>
```

The templates in http://www.jmedium.com/templates will be included via the HTTP protocol.

You can use a relative URI for the value of the href attribute. Before the document is included, the absolute URI is first computed using the base URI of the xsl:include element, which depends on the base URI of the document where it resides. The base URI of the document is assigned by the XSLT processor.

If you use an XSLT processor on the command line, the base URI for the XSLT document is probably the working directory in which you run the processor. For example, suppose you run this command in the directory C:\xslt

```
xt first.xml first.xsl
```

and the file *first.xsl* is

```
<?xml version='1.0'?>
<xsl:stylesheet version='1.0'
    xmlns:xsl='http://www.w3.org/1999/XSL/Transform'>

  <xsl:include href='second.xsl'/>
</xsl:stylesheet>
```

Then the file *second.xsl* in the directory C:\xslt will be included.

Suppose you have another XSLT document, *top.xsl*

```
<?xml version='1.0'?>
<xsl:stylesheet version='1.0'
    xmlns:xsl='http://www.w3.org/1999/XSL/Transform'>

  <xsl:include href='http://localhost:8080/first.xsl'/>
</xsl:stylesheet>
```

and you run this command.

```
xt top.xml top.xsl
```

Where would *second.xsl* be included? The same place as *first.xsl*—http://
localhost:8080. Therefore, the base URI of *second.xsl* is obtained from the
base URI of *first.xsl*.

An XSLT document cannot include itself because this recursion would
confuse the XSLT processor. Of course, if an XSLT document includes itself
directly, it is easy to spot. However, it is possible that an XSLT document
includes another XSLT document, and if so, it is difficult to determine if the
document does include itself.

9.2   The `xsl:import` Element

The other way to include templates declared in a different document is with the
`xsl:import` element. This element behaves differently from the `xsl:include`
element. When an `xsl:include` element is used, the templates in the included
file are inserted into the current XSLT document. However, it is possible that
one template in the included file may match the exact same pattern as a template
that is in the including file. For instance, suppose the including XSLT document
looks like this.

```
<?xml version='1.0'?>

<xsl:stylesheet
 xmlns:xsl='http://www.w3.org/1999/XSL/Transform'
 version='1.0'>

  <xsl:include href='http://www.jmedium.com/templates1'/>

  <xsl:template match='/'>
    <a><xsl:apply-templates/></a>
  </xsl:template>

  <xsl:template match='top'>
    <xsl:attribute name='href'>
      http://www.w3.org
    </xsl:attribute>
  </xsl:template>
</xsl:stylesheet>
```

And the file pointed to by `http://www.jmedium.com/templates1` looks like this.

```
<?xml version='1.0'?>
<xsl:stylesheet
 xmlns:xsl='http://www.w3.org/1999/XSL/Transform'
 version='1.0'>

  <xsl:template match='top'>
      Inside the top element.
  </xsl:template>
</xsl:stylesheet>
```

When you match a **top** element, two templates match the same **top** element, both with the same priority of 0. This is an error because the XSLT processor will not be able to choose which template to use. The specification states that the processor can either signal the error and stop or choose the template that is the last one defined in the XSLT document. Because it is not obvious that this is happening, suspect a matching conflict when you don't get the output you expected.

With the `xsl:import` element, however, the imported templates always have lower priorities than the templates declared in the importing document. In the preceding example, the including file is modified to be an importing file like this.

```
<?xml version='1.0'?>

<xsl:stylesheet
 xmlns:xsl='http://www.w3.org/1999/XSL/Transform'
 version='1.0'>

  <xsl:import href='http://www.jmedium.com/templates1'/>

  <xsl:template match='/'>
    <a><xsl:apply-templates/></a>
  </xsl:template>

  <xsl:template match='top'>
    <xsl:attribute name='href'>
      http://www.w3.org
    </xsl:attribute>
  </xsl:template>
</xsl:stylesheet>
```

Then the imported template has lower priority, and the template declared in the importing file will be used when you match a **top** element.

9.2.1   *Import Precedence*

In Section 6.7 we saw how to select the template that matched the current node. Before doing that, it is necessary to compute the **import precedence** of the matching templates. Only matching templates with the highest import precedence will be considered. In other words, the import precedence is always considered first, filtering out all but the templates that have the highest import precedence. Only then will the template priorities of the matching templates be compared.

The templates in the importing document always have higher precedence than the templates in the imported document. For instance, suppose there are three documents, Document A, Document B, and Document C. Document A imports Document B, and Document B imports Document C. If there is a conflict between a template in Document A and Document B or Document C, the template in Document A is always chosen. If there is a conflict between a template in Document B and a template in Document C, Document B is always chosen. Of course, if there is no template in Document A that matches an element and only templates in Document B match the element, the templates in Document B will be used.

The default templates provided by the XSLT processor always have the lowest import precedence. Any template in any document that has a conflict with one of the default templates is always chosen over the default template. So here is the complete algorithm for finding a template to match for this example.

1. If there is a template in Document A that matches the node, this template is used.

2. If there is no template in Document A but one in Document B that matches the node, this template is used.

3. If there is no template in Document A or B but one in Document C that matches the node, this template is used.

4. If no templates match the node in any document, use the default template that matches the node.

If Document A imports Document B and Document D, in that order

```
<xsl:import href='B'/>
<xsl:import href='D'/>
```

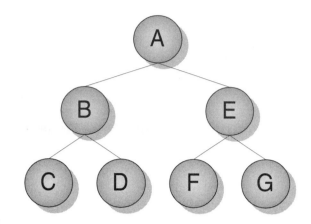

An import tree

and there is a conflict between a template in Document B and one in Document D, the template in Document D has the higher precedence because it occurs last in the import list.

Import Tree

The descriptions we have so far are not sufficient to handle a situation like the following. Suppose Document A imports

1. Document B, which imports
   a. Document C and
   b. Document D
2. Document E, which imports
   a. Document F and
   b. Document G

What is the order in terms of import precedence? We can draw an **import tree** for the above scenario (see Figure 9.1). The same depth-first traversal is used to find the import precedence. However, in our traversal procedure in Section 4.3.1, the label is output the moment a node is visited. This is called a **pre-order** depth-first traversal. For the import tree, the label of a node is not output until all the node's child nodes have been visited. It is called a **post-order** depth-first traversal of the tree.

It is easy to find both the pre-order and post-order depth-first traversals of a tree. Simply output the label whenever a node is visited. And it does not matter if a node has been visited before. For instance, for the import tree, the order of visit is A, B, C, B, D, B, A, E, F, E, G, E, and A. To get the pre-order traversal, simply remove all labels after the first occurrence of the labels. For instance, the node A has been visited three times, so remove the second and third labels. For nodes B and E—both visited twice—remove the second occurrence. The result is A, B, C, D, E, F, and G. For a post-order traversal, remove all but the last occurrence of the nodes. For Node A, remove the first and second occurrences. For nodes B and E, remove the first occurrence. The result is C, D, B, F, G, E, and A.

The import precedence of the example import tree is therefore C, D, B, F, G, E, and A, from the lowest to the highest. From the highest to the lowest, it is A, E, G, F, B, D, and C. Notice that although Document B is imported by Document A, it actually has a relatively low precedence compared to Documents G and F.

9.3   The `xsl:apply-imports` Element

You can partially override the import precedence of templates by using the `xsl:apply-imports` element. Suppose you have the following template to boldface some text defined in an XSLT document called *a.xsl*.

```
<xsl:template match='top'>
  <b><xsl:value-of select='.'/></b>
</xsl:template>
```

If you want to italicize the text too, you can define the following template.

```
<xsl:template match='top'>
  <i><xsl:apply-imports/></i>
</xsl:template>
```

Then in the document that has the above template, include the following `xsl:import` element.

```
<xsl:import href='a.xsl'/>
```

Suppose the input is

```
<?xml version='1.0'?>
<top>This is a text node in the top element.</top>
```

Then the first template would transform it into

```
<b>This is a text node in the top element.</b>
```

and the second template would transform it into

```
<i><b>This is a text node in the top element.</b></i>
```

The `xsl:apply-imports` element is useful only when you are not allowed to modify the imported template nor redefine the whole template. Granted, such a situation does not arise very often.

9.4   Summary

To write XSLT documents in a modular way, it is important to know how to include and import external XSLT documents. It also makes reuse possible. However, do not use these elements if it is not necessary. Defining one template in its own XSLT document, for instance, is overkill.

9.5   Looking Ahead

In the next chapter, we will talk about the extension mechanism in XSLT. Since different XSLT processors have different extensions, it is usually a good idea to steer clear of extension elements and functions unless there is absolutely no other way to do what you want without them.

⟨10⟩

Extensions

> Ancient men have limits on their knowledge.
> The limits are at the point when matter had not formed.
> They do not know anything extended beyond that point.
> —*Zhuang Zi*

XSLT is not designed to be a general programming language but is meant to provide facilities for performing transformations on XML documents. Specifically, XSLT provides features that will satisfy the transformation requirements in XSL. If other features are needed for some special purposes, XSLT provides a mechanism to allow developers of XSLT processors to incorporate extensions to XSLT.

There are two ways to extend XSLT. An XSLT processor can provide extension functions. For instance, if there is a reason for an XSLT document to use operating system facilities, an XSLT processor can provide a set of operating system functions. You can then use the functions inside your XSLT documents to access the operating system functions. An XSLT processor can also extend XSLT by providing extension elements. For example, if a `while` loop is desired, an XSLT processor can provide an extension element to provide the looping element.

It is important to remember that XSLT documents do not provide the extension elements or extension functions. They only use them. The XSLT processor used to run XSLT documents must provide the extension functions and elements. If an XSLT processor does not support an extension function, the extension function cannot be used in XSLT documents with that XSLT processor. An XSLT processor is not obligated to provide extension functions or elements provided by other XSLT processors.

The XSLT processors that provide extension functions and elements include XT, Saxon, Xalan, and the extension mechanisms are different. Consult the documentation of the processors to find the ones that provide the extension functions or elements that you need.

10.1 Declaring Extension Functions and Extension Elements

It is necessary to first declare the namespace for the extension elements and functions. The extension elements and function do not use the XSLT namespace. Their namespace prefixes are declared in the `xsl:stylesheet` element before they can be used, using the `extension-element-prefixes` attribute. For example, suppose there is a set of extension functions that use the prefix `os`; the stylesheet element will look like this.

```
<xsl:stylesheet
 extension-element-prefixes='os'
 version='1.0'
 xmlns:xsl='http://www.w3.org/1999/XSL/Transform'
 xmlns:os='http://www.jmedium.com/OS'>
<!-- the body of the stylesheet -->
</xsl:stylesheet>
```

The namespace prefix `os` must be declared before it is used. If more than one namespace for extension functions or elements are used, then the namespaces should be separated by a space in the `extension-element-prefixes` attribute.

10.2 Using Extension Functions

An extension function is used the same way as the default functions provided by XPath or XSLT. The namespace must be used in all such occurrences. For instance, to get the output of the operating system command `date` and put it in the output file using the `os` extension functions, the `xsl:value-of` element is used.

```
<xsl:value-of select='os:date()'/>
```

10.3 Using Extension Elements

Using an extension element inside a template is the same as using an XSLT element inside a template. For example, suppose a `while` element has been defined with the extension namespace `ext`. Here is an example of how it can be used.

```
<xsl:template match='/'>
  <xsl:variable name='var' select='100'/>
  <ext:while test='$var > 0'
       update='$var - 1'><P><xsl:value-of
       select='$var'/></P>
  </ext:while>
</xsl:template>
```

Here, the `P` element will be output 100 times, each with a text node bearing the value of the variable `var` at the time when the element is written to the output.

10.4 Checking Availability

To check if an element is available from the XSLT processor, the `element-available()` function can be used. The argument to the function is the name of the element to check. If the expanded name of the argument is available as an instruction element in the XSLT processor, the function returns true, otherwise, it returns false. This function can be used to check if an XSLT instruction element is available, too.

To check if an extension function or an XSLT function is available, `function-available()` can be used. Again, if the argument, converted to its expanded name, is available in the XSLT processor, then the function returns true, otherwise, it returns false.

When functions or elements are not available, XSLT has a rudimentary exception handling element called `xsl:fallback`. Fallback elements are put inside instruction elements. If the element containing the fallback elements is not available in the XSLT processor used to process the XSLT document, these fallback elements will be processed one by one in document order. If the element containing the fallback elements is available, then these fallback elements are simply ignored. In other words, the fallback element is most useful for extension elements.

10.5   Summary

We just examined the extension mechanism in XSLT that provides additional elements and functions outside of the XSLT and XPath specifications. Because of interoperability issues that arise, XSLT processor writers and vendors are discussing possible ways to add extensions to XSLT processors, to allow extensions to be used with any XSLT processor, and to create a common set of extensions for XSLT processors. Before these efforts bear fruit, however, be wary of extensions unless using only the elements and functions specified in the XSLT and XPath specifications is not sufficient for what you need to do.

10.6   Looking Ahead

We have now seen most of the XSLT elements. In the next chapter, we will switch gears and talk about how these elements can be used and how XSLT documents can be constructed in different situations, with useful tips you can use for your own projects as well.

PART III

⟨11⟩

Idioms and Tips

After a language has been used for a period of time, certain patterns and usages in the language become apparent. Users learn to recognize pitfalls as well as shortcuts and conveniences.

These features are called idioms and (design or software) patterns. Idioms are recurring programming practices—perhaps pertinent to a specific programming language only. Design patterns are called micro-architectures and are on a larger scale than idioms, useful for solving similar problems in any programming language.

Idioms are not always profound. Many of them are just plain common sense. Some are like warning signs or those handy tips you get from chefs on TV cooking programs. Most will become second nature after a while, but others will rescue you from unusual obstacles.

Patterns are components of a larger vision for an architecture that serves certain purposes. For instance, if you want your house to feel comfortable and hospitable, what do you do? There are many factors that you must consider. It's not enough to just make sure your guest has a place to sit. It may be necessary to plan details for every moment that guest is in your house.

XSLT is still young, and its paradigm is unfamiliar. Patterns for XSLT are still being mined. However, there are XSLT idioms that are useful for XSLT developers right now. This chapter presents some of them.

11.1   Table Generation

The general layout of a Web page is usually designed by a graphics designer or a producer before it is given to an HTML developer to handle the dynamic aspects of the Web page. The job of the HTML developer is to carve up the different components on a Web page and put them into different XSLT templates to be generated. The only time an HTML developer may have to generate a table on the fly is when there is a component on the Web page that has requirements such as these.

1. A middle column with a headline, a photo, and the first paragraph of the main story.
2. A two-column layout of the day's stories.

Because the HTML developer does not know until publication time how many stories are available, the second requirement must be designed with insufficient information. In this particular case, the developer doesn't know how many rows are needed. All of these design problems, however, have the same solution.

To generate a table with XSLT, a template must first be used to produce the table's features. Then, using the `xsl:for-each` element, it must iterate over the elements—in our example, stories. Fill in the necessary empty cells to pad the last row of the table.

The number of columns is set to 2 in this example, because we have a two-column layout; you can set it to 3 if you have a three-column layout, and so on.

```
<xsl:template match='stories'>
  <table>
    <xsl:for-each select='story'>
      <!-- generate cells and rows -->
    </xsl:for-each>
  </table>
</xsl:template>
```

To ensure the elements are nested properly, a named template is used to generate one row of the table. As the named template handles the same number of stories as the number of columns in the table, the named template is called only for the first story in a row. The first story in a row is determined by finding the remainder after dividing the position of the current story by the number of columns in the table (2). If the remainder is 1, then the story is the first story of a row. Otherwise, it is not.

```
<xsl:template match='stories'>
  <table>
    <xsl:for-each select='story'>
      <xsl:if test='position() mod 2 = 1'>
        <tr>
          <!-- generate a row here -->
        </tr>
      </xsl:if>
    </xsl:for-each>
  </table>
</xsl:template>
```

The number 2 in this code is the number of columns.

Call the named template by replacing

```
<!-- generate a row here -->
```

with this xsl:call-template (the named template is called row).

```
<xsl:call-template name='row'>
  <xsl:with-param name='position' select='position()'/>
  <xsl:with-param name='parent' select='..'/>
  <xsl:with-param name='times' select='2'/>
</xsl:call-template>
```

There are three parameters for the named template. The position parameter is the context position of the first column. The parent parameter contains the parent of the story element. The times parameter is the number of columns in a row.

The named template iterates as many times as necessary to produce a row.

```
<xsl:template name='row'>
  <xsl:param name='position'/>
  <xsl:param name='parent'/>
  <xsl:param name='times'/>
  <xsl:if test='$times > 0'>
    <xsl:choose>
      <xsl:when test='$position > last()'>
        <td> </td>
      </xsl:when>
```

```
        <xsl:otherwise>
          <td><xsl:value-of select='$parent/story[$position]'/>
          </td>
        </xsl:otherwise>
      </xsl:choose>
      <xsl:call-template name='row'>
        <xsl:with-param name='position' select='$position + 1'/>
        <xsl:with-param name='parent' select='$parent'/>
        <xsl:with-param name='times' select='$times - 1'/>
      </xsl:call-template>
    </xsl:if>
  </xsl:template>
```

As you can see, a hardspace (or   in a character reference) is
used for an empty cell because some browsers still do not render empty cells
properly.

The `xsl:if` element determines if the columns have been filled. If they
are filled, nothing is done. If all the stories have not been used, add one story
to the column. If all the stories are used, fill the column with an empty space.
Continue to the next story by incrementing the column number and decreasing
the number of columns to fill. The named template is similar for all cases,
regardless of the number of columns in a row.

If we have this input file

```
<?xml version='1.0'?>
<stories>
  <story>1</story>
  <story>2</story>
  <story>3</story>
  <story>4</story>
  <story>5</story>
  <story>6</story>
  <story>7</story>
  <story>8</story>
  <story>9</story>
</stories>
```

the output will look like this.

```
<html>
<body>
<table>
```

```
<tr>
<td>1</td><td>2</td>
</tr>
<tr>
<td>3</td><td>4</td>
</tr>
<tr>
<td>5</td><td>6</td>
</tr>
<tr>
<td>7</td><td>8</td>
</tr>
<tr>
<td>9</td><td> </td>
</tr>
</table>
</body>
</html>
```

But you must have a template that matches the document template like this.

```
<xsl:template match='/'>
  <html>
  <body>
    <xsl:apply-templates/>
  </body>
  </html>
</xsl:template>
```

11.2 Character Replacement

It is often necessary to replace the same string throughout a text node. For example, you might have to replace newline characters with BR elements. The following is the named template that can be used to replace any substring contained in a string by another string or an element, maybe even a subtree.

```
<xsl:template name='replace-substring'>
  <xsl:param name='text'/>
  <xsl:param name='from'/>
  <xsl:param name='to'/>
  <xsl:choose>
    <xsl:when test='contains($text, $from)'>
```

```
                    <xsl:value-of select='substring-before($text, $from)'/>
                    <xsl:copy-of select='$to'/>
                    <xsl:call-template name='replace-substring'>
                      <xsl:with-param name='text'
                            select='substring-after($text, $from)'/>
                      <xsl:with-param name='from' select='$from'/>
                      <xsl:with-param name='to' select='$to'/>
                    </xsl:call-template>
                  </xsl:when>
                  <xsl:otherwise>
                    <xsl:copy-of select='$text'/>
                  </xsl:otherwise>
                </xsl:choose>
              </xsl:template>
```

To replace all the newline characters in a text node by the BR element, call the template like this.

```
<xsl:call-template name='replace-substring'>
  <xsl:with-param name='text' select='text()'/>
  <xsl:with-param name='from'>&#xA;</xsl:with-param>
  <xsl:with-param name='to'><BR/></xsl:with-param>
</xsl:call-template>
```

11.3   Using xsl:include for Project Reuse

When you develop XSLT documents in a project, the shared templates are usually put into one or more documents. It is usually a good idea to use xsl:include rather than xsl:import to reuse these XSLT documents.

Including documents ensures that any duplicate templates can be identified. Templates matching the same elements with the same priority are usually troublesome in a project. They may have been written by different developers with different results for the same elements. These templates should be flushed out as early as possible in the development process.

If you need to use xsl:import to ensure that the imported templates have lower priorities, perhaps you should reorganize the documents that contain shared templates. You may want to find out whether the templates you need to override should be in the shared documents at all.

Because it is a good idea to test all the templates you design individually, you should design a root template for testing purposes only. To ensure that the XSLT processor will not use this testing root template, whenever you include an XSLT document, make sure the document does not have any root template. Indeed, make sure the included document does not have templates that will disrupt the including XSLT document.

11.4 Using `xsl:import` for Reuse from Different Projects

To reuse XSLT documents from other projects, use `xsl:import` rather than `xsl:include.` If you use `xsl:import`, you can be comfortable that the templates you reuse have lower import priorities than the templates you define in the importing document. You can easily override an undesired template in an imported document by defining a new template in the importing template with the same value in the `match` attribute of the template.

Usually when you use `xsl:import`, you really only need some of the templates in the imported document. This is usually the motivation for reusing templates from other projects.

11.5 Using the mode Attribute to Organize Templates

When you have to define two or more templates to match the same element, you should reorganize the templates you already have. This situation may arise when you have to handle the same element in two or more ways, depending on the project. The usual impulse is to combine all the templates that match the same element and use an `xsl:choose` element to handle each situation.

But when it comes to XSLT, using `xsl:choose` elements to combine templates is not always a good idea. You might need a new way to handle the element later on, and you will have to find out where you encountered it before.

Since you have `xsl:include` and `xsl:import` elements, it is not always obvious which is the proper template to modify. It's best to first determine the different ways that elements need to be handled and divide the templates into groups, with each group used for one way. If the template contains an `xsl:choose` element for each way, break a template into independent templates. Finally, assign each group a different `mode` string. Then when a new way is needed, it will be clear how many new templates are required.

11.6   The xsl:include and xsl:import Elements

Of course, xsl:import elements must always be the first elements of an XSLT document, followed by any xsl:include elements.

You may put xsl:include elements in any location of an XSLT document as long as they are top-level elements. The positions of templates are not important unless there are two or more templates that match the same element. The last template is always chosen.

However, it is almost always a bad idea to rely on tie-breaking. You should examine the templates to find out why two templates that match the same element have the same priority. For example, this XSLT document has an xsl:include element in the beginning of the document.

```
<xsl:stylesheet
    xmlns:xsl='http://www.w3.org/1999/XSL/Transform'
    version='1.0'>
  <xsl:include href='included.xsl'/>

  <xsl:template match='ticket'>
    <!-- body of the template in the including
         document -->
  </xsl:template>
</xsl:stylesheet>
```

the included.xsl element is

```
<xsl:stylesheet
    xmlns:xsl='http://www.w3.org/1999/XSL/Transform'
    version='1.0'>
  <xsl:template match='ticket'>
    <!-- the body of the template in the included
         document -->
  </xsl:template>
</xsl:stylesheet>
```

According to the XSLT specification, the template in the including document will be the template used, even though the priority of the two templates is the same.

However, if you put the xsl:include element behind the template defined in the including document like this

```
<xsl:stylesheet
    xmlns:xsl='http://www.w3.org/1999/XSL/Transform'
```

```
     version='1.0'>
  <xsl:template match='ticket'>
    <!-- body of the template in the including
         document -->
  </xsl:template>

  <xsl:include href='included.xsl'/>
</xsl:stylesheet>
```

then the template in the included document is used instead. Therefore, don't depend on the location of the declaration to determine which template to use in your XSLT documents.

11.7   Using a Global Parameter to Seed Configuration

In XSLT, you can specify as many parameters as you want to an XSLT document on the command line. However, you should probably limit the number of parameters you pass to an XSLT document on the command line. You need 10 global `xsl:param` elements if you want to specify 10 command-line parameters.

If you need a lot of configuration parameters, put them in an XML document and design the XSLT document to read the configurations from the XML document. Then only the file name needs to be specified on the command line. Since you can only pass in numbers and strings anyway, the command line option is not the most flexible.[1]

11.8   Absolute Paths and Template Patterns

When designing your first XSLT templates, it is tempting to use absolute paths for the value of the `match` attribute of the templates, thinking that it helps the XSLT processor find the proper templates faster and more efficiently. But, depending on the implementations, it could make it less efficient and it might make your templates rigid and hard to reuse.

---

1. It is true some XSLT processors allow you to convert a string into a node-set by extension elements, but I don't like to use extension elements unless I have no other choice. In this case, I do have an alternative that does not use extensions.

We already saw how to match patterns with the current node. We saw that the more steps the pattern has, the more work the XSLT processor has to find the most appropriate template. If you have absolute paths, the XSLT processor has to match all the way to the root of the tree. It also makes life harder because if the same elements are in different levels inside different elements—like a `date` element is prone to be—there must be one template that uses an absolute path for each different place the element can occur.

It is also harder to reuse templates with absolute paths as patterns because different projects usually do not share the same XML documents. Here is an example of a template using an absolute path.

```
<xsl:template match='/book/author/lastname'>
</xsl:template>
```

11.9   Steps for Template Patterns

Instead of using absolute paths for template patterns, limiting your patterns to one or two steps makes the template more versatile. Then you can reuse the template in more places. Another reason why one or two steps are enough is that you use XSLT to perform half of the transformation process and guide the other half by using appropriate `xsl:apply-templates` elements. Patterns with many steps mean that you are not guiding the transformation enough.

Of course, matching patterns with one or two steps is much faster. Furthermore, the priorities of templates are straightforward for patterns with one or two steps. When two patterns with more than one step match the same element, they have the same priorities, so it does not help to specify too many steps when there are ambiguities.

Although one step is the best for template patterns, you sometimes need two levels. There are two common situations when you need two steps.

1. When you need to specify what the parent element is. This situation arises when you have elements with the same name in different parts of the same XML tree.

2. When you want to match an attribute of a specific element.

Again, 80 percent of the time you will need only one or at most two steps in your template patterns. This is one of the strengths of XSLT. Take advantage of it.

You can limit the number of steps for patterns by specifying more specific location paths for the `select` attribute of the `apply-templates` elements. It is cheaper to evaluate a location path there.

11.10   Using Simple Predicates in Template Patterns

Templates are not just for the XSLT processors. You should be able to read and understand them because you may want to use some templates for more than one project. Whether the template can be used verbatim (by `xsl:import`) or with cutting and pasting, you should be able to understand what you are reusing.

Using simple predicates is one way of ensuring readability. Simple predicates produce a faster matching process, and the templates handle the right granularity of nodes. You want templates that match the right amount of nodes—not too narrow, not too broad. Templates with complicated predicates usually match too few nodes. These templates are not very versatile and cannot be easily reused. Most templates do not have predicates, and those that do have simple predicates like

```
story[1]
```

to handle the first story in a special way and perhaps

```
story[position() < 10]
```

to handle only the first 10 stories. Be careful about the priorities of templates though; the above two patterns have the same priority.

11.11   Using `translate()` to Convert Cases

Sometimes you have to compare a string but you are not sure about whether it is in upper case, lower case, or a combination of both. It's best to convert the string into all upper case or all lower case with the XPath `translate()` function. (See Section C.2.34 for more details about the `translate` function.)

Suppose the string to be compared is `Final`, but it is unclear whether the string will turn out to be `FINAL` or `final`. Let's convert the string to `FINAL`, using the `translate()` function.

```
translate($word, 'final', 'FINAL')
```

This is assuming the variable `$word` holds the string to be compared. This is more a pragmatic tip than anything else. We do not live in a perfect world, so it's good sometimes to be suspicious of the input.

11.12   Short Templates

A template should be about one screenful so you can see the whole template without moving the mouse or using the keyboard. How much information that is depends on how big your screen is. It is difficult to read a template that cannot all fit on the screen.

11.13   Identifying Your XML Data

Strictly speaking, this is not an XSLT idiom but an XML idiom. This idiom arises from the difficulty encountered when dated HTML documents must be replaced. With unique identification, you can write tools to find obsolete pages. Unique identifications are especially useful in cases where pages become dated after each publication period, like a news site.

Suppose we have a site that provides the schedule for a basketball league, and suppose the schedule and updates to the schedule are in an XML document. If the games in the XML document do not have unique identification, each update will have to contain the entire schedule. You can't send only the updated games because you won't know for sure which games in the original schedule must be changed. This is not a problem if the schedule is small. If the schedule contains more than 1,000 games—as major sports leagues do—handling the updates will take too much time and effort.

11.14   Using `xsl:apply-templates`

My personal preference is to use the `xsl:apply-templates` element instead of the `xsl:for-each` element. It just makes more sense to use templates that allow flexibility in development of XSLT documents for transformation (which is what this book is about). Let's look at templates with this structure

```
<xsl:template match='...'>
   .
   .
   <xsl:apply-templates select='target'/>
   .
   .
</xsl:template>

<xsl:template match='target'>
```

```
         .
         .
         .
</xsl:template>
```

compared to this template.

```
<xsl:template match='...'>
     .
     .
     .
  <xsl:for-each select='target'>
       .
       .
       .
  </xsl:for-each>
     .
     .
     .
<xsl:template>
```

Obviously, the template with `target` as its `match` value can be reused with `xsl:import`, whereas the content contained by the `xsl:for-each` cannot be.

The template with the `xsl:for-each` element is also less likely to be reused because its reusability depends on both the usefulness of the template itself and the usefulness of the handling of the `target` elements in the `xsl:for-each` element. The template with `xsl:apply-templates` makes it easy to define another template that matches `target` to override the imported template. Also, it is harder to do incremental development with `xsl:for-each` elements than `xsl:apply-templates`.

11.15   One Page at a Time

It is tempting to write a single XSLT document to generate multiple HTML documents. The usual excuse is efficiency. The rationale goes like this: If I can generate two kinds of documents with one XSLT document, I will save development time, or if I can generate more than one kind of HTML document with one XSLT document, I won't have to parse the XML document more than once.

This idiom covers both the case that one XSLT document can generate two different kinds of documents with a command line parameter, and the case that one XSLT document generates more than one HTML document at the same time.

It is difficult to argue with the first reason. The `xsl:import`, `xsl:include` and `xsl:apply-templates` elements allow you to factor out commonly used templates into separate XSLT documents. You can write two XSLT documents sharing many common templates to generate two kinds of related documents.

The second reason, however, has a lot of merit right now. Currently the available XSLT processors must go through the same XML document over and over again to generate different documents in different XSLT documents. In the future, this may not be the case. Instead of an XML document as the input, there will be an XML database. In other words, you may never again have to go through the same XML document more than once because the XML database will have the XML data parsed and stored so you can access it multiple times. In addition, future XSLT processors may allow you specify one XML document and more than one XSLT document. With such an XSLT processor, obviously it will not be necessary to parse the XML document more than once. The XSLT processor will be able to analyze all the XSLT documents as one unit and then find out the best way to generate the result documents.

Until XML databases and optimizing XSLT processors are available, the temptation will be there. If the efficiency gained is not significant for the job at hand, the inherent complexity is probably not worthwhile.

11.16   Mockup, Generalize, Write

If there is a pattern for XSLT document development to generate HTML documents, it is probably a process pattern that graphics designers, usability architects, and Web developers all work with to create Web sites. Here is a good process pattern.

1. The usability architects design the navigation of the site and the layouts of the various pages of the Web site.

2. The graphics designers design all the graphics, colors, and all the other creative elements.

3. With the help of the Web developers, mockups of the Web sites are developed. One mockup for each kind of HTML document is done by the Web developers to implement the usability architecture and the various creative elements.

4. When the HTML mockups have been approved, the HTML documents are given to the XSLT designers to be carved up into parts.

5. The parts that contain dynamic content are parameterized. The parameters contain XML elements from the input XML document(s). Common templates for the Web pages are developed first.

6. The XSLT developers design all the templates that generate the different parts for the Web pages, with one XSLT document for each kind of document.

Programmers may come into the picture. They usually talk to the XSLT developers to ensure the HTML documents are generated in the right directories and the XML documents get into the right directories to be used by the XSLT developers. The programmers are also responsible for obtaining data from the database and generating the XML documents to represent the data.

11.17 Working Directory

The working directory of the XSLT document being processed by the XSLT processor is important if `xsl:import` and `xsl:include` are used and the HTTP protocol is not desired to obtain the included or imported documents.

There are a few solutions to ensure the XSLT developers do not have to put fixed and hard-coded URLs into the XSLT documents. One solution is to ensure that all related XSLT documents are in the same directory. Another is to impose a discipline on the names of the directories to use, even though this is usually system-dependent and hence not very practical for those who develop on one kind of system and deploy on another. Another solution is to write an XSLT document to preprocess all XSLT documents when they are moved from one system to another.

This is a small XSLT document that takes a directory and modifies the `xsl:include` and `xsl:import` elements in an XSLT document to include (or import) from that directory.

```
<?xml version='1.0'?>
<xsl:stylesheet version='1.0'
    xmlns:xsl='http://www.w3.org/1999/XSL/Transform'>

  <xsl:output method='xml'/>

  <!-- To allow the prefix to be specified on
       command line -->
  <xsl:param name='prefix'/>

  <!-- only one template, not intended to be reusable. -->
  <xsl:template match='/'>
    <xsl:choose>
```

```
<!-- So the stylesheet element is there and its
     namespace is indeed that of XSLT's -->
<!-- The value of the test attribute must be
     on the same line. I break it up to show it
     here -->
<xsl:when
    test='local-name(*) = "stylesheet" and
          namespace-uri(*) = "http://www.w3.org/1999/XSL/Transform"'>
  <!-- Must copy everything before and after the document
       element too. -->
  <xsl:for-each select='node()'>
    <xsl:copy>
      <!-- Copy everything other than the import and include
           elements too. -->
      <xsl:for-each select='node()'>
        <xsl:choose>
          <!-- Attach the prefix if it is an import or include
               element. -->
          <!-- The value of the test attribute must be
               on the same line. I break it up to
               show it here -->
          <xsl:when
              test='(local-name(.) = "import" or
                     local-name(.) = "include") and
                     namespace-uri(.) =
                        "http://www.w3.org/1999/XSL/Transform"'>
            <xsl:copy>
              <xsl:attribute name='href'>
                <xsl:value-of select='$prefix'/>
                <xsl:value-of select='@href'/>
              </xsl:attribute>
            </xsl:copy>
          </xsl:when>
          <!-- Just copy if it is not an import or include
               element. -->
          <xsl:otherwise>
            <xsl:copy-of select='.'/>
          </xsl:otherwise>
        </xsl:choose>
      </xsl:for-each>
    </xsl:copy>
```

```
        </xsl:for-each>
      </xsl:when>
      <xsl:otherwise>
        <!-- Not even an XSLT document.
             Simply copy everything to the  output. -->
        <xsl:copy-of select='.'/>
      </xsl:otherwise>
    </xsl:choose>
  </xsl:template>

</xsl:stylesheet>
```

This XSLT document seems to have violated some of the idioms presented in this chapter. It deliberately has no flexibility so it is not reusable. It has only the template that matches the root node and the template that matches each and every node in the input document, so it has only one purpose. Sometimes you need to ensure that a template cannot be reused for whatever reason. This is called **throwaway** programming.

11.18   Inside-Out XSLT Template Application

XSLT documents can be designed in a simple way. You just design one skeleton template for each kind of node on each level of the input XML document. Using `xsl:apply-templates` elements inside the templates to select how the transformation process should continue, you can handle most transformations that you encounter. Here is a hypothetical XML document.

```
<level1>1
  <level2.1>2.1
    <level3.1.1>3.1.1
    </level3.1>
  </level2.1>
  <level2.2>2.2
    <level3.2.1>3.2.1
    </level3.2.1>
  </level2.2>
</level1>
```

Suppose you want the output to look like this.

```
<HTML>
  <HEAD><TITLE>An Example</TITLE></HEAD>
```

```
<BODY>
  <H1>3.2.1</H1>
  <H2>2.1</H2>
  <H1>2.2</H1>
  <H2>3.1.1</H2>
  <H3>1</H3>
</BODY>
</HTML>
```

First, write one template for each element and have one `xsl:apply-templates` element for each template.

```
<xsl:template match='level1'>
  <xsl:apply-templates/>
</xsl:template>

<xsl:template match='level2.1'>
  <xsl:apply-templates/>
</xsl:template>

<xsl:template match='level3.1.1'>
  <xsl:apply-templates/>
</xsl:template>

<xsl:template match='level2.2'>
  <xsl:apply-templates/>
</xsl:template>

<xsl:template match='level3.2.1'>
  <xsl:apply-templates/>
</xsl:template>
```

Then output the HTML elements for each of the templates by filling in the skeletons.

```
<xsl:template match='level1'>
  <H3><xsl:value-of select='text()'/></H3>
  <xsl:apply-templates/>
</xsl:template>

<xsl:template match='level2.1'>
  <H2><xsl:value-of select='text()'/></H2>
  <xsl:apply-templates/>
```

```
</xsl:template>

<xsl:template match='level3.1.1'>
  <H2><xsl:value-of select='text()'/></H2>
  <xsl:apply-templates/>
</xsl:template>

<xsl:template match='level2.2'>
  <H1><xsl:value-of select='text()'/></H1>
  <xsl:apply-templates/>
</xsl:template>

<xsl:template match='level3.2.1'>
  <H1><xsl:value-of select='text()'/></H1>
  <xsl:apply-templates/>
</xsl:template>
```

Finally, use the `xsl:apply-templates` elements to direct the transformations.

```
<?xml version='1.0'?>

<xsl:stylesheet version='1.0'
    xmlns:xsl='http://www.w3.org/1999/XSL/Transform'>

  <xsl:output method='html'/>

  <xsl:template match='/'>
    <HTML>
      <HEAD><TITLE>An Example</TITLE></HEAD>
      <BODY>
        <xsl:apply-templates select='level1/level2.2/level3.2.1'/>
      </BODY>
    </HTML>
  </xsl:template>

  <xsl:template match='level1'>
    <H3><xsl:value-of select='text()'/></H3>
  </xsl:template>

  <xsl:template match='level2.1'>
    <H2><xsl:value-of select='text()'/></H2>
```

```
      <xsl:apply-templates select='../level2.2'/>
    </xsl:template>

    <xsl:template match='level3.2.1'>
      <H2><xsl:value-of select='text()'/></H2>
      <xsl:apply-templates select='../../level2.1'/>
    </xsl:template>

    <xsl:template match='level2.2'>
      <H1><xsl:value-of select='text()'/></H1>
      <xsl:apply-templates select='../level2.1/level3.1.1'/>
    </xsl:template>

    <xsl:template match='level3.1.1'>
      <H2><xsl:value-of select='text()'/></H2>
      <xsl:apply-templates select='../../../level1'/>
    </xsl:template>

  </xsl:stylesheet>
```

The template that matches level1 elements has no xsl:apply-templates elements in it. Most XSLT documents can be written this way in the beginning, though refinements will be needed.

11.19   Removing an Element

One way to stop processing an element is to have an empty template for the element. For instance, this empty template effectively prevents any processing for the comment elements.

```
    <xsl:template match='comment'/>
```

This is usually not a good idea, however, because it is too powerful. Overriding it requires defining other templates with higher priority.

It is better to ignore the comment elements while their parent is being handled. Suppose a part of the XML document looks like this.

```
<picture>
  <comment>This caption was modified by John Porter.</comment>
  <image .../>
  <caption>...</caption>
</picture>
```

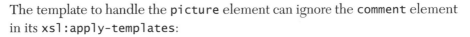

The template to handle the `picture` element can ignore the `comment` element in its `xsl:apply-templates`:

```
<xsl:template match='picture'>
   .
   .
   .
   <xsl:apply-templates select='image | caption'/>
   .
   .
   .
</xsl:template>
```

This way, the `comment` element is ignored, but the powerful template that removes the `comment` elements is not defined in the XSLT document. You never know where the `comment` element must or must not be handled.

11.20   Using XML Configuration Files

XML documents are wonderful as configuration files. Although parameters can be applied on the command line, if the parameters are numerous or have structures, XML documents are the best way to contain configuration information.

A simple example is the association of advertising with Web pages. If you use an XML document to contain all the information about the advertisement, your XSLT document can generate Web pages with ads that are most appropriate for the pages. You can define such a configuration this way.

```
<ads>
  <politics><!-- For politics-related pages -->
    <ad href='http://www.tripleclick.com/politics' width='200' height='50'>
      Politics Ads
    </ad>
    .
    .
    .
  </politics>
  <sports><!-- For sports-related pages -->
    <ad href='http://www.sportsthings.com/general' width='200' height='50'>
      Sports things Ads
    </ad>
    .
    .
    .
  </sports>
</ads>
```

This kind of configuration file is easy to maintain.

11.21   Using Lineup Files

When it comes to news sites, you have two basic options from which to choose. All the news stories can be placed in one file, or individual stories can go in separate files. If all the stories are in one file, the file can be very large and processing time can be significant unless the file is in an XML database. If the stories are in individual files, the files must be properly maintained.

For both options, lineup files are very useful. A lineup file contains references to the stories that should appear on a page. In a sense, a lineup file is simply a configuration file containing the references to the content of a page.

11.22   One Subtree at a Time

Templates that handle only one subtree are easier to understand than templates that handle multiple subtrees. The subtree handled by a template can be simply the subtree rooted at the node matched by a template.

It is quite easy to convert a template that handles more than one subtree to a template that handles only one template.

1. Take the elements that handle different subtrees out and define templates for them.
2. Use `xsl:apply-templates` to replace the removed elements.

11.23   Using `xsl:copy-of`

We tend to use too many `xsl:value-of` elements and not enough `xsl:copy-of` elements. This might be because we think "value-of" means "whatever the value is." Of course, we get only the string value when we use the `xsl:value-of` element.

This misuse is especially prominent when we have result tree fragments as parameters of a named template. The result is that we define more templates than we have to. This template shows what happens when we think in terms of `xsl:value-of` elements.

```
<xsl:template match='story'>
  <!-- 'image', 'anchor', or 'both' -->
  <xsl:param name='linkType'/>
  <xsl:param name='imageName'/>
  <xsl:param name='imageAlt'/>
  <xsl:param name='anchorHRef'/>
```

```
    <xsl:param name='anchorText'/>
    <p><xsl:value-of select='.'/> You can find more about the story in
      <xsl:choose>
        <xsl:when test='$linkType = "image"'>
          <img src='{$imageName}' alt='{$imageName}'/>
        </xsl:when>
        <xsl:when test='$linktype = "anchor"'>
          <a href='{$anchorHRef}'><xsl:value-of
              select='$anchorText'/></a>
        </xsl:when>
        <xsl:otherwise>
          <a href='{$anchorHRef}'><img src='{$imageName}'
                                        alt='{$imageName}'/></a>
        </xsl:otherwise>
      </xsl:choose></p>
  </xsl:template>
```

This is a simpler way.

```
<xsl:template match='story'>
  <xsl:param name='link'/>
  <p><xsl:value-of select='.'/> You can find more about the story in
    <xsl:copy-of select='$link'/></p>
</xsl:template>
```

And this way is even more useful if the next version of XSLT allows the treatment of result-tree fragments as node-sets.

11.24 Overriding Default Templates

Although default templates are good as safety nets, sometimes we rely on them too much. The default templates for comments and processing instructions are not usually a problem, but the default templates for elements and attributes can be.

Defining templates that handle elements and attributes that are not handled by explicit templates is a good way to find out if your XSLT documents are doing mysterious things. You can define a template to handle all elements.

```
<xsl:template match='*'>
  <xsl:message>Matching unmatched element:
    <xsl:value-of select='name(.)'/></xsl:message>
</xsl:template>
```

11.25   Avoiding the Descendant Axis

The descendant axis is a very expensive axis. Often this axis is used when an XSLT developer is too lazy to figure out how to get to certain elements or doesn't know how to get to the elements. This is the most frequently used pattern.

```
<xsl:apply-templates select='//story/@title'/>
```

Nothing is wrong with this element if, for example, the titles of the stories are compiled for a table of contents. But too often the current node-set contains all the `story` elements in the document. Here is a much simpler and less misleading element.

```
<xsl:apply-templates select='@title'/>
```

It will be much more efficient for most processors, and it won't confuse the reader. The second way is geared toward selecting the `title` attribute of the current collection of `story` elements, not all the `title` attributes of all the `story` elements in the whole XML document. Likewise, the descendant axis is overused in template patterns as well. That is also an overspecification.

11.26   Reducing the Size of Node-Sets

The more steps an XPath expression has, the more expensive it is. And the more nodes the result node-set for each step has, the more expensive the XPath expression is.

The best way to write an XPath is to make sure the first step has an efficient axis that produces only a small number of nodes. Then reduce the number by using a good node test. Finally, use a predicate that does not have embedded location paths to cut down the node-set to the smallest size.

In other words, if you know the structure of the XML tree, use it. Don't be lazy. Compare the following two location paths.

```
bookCollection//author
bookCollection/book/author
```

Both location paths produce the same node-set in most cases. But the first location path examines all the descendants of the `bookCollection` element. The second includes only the `book` child nodes of the `bookCollection` element. Some XSLT and XML processors will probably pick this up, and both will be handled in the same way. Other processors will spend much more time for the first location path than for the second location path.

11.27   Avoiding Multiple Predicates

You can even reduce the processing within a step. For instance, you won't usually use more than one predicate in a step like this

```
story[@type='new'][@year=$thisyear]
```

because it can be replaced by this.

```
story[@type='new' and @year=$thisyear]
```

You need more than one predicate only if you want to reuse the positions of the nodes in the result node-set after evaluating a predicate. For example,

```
story[@type='new' and position()=1]
```

chooses the element if its type attribute has the value new and is the first story element of its parent. On the other hand, if you want to choose the first story element with the type attribute being new (a more likely scenario), then you need

```
story[@type='new'][1]
```

In fact, 90 percent of the time this is the reason you have multiple predicates in a step. Embedded location paths inside predicates are very expensive unless the paths have one step with the child or parent axes.

11.28   Summary

In the course of using XSLT for the past year, I have realized that some ways of doing things are better than others. I have also found that some tasks have to be done over and over again. Other times, I ran into problems because I used XSLT in certain ways. This chapter has documented some of the idioms I discovered. It has also given you some tips that should be useful in your XSLT document-writing.

11.29   Looking Ahead

We have discussed the XSLT elements and tips for writing XSLT documents. The next chapter presents a full example of how to use XSLT to construct a Web site. All the messy and ugly details will be displayed. You will see that you do not have to switch contexts from HTML to Java (or C++ or Perl or C) and back again. And you don't have to worry about generating invalid HTML pages.

⟨12⟩

A Case Study

The butcher says:
"What I am good at is the truth between things;
it is more than just techniques.
When I first started butchering,
I saw the whole cattle.
Now, I use my mind
to touch the body of the cattle;
using the structure of the cattle
to insert the knife at the joints."
—*Zhuang Zi*

In this chapter, we will look at an XSLT project. A real-life project has several stages. Many of the initial stages are business-related. We will skip these initial stages and go directly to the point where the business side has decided to go with XML and XSLT.

Our aim is to produce a Web site that serves only HTML pages with minimal database access. We want the Web site to be as static as possible so that we can host the Web site on ordinary hardware to handle large numbers of hits. The dynamic elements will be handled by servlets, and even they will be straightforward with little processing capacity.

To be able to serve only HTML pages, we must use XML documents as the sources and XSLT as the transformation technology (surprise!). We will use XML to represent everything that will be shown on the Web site. The XML documents will be produced by the producers of the Web site and stored on a project machine away from the Web server. Whenever there is a need to generate new content, the appropriate XML documents and their XSLT documents are combined to produce HTML documents. These HTML documents are then moved to the Web server. No processing will be performed on the Web server.

As you can see from this description, you need other technologies to develop a Web site using XML and XSLT. For instance, you need a content management tool to check page dependency and to schedule the replacement of old pages with new pages. You also need to provide tools to the producers of the Web site to create, edit, select, and remove stories. In other words, you need a publishing tool.

These tasks do not concern you as an XSLT developer. We will look at what is needed outside XSLT, but we will not get into the procedures here.

12.1   The Web Site

Our Web site is a vertical portal site intended as a meeting place for Java programmers in the Greater Toronto area. Phase one of the development deals with presenting information that is of interest to the Java programmer community. It features advertisements, departments, news stories about the community, industry, education, and information about the Toronto area.

Initially, the Web site will have only simple navigation. It has a similar structure for most departments, so it has only three basic designs.

12.1.1   *The Home Page*

The home page is a simple page showing the name of the site. This page will be replaced by a logon page later on. Although it is not useful right now, it will stay in the project. Its mockup is shown in Figure 12.1. At the bottom of the page are the links to the departments of the Web site.

The source of the page is shown here since we will be using this mockup as the basis for our templates.

```
<html>
<head>
<meta http-equiv="Content-Language" content="en-us">
<title>torontojava.com</title>
</head>
<body bgcolor="#000035" text="white" link="white"
  vlink="white">
<TABLE WIDTh=100% HEIGHT=90%>
```

FIGURE

12.1 The home page of the Web site

```
<TR><TD><center><font face="Impact" size="10"
color="#FFFFFF">torontojava.com</font></center>
</TR></TD>
</TABLE>
<HR>
<font face="Arial" size=2 color="#FFFFFF"><CENTER>
<B><A HREF="main/index.html">START</B></A>
  |
  <A HREF="career/index.html">career</A>
  |
  <A HREF="industry/index.html">industry</A>
  |
```

```
<A HREF="education/index.html">education</A>
|
<A HREF="just_java/index.html">just java</A>
|
<A HREF="community/index.html">community</A>
|
<A HREF="fyi_toronto/index.html">fyi toronto</A>
|
<A HREF="about_us/index.html">about us</A>
</CENTER></font>
</body>
</html>
```

In each department we will have one summary page with links to the full stories, and we will have one detail page for each story featured on the summary page.

12.1.2   *The Summary Page*

A mockup of the main summary page is shown in Figure 12.2. We will break down the page into parts, which will be independent of each other. Each part will be generated by one or more templates, which can be shared if necessary.

Overall Structure of the Summary Page

The summary page has a header, a main body, and a footer. The main body can be divided into two parts. The left bar is meant for links, polls, and advertisements. The right side contains the lineup—summaries of stories for the department.

We also need the declaration of the scripts used in the page. This is the declaration.

```
<!-- hide from non-JavaScript Browsers
ImageAbout= new Image(70,30)
ImageAbout.src = "images/about_us.gif"
ImageAbout_f = new Image(70,30)
ImageAbout_f.src = "images/about_us_f.gif"
<!-- similar Javascript for the images of career,
     industry, education, fyi, community,
     just_java departments -->
```

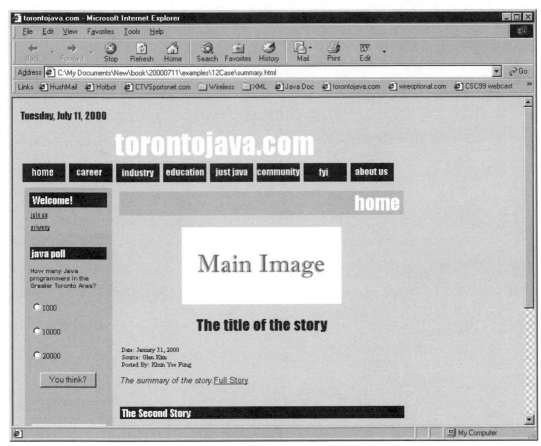

FIGURE

12.2 The summary page for the main department

```
function getMouseOver(imName){
  document.images[imName].src = eval("Image" + imName + "_f.src");
}
function getMouseOut(imName){
  document.images[imName].src = eval("Image" + imName + ".src");
}
function dayName(day) {
  var days = new Array("Sunday", "Monday", "Tuesday",
                       "Wednesday",
                       "Thursday", "Friday", "Saturday");
  return days[day];
}
```

```
function numString(num) {
  if (num < 10)
    sNum = "0" + String(num);
  else
    sNum = String(num);
  return sNum;
}
function monthName(month) {
  var months - new Array("January", "February",
                         "March", "April", "May",
                         "June", "July", "August",
                         "September",
                         "October", "November", "December");
  return months[month];
}
function yearString(theyear) {
  if (theyear == 99 | theyear == 1999){
    year = 1999;
  }
  else if (theyear < 99){
    year = theyear + 2000;
  }
  else if (theyear >= 2000){
    year = theyear;
  }
  else if (theyear > 99) {
    year = theyear + 1900;
  }
  return year;
}
function getToday() {
  var today = new Date();
  return today;
}
function getTheDate(year, month, date) {
  var thedate = new Date(year, month, date);
  return thedate;
}
function displayDate(thedate) {
  var displayedDate = dayName(thedate.getDay()) + ", " +
                      monthName(thedate.getMonth()) + " " +
```

```
                            thedate.getDate() + ", " +
                            yearString(thedate.getYear());
        document.write(displayedDate);
    }
```

This is the HTML source (minus the script declaration) for the skeleton of a summary page.

```html
<html>
<head>
    <meta http-equiv="Content-Type"
      content="text/html; charset=iso-8859-1">
    <title>torontojava.com</title>
    <SCRIPT LANGUAGE="JavaScript">
      <!-- put the declaration shown above here -->
      // - stop hiding -->
    </SCRIPT>
</head>

<body text="#000035" bgcolor="#dddddd" link="#000035" vlink="#000035"
      alink="#000035">
  <table>
    <!-- Header -->
    <!-- The Main body -->
    <table>
      <tr>
        <td><!-- The left bar --></td>
        <td><!-- The main bar --></td>
      </tr>
    </table>
    <!-- Footer -->
  </table>
</body>
</html>
```

The skeleton has the document element of the page, the JavaScript declarations, and the layout for the page. The comments are the placeholders for the different components on the page.

The Header

The header of the page has the name of the Web site, the date of the day it is viewed, and a list of buttons to the departments of the Web site. This is the HTML source for the header.

```
<table bgcolor="#dddddd">
  <!--DATE HEADER-->
  <tr>
    <td>
      <font face="Impact">
          <script language="JavaScript">
          displayDate(getToday());</script>
      </font><br>
    </td>
  </tr>
  <tr>
    <td>
      <!-- TORONTOJAVA.COM BANNER-->
      <table border=0 cellspacing=0 cellpadding=0 width="630">
        <tr>
          <td>
            <center>
              <font face="Impact" size="7"
                    color="white">torontojava.com</font>
            </center>
          </td>
        </tr>
      </table>
      <table>
        <tr>
          <td width='72' valign='top'>
          <a href="main_back.html"
            onMouseOver="getMouseOver('Home')"
              onMouseOut="getMouseOut('Home')">
            <img name="Home"
                src="images/main.gif" border=0 width="70"
                height="30">
            </a>
          </td>
          <td width='72' valign='top'>
          <a href="career/index.html"
              onMouseOver="getMouseOver('Career')"
              onMouseOut="getMouseOut('Career')">
            <img name="Career"
                src="images/career.jpg" border=0 width="70"
```

```
                   height="30">
          </a>
        </td>
        <!-- the same thing for industry, education, just_java,
             community, fyi_toronto, and
             about_us departments too -->
      </tr>
    </table>
  </td>
 </tr>
</table>
```

The buttons have similar code. For the pages in phase one, the button bar will be the same for all the pages, except for the home page.

The Left Bar

The left bar of the main body contains links to pages that are associated with the summary page. It contains advertisements. For the main summary page of the site, the left bar also contains a poll.

The mechanism of the poll will not be discussed here, but it is a nice example of how a form can be generated using XSLT. This is the HTML source for the left bar.

```
<td bgcolor="silver">
  <!--Menu ITEMS-->
  <table border=0 cellspacing=0 cellpadding=0 bgcolor="silver"
         width=120 height=100% bordercolor="#000035">
    <tr>
      <td>
        <table width="100% border=0 cellspacing=2 cellpadding=2
               bgcolor="#BEC8B9" width=120>
          <tr>
            <td bgcolor="#000035">
              <font face="IMPACT"
                    color="WHITE"> items</font>
            </td>
          </tr>
          <!-- similar for welcome, faqs, contact, join, host,
               advertise menus. -->
          <tr valign=top><td> </td></tr>
```

```
            </table>
          </td>
      </tr>
      <!--SPACER-->
      <tr><td> </td></tr>
      <!--JAVA POLL-->
      <tr>
        <td>
          <table border="0" width="100%">
            <tr>
              <td width="100%">
                <form method="GET" action="servlet/pollSSI">
                  <table  border=0 cellpadding=0 cellspacing=0
                          bgcolor=#BEC8B9 width="100%">
                    <tr>
                      <td bgcolor="#000035" width=125 valign='top'>
                        <font face="IMPACT" color="white">
                           java poll
                        </font>
                      </td>
                    </tr>
                    <tr>
                      <td width=125>
                        <font face="ARIAL" size=-2>
                          <b><br>
                          How many Java Developers do you
                          think there are in Toronto?
                          </b>
                        </font>
                      </td>
                    </tr>
                    <tr>
                      <td><br>
                        <input name=1 type=radio
                               value=1000><!--
                        --><font size=-1>1000</font>
                      </td>
                    </tr>
                    <!-- similar for other choices: 5000,
                         10000, 25000 -->
                    <tr>
```

```
            <td><br>
              <center>
                <font size=-1>
                  <input name=Vote type=submit value=VOTE>
                </font>
              </center>
            </td>
          </tr>
          <tr><td> </td></tr>
        </table>
      </form>
    </td>
  </tr>
</table>
</td>
</tr>
<!--END JAVA POLL-->
<tr><td> </td></tr>
<!--SPONSOR TABLE-->
<tr>
  <td>
    <table border=0 width="100%" cellspacing=0 cellpadding=0>
      <!-- Ad 1 -->
      <tr>
        <td align=center valign=top>
          <a href="#">
            <img src="images/ad1.jpg" width=120 height=72
                 border=0 ALT="First Ad">
          </a>
        </td>
      </tr>
      <!--END AD1-->
      <tr><td> </td></tr>
      <!-- for other ads as well -->
    </table>
  </td>
</tr>
<!--END SPONSOR TABLE-->
<!--END LEFT NAV BAR-->
</table>
</td>
```

Again, most structures recur in the component. This is very normal in this kind of Web site.

The Main Column

The main column has one main story and as many secondary stories as desired. Its main story has a bigger image than the secondary stories. Also, the main story's layout is different than the second stories'.

This is the HTML source for the main column.

```
<!--Story BAR-->
<td COLSPAN=2 align=top>
  <!--STORY 1-->
  <!--TOP STORY MORE REAL ESTATE-->
  <table width="100%" border=0 cellspacing=0 cellpadding=0 >
    <tr>
      <td colspan=2 align="right" bgcolor="#BEC8B9">
        <font face="IMPACT" size="6" color="white">home 
        </font>
      </td>
    </tr>
    <tr>
      <td width="100%"  >
        <font face="impact" color="#000035" size="5">
          <b><center> The Main Story </center></b>
        </font>
      </td>
    </tr>
    <tr><td width="100%"> </font></td></tr>
    <tr>
      <td width="100%" align=top>
        <center>
          <img src="images/big.jpg" width="260" height="125">
        </center>
      </td>
    </tr>
    <tr><td width="100%"> </td></tr>
    <tr>
      <td width="100%" align=top>
        <font size="-2">
           Date: December 1, 1999<br>
           Source: Glen Kim<br>
           Posted By: Glen Kim<br><br>
```

```
          </font>
          <font size="-1" face="Arial">
            This is the summary paragraph for the main story.
            To make it look like a story, more words will have
            to be put here. This is difficult because making up stories
            is not my strength. That begs the question: people
            who can make up stories are obviously talented,
            or are they?
            <a href='main_story.html'>Full Story</a>
          </font>
        </td>
    </tr>
    <tr><td height=10 width="100%"> </td></tr>
</table>
<!--STORY 2-->
<table width="461" border=0 cellspacing=0 cellpadding=0 >
    <tr>
        <td colspan=2 BGcolor="#000035" width="459" >
          <font face="impact" color="WHITE" size="3">
             Second Story
          </font>
        </td>
    </tr>
    <tr><td><font size="-5"> </font></td></tr>
    <tr valign=top>
        <td align=top width=51 height=50>
          <img src="images/small.jpg" width=50 height=50>
        </td>
        <td align=top width="406">
          <font size="-2" face="Arial">
             Date: December 1, 1999<br>
             Source: Glen Kim<br>
             Posted By: Glen Kim<br>
          </font>
          <font size="-1" face="Arial"><br>
              The second story has about the same things as the main
            story. However, the image is supposed to be smaller.
            The summary, on the other hand, should be the same as
            the main story.
            <a href='second_story.html'>Full Story</a>
            <br>
          </font><br>
```

```
        </td>
      </tr>
    </table >
    <!-- End of Story 2 -->
    <!-- Other secondary stories here -->
  </td>
```

There are one main story and two secondary stories in this example.

The Footer

The footer contains links to the departments again. At the end of the page is the copyright notice. This is the HTML source for the footer.

```
<table border=0 cellspacing=0 cellpadding=0 width="630"
        bgcolor="#BEC8B9">
  <tr><td><hr width=95%></td></tr>
  <tr>
    <td >
      <font face="Arial" size=2 color="#000035">
        <center>
          <a href="main.html">home</a>
          |
          <a href="career/index.html">career</a>
          |
          <a href="industry/index.html">industry</a>
          |
          <a href="education/index.html">education</a>
          |
          <a href="just_java/index.html">just java</a>
          |
          <a href="community/index.html">community</a>
          |
          <a href="fyi_toronto/index.html">fyi toronto</a>
          |
          <a href="about_us/index.html">about us</a>
        </center>
      </font>
    </td>
  </tr>
  <tr>
    <td>
```

```
<font face="Arial" size=1 color="#000035">
  <center>
  <br>Copyright &copy;2000, torontojava.com inc.</center>
  <br>
  </font>
    </td>
  </tr>
</table>
```

12.1.3 *The Detail Page*

The design for a detail page is similar to the summary page except that the whole detail page is devoted to one story whereas the summary page has multiple stories with only a summary for each of them.

The screen shot for an example of a detail page is shown in Figure 12.3. The HTML is very similar to that of the summary page.

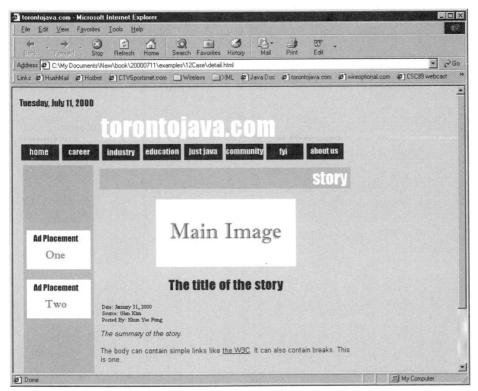

FIGURE

12.3 The design for a detail page

12.1.4   *Non-XSLT Tasks*

After the mockups are done, more tasks must be performed that are not XSLT-related—for example, the mechanism used by the poll, how the stories will be produced, and so forth. Let's fast-forward to the point where we must decide how to generate HTML documents.

12.2   Designing the XML Files

Because this Web site is being developed from scratch with no legacy data source, we can design the XML files any way we like. But what is important is how to design the XML document types. Then we will assume that the appropriate XML files will be deposited in the right place before the transformation takes place. This is what is needed in the XML document for one story.

1. A title for the story

2. The date the story is composed

3. The reporter or writer of the story

4. The source of the story

5. A large photo if the story is the main story. This is optional.

6. The lead paragraph as the summary of the story

7. A small photo if the story is not the main story. This is optional. The story is assumed to contain only text and links to URLs. The URLs will not be checked by the transformation and assumed to be valid links

8. The body of the story

Here is a sample XML document.

```
<?xml version='1.0'?>
<story>
  <title>The title of the story</title>
  <source>Source of the story.</source>
  <date>Date the story is composed. Whatever the format of the date
is.</date>
  <writer>The person who wrote the story.</writer>
  <images main='URL' side='URL'/>
  <body>
    <summary>The summary of the story.</summary>
    The body can contain simple links like
    <link url='url'>text</link>.
```

```
    </body>
</story>
```

We design our story XML document from the mockups. In general, we have to think about what will be needed in the longer term as well. For instance, a unique identification number for each story will come in handy for organizing the XML documents in the content management tool and the publishing tool. But let's look at what we need right now instead.

The other two XML documents needed directly for the Web pages are for the polls and the advertisements. This is the XML document for a poll.

```
<?xml version='1.0'?>
<poll name='the name'>
  <question>The question for the poll.</question>
  <response value='value1'>The first possible response</response>
  <response value='value2'>The second possible response</response>
  <response value='value3'>The third possible response</response>
  <!-- repeat as many as the number of possible
       responses. -->
  <button name='name of the button'>The label for the button.</button>
  <method name='name of the method for the poll'/>
  <action>The action for the poll</action>
</poll>
```

This XML document type for the advertisements is the simplest of the three.

```
<?xml version='1.0'?>
<ads>
  <ad>
    <image url='images/ad1.jpg'/>
    <link url='#'/>
    <text>First Ad</text>
  </ad>
  <ad>
    <image url='images/ad2.jpg'/>
    <link url='#'/>
    <text>Second Ad</text>
  </ad>
</ads>
```

The URLs will be replaced by the URLs to the advertisers' home pages.

Finally, each department needs an XML document to specify the story lineup. Here is an example of a lineup document.

```
<?xml version='1.0'?>
<lineup>
  <department>The name of the department.</department>
  <story>The URL of the main story of the department.</story>
  <story>The URL of the second story of the department.</story>
  <!-- Repeat as many times as there are stories in the
       department -->
  <leftbar>
    <name>Name for the leftbar.</name>
    <item link='url'>The label for the item.</item>
    <item link='url'>The label for the item.</item>
    <!-- Repeat as many as needed for the items. -->
  </leftbar>
</lineup>
```

The stories are listed by their URLs. Usually the lineup of stories in a department is produced by a publishing tool. For a small Web site, the lineups can be produced manually, too.

Finally, there is the left bar of the detail pages. For the Web site, we need the advertisements on the left bar, but we will take a shortcut and omit the advertisements in this chapter.

12.2.1   *The Publishing Process*

When you have to generate the HTML documents, the location of all the XML documents should be apparent. There should be a scheduler in place during the transformation process that knows when to generate new HTML pages and which XML documents should be used with which XSLT document.

Alternatively, you can generate all the Web pages of the Web site every time you need to update the content. This is a simple process for deploying HTML pages. Simply generate the whole Web site, remove all the pages from the Web server, and copy all the new pages to the Web server. You won't have to worry about the dependability of the pages or garbage pages on the Web server. Of course, you cannot use this strategy for large Web sites, but you can certainly use it for smaller ones. Either way, the XML and XSLT documents do not change.

12.3   Organizing the XSLT Documents

Now we will design the XSLT document to generate the home page and then the XSLT document to generate all the summary pages for the departments.

Finally, we will design the XSLT document to generate all the detail pages for the departments.

After this, we'll look at how to cut up the mockups to organize the XSLT documents. In our case, we need to distinguish the common elements in the pages.

Later we will see the cut-up components with placeholders that will be replaced by XSLT elements. Components that do not contain XSLT elements will not be shown again.

12.3.1 *The Home Page*

The home page always looks the same, and there is no shared element on the page. It is not necessary to use an XSLT document to generate it, but in our case we will use it because we may want to modify it later on.

12.3.2 *The Summary Page*

A summary page shares a few elements with the detail page. Each of these shared elements will be generated by one XSLT document. These XSLT documents will be included by the main department XSLT documents and by the detail pages.

The Header

The same header is used for all the summary pages. The template that generates it will be in a document by itself. In this way, the template can be shared and modification of the header is also easier. The header itself will be shared, but the header does not have any components that will be replaced by XSLT elements.

The Left Bar

The links shown on the left bar are different from department to department. Using placeholders, the left bar HTML is shown here.

```
<table width="100%" border=0 cellspacing=2 cellpadding=2
       bgcolor="#BEC8B9" width=120>
  <tr>
    <td bgcolor="#000035">
      <font face="IMPACT"
              color="WHITE"> <bar-name/>
      </font>
    </td>
```

```
        </tr>
      <repeat>
        <tr valign=top>
          <td valign=top width="120">
            <font face="IMPACT" size="-1" color="#000035" >
              <a href="item url">Item Label</a>
            </font>
          </td>
        </tr>
      </repeat>
      <tr valign=top><td> </td></tr>
    </table>
```

There are three placeholders in the code fragment.

> The placeholder bar-name is the name for the left bar.

> The placeholder repeat is an indication that the content of the place-holder can be repeated as many times as needed.

> The href attribute and the Item Label text node are for the URL for the link of an item and the label for that link.

The Poll

The poll on the main summary page will also be in its own file. This is done because not all summary pages will have the poll. With placeholders, the poll looks like this.

```
<table border="0" width="100%">
  <tr>
    <td width="100%">
      <form method="form method" action="form action">
        <table  border=0 cellpadding=0 cellspacing=0
                BGcolor=#BEC8B9 width="100%">
          <tr>
            <td bgcolor="#000035" width=125 valign='top'>
              <font face="IMPACT" color="white">
                 <poll-name/>
              </font>
            </td>
          </tr>
          <tr>
            <td width=125>
```

```
        <font face="ARIAL" size=-2>
          <b><br>
            <poll-question/>
          </b>
        </font>
      </td>
    </tr>
    <repeat>
      <tr>
        <td><br>
          <input name=1 type=radio
            value='choice-value'><!--
          --><font size=-1><choice-label/></font>
        </td>
      </tr>
    </repeat>
    <tr>
      <td><br>
        <center>
          <font size=-1>
            <input name='button name' type='submit'
                   value='button value'>
          </font>
        </center>
      </td>
    </tr>
    <tr><td> </td></tr>
  </table>
</form>
      </td>
    </tr>
  </table>
```

The poll has more placeholders.

> The placeholder form method is for the form method for the poll.

> The placeholder form action is for the form action for the poll.

> The placeholder poll-name is used for the name of the poll.

> The placeholder poll-question holds the question of the poll.

> The placeholder choice-value holds the value of a particular choice for the poll.

> The placeholder `choice-label` holds the label for a choice.

> The placeholder `button name` holds the name of the submit button for the poll.

> The placeholder `button value` holds the value of the submit button.

The Footer

The footer, like the header, is also the same for all the pages. The template that generates it is in its own file. No placeholders are needed for the footer.

The Main Story

The main story on a summary page has the story title, the main image, the story summary, and the story link to the full page.

```
<table width="100%" border=0 cellspacing=0 cellpadding=0 >
  <tr>
    <td colspan=2 align="right" bgcolor="#BEC8B9">
      <font face="IMPACT" size="6" color="white">
            <page-name/> </font>
    </td>
  </tr>
  <tr>
    <td width="100%">
      <font face="impact" color="#000035" size="5">
        <b><center><main-story-name/></center></b>
      </font>
    </td>
  </tr>
  <tr><td width="100%"> </font></td></tr>
  <tr>
    <td width="100%" align=top>
      <center>
        <img src="main.image" width="260" height="125">
      </center>
    </td>
  </tr>
  <tr><td width="100%"> </td></tr>
  <tr>
    <td width="100%" aling=top>
      <font size="-2">
         Date: <date/><br>
```

```
       Source: <source/><br>
       Posted By: <writer/><br><br>
    </font>
    <font size="-1" face="Arial">
      <main-story-summary/>
      <a href='main_story.html'>Full Story</a>
    </font>
  </td>
</tr>
<tr><td height=10 width="100%"> </td></tr>
</table>
```

These are the placeholders.

> The placeholder page-name has the name of the page.

> The placeholder main-story-name holds the name of the main story.

> The placeholder main.image holds the URL of the main image of the story.

> The placeholder date holds the date the story is written.

> The placeholder source holds the source of the story.

> The placeholder writer holds the name of the writer of the story.

> The placeholder main-story-summary holds the summary of the story.

> The placeholder main_story.html holds the detail page of the story.

The Secondary Story

A secondary story has almost as many placeholders as the main story.

```
<table width="461" border=0 cellspacing=0 cellpadding=0 >
  <tr>
    <td colspan=2 BGcolor="#000035" width="459" >
      <font face="impact" color="WHITE" size="3">
         <secondary-story-title/>
      </font>
    </td>
  </tr>
  <tr><td><font size="-5"> </font></td></tr>
  <tr valign=top>
    <td align=top width=51 height=50>
      <img src="secondary.image" width=50 height=50>
    </td>
```

```
<td align=top width="406">
  <font size="-2" face="Arial">
     Date: <date/><br>
     Source: <source/><br>
     Posted By: <writer/><br>
  </font>
  <font size="-1" face="Arial"><br>
    <secondary-story-summary>
    <a href='full-story.html'>Full Story</a>
    <br>
  </font><br>
</td>
</tr>
</table>
```

These are the placeholders.

> The placeholder `secondary-story-title` holds the title of the secondary story.

> The placeholder `secondary.image` holds the secondary image for the story.

> The placeholders `date`, `source`, and `writer` have been explained previously.

> The placeholder `secondary-story-summary` holds the summary of the secondary story.

> The placeholder `full-story.html` holds the link to the full story.

12.3.3   *The Detail Page*

The detail page looks similar to the summary page, except that it contains only one story and its left bar has only advertisements. A better detail page probably has a separate left bar for some of the stories so different audiences can be targeted.

```
<table width="100%" border=0 cellspacing=0 cellpadding=0 >
  <tr>
    <td colspan=2 align="right" bgcolor="#BEC8B9">
      <font face="IMPACT" size="6" color="white">story </font>
    </td>
  </tr>
  <tr>
```

```
<td width="100%">
  <font face="impact" color="#000035" SIZE="5">
    <b><center><story-title/></center></b>
  </font>
</td>
</tr>
<tr><td width="100%"> </font></td></tr>
<tr>
  <td width="100%" align=top>
    <center><img src="main.image" width="260" height="125"></center>
  </td>
</tr>
<tr><td width="100%"> </td></tr>
<tr>
  <td width="100%" align=top>
    <font size="-2">
       Date: <date/><BR>
       Source: <source/><BR>
       Posted By: <writer/><BR><BR>
    </font>
    <font size="-1" face="Arial">
      <i><story-summary/></i>
      <p><full-story/>
    </font>
  </td>
</tr>
<tr><td height=10 width="100%"> </td></tr>
</table>
```

These are the placeholders in the code fragment.

> The placeholder `story-title` holds the title of the story.

> The placeholders `main.image`, `date`, `source`, `writer`, and `story-summary` have been explained previously.

> The placeholder `full-story` holds the full story.

12.4 Designing the XSLT Templates

After the mockups have been cut up into units, the next step is to design the actual templates that will generate the units. There are different ways to develop the templates. One way is to start from the three major pages: the home page, the summary page, and the detail page. First, develop the main templates for these pages. Then develop the templates needed in the major templates. Continue this process until all the templates have been developed. This is the top-down strategy.

The other way is to first design templates for the parts that are nested deepest inside other parts. Then design templates for the next deepest nested parts. Continue this process until all templates are designed. This is the bottom-up approach.

We will use both approaches in the development. That is, we will use the top-down approach when it makes sense and use the bottom-up approach otherwise. We will see how to determine which is appropriate when.

12.4.1   *Division of Labor*

For a simple Web site like ours, one XSLT developer is sufficient to design all the templates. For larger Web sites, more than one XSLT developer may be needed. When we have more than one XSLT developer, the work must be divided among them.

Initially, use the top-down approach. The more senior members of the team should start working from the major pages. Once they have developed the top-level templates and determine which templates they use, they can assign each of the templates needed for the top-level to other XSLT developers.

Each developer can then develop a template in the bottom-up fashion. When the template is finished, it is integrated with the top-level templates to produce a Web page.

The bottom-up approach is good for when there is more than one developer because the developers can work independently until there is a need for integration. Developing a Web site is faster this way. The major templates are needed in the beginning because without the major templates, the basic organization of the templates is not known. The developers will not be able to integrate their work.

The Web site we are developing is simple enough that we can use the bottom-up approach only. We will start from the deepest nested templates.

12.4.2   *Advertisements*

One of the deepest nested parts is the advertisement component. The advertisement document name is contained in a lineup document. Since only the document name is needed to generate the advertisements, a template is used

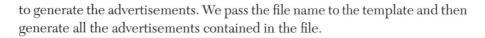

to generate the advertisements. We pass the file name to the template and then generate all the advertisements contained in the file.

```
<xsl:template name='generateAd'>
  <xsl:param name='fileName'/>
  <table border='0' width="100%" cellspacing='0' cellpadding='0'>
    <xsl:apply-templates
        select='document($fileName)/ads/ad' mode='ad'/>
  </table>
</xsl:template>
```

Because there may be more than one template matching an **ad** element, a **mode** attribute is used to specify the template designed for advertisements.

Now we want to generate one advertisement. This is the template to generate an advertisement in the table.

```
<xsl:template match='ad' mode='ad'>
  <tr>
    <td align='center' valign='top'>
      <a href="{link/@url}">
        <img src="{image/@url}" width='120' height='72'
                 border='0' ALT="{text}"/>
      </a>
    </td>
  </tr>
  <tr><td> </td></tr>
</xsl:template>
```

The template uses attribute-value templates. (Details for attribute-value templates are in Section 8.2.1). Basically they allow you specify the value of an XPath expression in an attribute of an element.

Finally, since the templates for the advertisements will be included in other XSLT documents, the templates are included in an XSLT document by themselves.

```
<?xml version='1.0'?>
<xsl:stylesheet
 xmlns:xsl='http://www.w3.org/1999/XSL/Transform'
 version='1.0'>
 <!-- the templates inserted here. -->
</xsl:stylesheet>
```

For debugging purposes, it is usually a good idea to include the template matching the root in an XSLT document so that the individual documents can be tested separately. This template will be overridden when the document is imported by another XSLT document.

```
<xsl:output method='html'/>

<xsl:template match='/'>
  <html>
  <xsl:call-template name='generateAd'>
     <xsl:with-param name='fileName'>ad.xml</xsl:with-param>
  </xsl:call-template>
  </html>
</xsl:template>
```

In the beginning, it is also useful to set the indent attribute of the xsl:output element to yes so that you can inspect the output easily. Just make sure to turn it off later.

12.4.3   *Header and Footer*

The templates for the header and the footer are very simple because the header and the footer used in the Web site are static. We will provide the templates for the header here. The templates for the footer are very similar.

The main template to generate the header is a named template. The template generates a table with the buttons in the header generated by another template.

```
<xsl:template name='generateHeader'>
  <table border='0' cellspacing='0' cellpadding='0' width="630">
    <tr>
      <td>
        <center>
          <font face="Impact" size="7"
                color="white">torontojava.com</font>
        </center>
      </td>
    </tr>
  </table>
  <table>
    <tr>
```

```
          <xsl:call-template name='oneButton' mode='header'>
            <xsl:with-param
                  name='link'>main_back.html</xsl:with-param>
            <xsl:with-param name='name'>Home</xsl:with-param>
            <xsl:with-param
                  name='image'>images/main.gif</xsl:with-param>
          </xsl:call-template>
          <!-- the same for career, industry, education,
               just_java, community, fyi_toronto, and
               about_us -->
        </tr>
      </table>
    </xsl:template>
```

To avoid repetitive code, each button is generated by calling a template. When the look and feel of the buttons need to be modified, only one template must be modified. This is less error-prone than having the code for each button repeated in the main template. This is the template for generating one button in the header.

```
    <xsl:template name='oneButton' mode='header'>
      <xsl:param name='link'/>
      <xsl:param name='name'/>
      <xsl:param name='image'/>
      <td width='72' valign='top'>
        <a href="main_back.html"
           onMouseOver="getMouseOver('{$name}')"
           onMouseOut="getMouseOut('{$name}')">
          <img name="{$name}"
               src="{$image}" border='0' width="70"
               height="30"/>
        </a>
      </td>
    </xsl:template>
```

JavaScript calls are used in the template. We will declare them in the header.

We can expect error dialogs when the following template is used to test the template for the header because the script declaration is nowhere to be found. However, we just want to find out whether the template for the header generates the correct HTML code. We can ignore the error dialogs for now.

```
<xsl:template match='/'>
  <html>
    <xsl:call-template name='generateHeader'/>
  </html>
</xsl:template>
```

This is the template for the footer.

```
<xsl:template name='generateFooter'>
  <table border='0' cellspacing='0' cellpadding='0' width="630"
         bgcolor="#BEC8B9">
    <tr><td><hr width='95%' /></td></tr>
    <tr>
      <td>
        <font face="Arial" size='2' color="#000035">
          <center>
            <a href="main.html">home</a>
            |
            <a href="career/index.html">career</a>
            |
            <a href="industry/index.html">industry</a>
            |
            <a href="education/index.html">education</a>
            |
            <a href="just_java/index.html">just java</a>
            |
            <a href="community/index.html">community</a>
            |
            <a href="fyi_toronto/index.html">fyi toronto</a>
            |
            <a href="about_us/index.html">about us</a>
          </center>
        </font>
      </td>
    </tr>
    <tr>
      <td>
        <font face="Arial" size='1' color="#000035">
          <center><br/>Copyright &#169;2000, torontojava.com inc.
          </center><br/>
        </font>
      </td>
```

```
      </tr>
    </table>
  </xsl:template>
```

12.4.4   *Full Story*

The detail page contains the header, the footer, the left side bar, and a full story.
The template for the full story requires the story file name.

```
<xsl:template name='generateFullStory' mode='fullStory'>
  <xsl:param name='fileName'/>
  <table width="100%" border='0' cellspacing='0' cellpadding='0' >
    <tr>
      <td colspan='2' align="right" bgcolor="#BEC8B9">
        <font face="IMPACT" size="6" color="white">story </font>
      </td>
    </tr>
    <xsl:apply-templates
        select='document($fileName)/story' mode='fullStory'/>
  </table>
</xsl:template>
```

If the XML tree for the story is the default XML tree, we will not need the
document function to get the **story** branch of the tree. Even then, this template
is still useful for testing purposes.

This is the template matching the **story** element.

```
<xsl:template match='story' mode='fullStory'>
  <xsl:apply-templates select='images/@main' mode='fullStory'/>
  <xsl:apply-templates select='title' mode='fullStory'/>
  <tr>
    <td width="100%" align='top'>
      <xsl:call-template name='byLine' mode='fullStory'>
        <xsl:with-param name='date' select='date'/>
        <xsl:with-param name='source' select='source'/>
        <xsl:with-param name='writer' select='writer'/>
      </xsl:call-template>
      <xsl:apply-templates select='body' mode='fullStory'/>
    </td>
  </tr>
</xsl:template>
```

This is the template for generating the title.

```
<xsl:template match='title' mode='fullStory'>
  <tr>
    <td width="100%  >
      <font face="impact" color="#000035" size="5">
        <b><center><xsl:value-of select='.'/></center></b>
      </font>
    </td>
  </tr>
  <tr><td> </td></tr>
</xsl:template>
```

And this is the template for generating the image placement.

```
<xsl:template match='images/@main' mode='fullStory'>
  <tr><td width="100%"> </td></tr>
  <tr>
    <td width="100%" align='top'>
      <center>
        <img src="{.}" width="260" height="125"/>
      </center>
    </td>
  </tr>
  <tr><td width="100%"> </td></tr>
</xsl:template>
```

This template matches only the attribute that is called main of an element called images.

The byline of the article is generated by a named template that takes the date, the source, and the writer and formats it in the desired way.

```
<xsl:template name='byLine' mode='fullStory'>
  <xsl:param name='date'/>
  <xsl:param name='source'/>
  <xsl:param name='writer'/>
  <font size="-2">
     Date: <xsl:value-of select='$date'/><br/>
     Source: <xsl:value-of select='$source'/><br/>
     Posted By: <xsl:value-of select='$writer'/><br/><br/>
  </font>
</xsl:template>
```

This is the template that handles the body of the full story.

```
<xsl:template match='body' mode='fullStory'>
  <font size="-1" face="Arial">
    <xsl:apply-templates mode='fullStory'/>
  </font>
  <tr><td height='10' width="100%"> </td></tr>
</xsl:template>
```

It is important to use the `xsl:apply-templates` element instead of a possible `xsl:value-of` element.

```
<xsl:template match='body' mode='fullStory'>
  <font size="-1" face="Arial">
    <xsl:value-of select='.'/>
  </font>
  <tr><td height='10' width="100%"> </td></tr>
</xsl:template>
```

Using the `xsl:apply-templates` element rather than the `xsl:value-of` element makes it possible for the body of the story to contain elements that need to be processed further. This is especially common for a production Web site because there are always more features to be incorporated after the site has been launched. Using the `xsl:apply-templates` element, these new elements can be incorporated more easily, whereas the `xsl:value-of` element returns only the string value of the element.

Right now, there are three possible elements inside a body element: the summary element, the link element, and the break element. The summary element is always the first element inside a body element. This is the template for rendering it in italics.

```
<xsl:template match='summary' mode='fullStory'>
  <i><xsl:value-of select='.'/></i><br/><br/>
</xsl:template>
```

Similarly, the choice between using an apply-templates element or an `xsl:value-of` element applies for this template as well. However, in this case, we choose `xsl:value-of`, trusting that the summary of a story will not have markups.

This is the template to handle links.

```
<xsl:template match='link' mode='fullStory'>
  <a href='{@url}'><xsl:value-of select='.'/></a>
</xsl:template>
```

Finally, we will develop the template to handle the **break** element, which is used to separate paragraphs. Perhaps a paragraph element would have been better. If such an element is necessary later, additional templates can be written to format a paragraph differently. This is the template.

```
<xsl:template match='break' mode='fullStory'>
  <br/><br/>
</xsl:template>
```

A break in the story is simply two break elements in the HTML document.

12.4.5   *Left Side Bar of a Detail Page*

The final piece of the puzzle before we can format a detail page is the left side bar of a detail page. The left side bar contains the advertisements for a detail page. This is the template.

```
<xsl:template name='generateDetailLeft'>
  <xsl:param name='fileName'/>
  <table border='0' cellspacing='0' cellpadding='0' BGcolor="silver"
         width='120' height='100%' bordercolor='#000035'>
    <tr>
      <td>
        <xsl:call-template name='generateAd'>
            <xsl:with-param name='fileName' select='$fileName'/>
        </xsl:call-template>
      </td>
    </tr>
  </table>
</xsl:template>
```

The XSLT document for a detail page looks like this.

```
<?xml version='1.0'?>
<xsl:stylesheet
 xmlns:xsl='http://www.w3.org/1999/XSL/Transform'
 version='1.0'>
  <xsl:output method='html'/>

  <xsl:include href='ad.xsl'/>

  <!-- the templates for the left side bar for the
       detail page -->
```

We assume that the name for the XSLT document containing templates for the advertisements is *ad.xsl*.

12.4.6   Header

Every HTML page has the same JavaScript declarations. This is the template used to generate the header.

```
<xsl:template name='generateHtml'>
  <head>
    <meta http-equiv="Content-Type"
          content="text/html; charset=iso-8859-1"/>
    <title>torontojava.com</title>
    <script language="Javascript">
     <xsl:comment> hide from non-Javascript Browsers
       ImageAbout= new Image(70,30)
       ImageAbout.src = "images/about_us.gif"
       ImageAbout_f = new Image(70,30)
       ImageAbout_f.src = "images/about_us_f.gif"
       <!-- similar for the other buttons as well. -->

       function getMouseOver(imName){
         document.images[imName].src =
                   eval("Image" + imName + "_f.src");
       }
       <!-- the rest of the Javascript declaration -->
       // - stop hiding </xsl:comment>
    </script>
  </head>
</xsl:template>
```

You can see how a comment can be generated by using an `xsl:comment` element.

12.4.7   Detail Page

Finally, we can generate a detail page. We must include all the XSLT documents for the detail page. We also want the name of the XML file containing advertisements passed in when the detail page is generated.

```
<?xml version='1.0'?>
<xsl:stylesheet
 xmlns:xsl='http://www.w3.org/1999/XSL/Transform'
```

```
               version='1.0'>
                <xsl:output method='html'/>

                <xsl:import href='ad.xsl'/>
                <xsl:import href='detail_left.xsl'/>
                <xsl:import href='footer.xsl'/>
                <xsl:import href='header.xsl'/>
                <xsl:import href='full.xsl'/>
                <xsl:import href='htmlhead.xsl'/>

                <xsl:param name='adFile'/>

                <!-- The templates. -->

        </xsl:stylesheet>
```

The interesting feature is the way that the file name for the advertisement is
passed in by a global **xsl:param** element.

It happens that there is only one template written for the detail page. This
template is the root template, and it generates everything in a detail page.

```
        <xsl:template match='/'>
          <html>
            <xsl:call-template name='generateHtml'/>
            <body text="#000035" bgcolor="#dddddd" link="#000035" vlink="#000035"
                  alink="#000035">
              <table bgcolor="#dddddd">
                <tr>
                  <td>
                    <font face='Impact'>
                      <script language="Javascript">displayDate(getToday());
                      </script>
                    </font><br/>
                  </td>
                </tr>
                <tr>
                  <td>
                    <xsl:call-template name='generateHeader'/>
                    <table border='0' cellspacing='6' cellpadding='6'
                           width="630"
                           bgcolor="#dddddd" bordercolor="#000066" >
                      <tr valign='top'>
                        <td bgcolor="silver">
```

```
            <xsl:call-template name='generateDetailLeft'>
              <xsl:with-param name='fileName' select='$adFile'/>
            </xsl:call-template>
          </td>
          <td colspan='2' align='top'>
            <table width="100%" border='0'
                    cellspacing='0' cellpadding='0' >
              <tr>
                <td colspan='2' align="right" bgcolor="#BEC8B9">
                  <font face="IMPACT" size="6"
                        color="white">story </font>
                </td>
              </tr>
              <xsl:apply-templates select='/story'
                    mode='fullStory'/>
            </table>
          </td>
        </tr>
      </table>
      <xsl:call-template name='generateFooter'/>
    </td>
  </tr>
</table>
</body>
</html>
</xsl:template>
```

The full story is generated by calling the template that matches story rather than the template that uses a file name as the parameter. We do this because the default XML file is the story file itself.

Many of the elements will be reused when the XSLT document for the summary page is designed. The templates that are needed for the summary page are the templates for the poll for the left side bar of a summary page, the templates for the left side bar itself, the templates for the main story on the page, and the templates for the secondary stories. Again, we will present the deepest nested elements first.

12.4.8   *Link Items*

To format the link items in the left side bar, we need the name for the collection of the items and the URL and labels for the links. The main template will generate the table containing the links. The information needed is from the lineup XML file (see Section 12.2).

```
<xsl:template match='leftbar' mode='leftbar'>
  <table width="100%" border='0' cellspacing='2' cellpadding='2'
        bgcolor="#BEC8B9">
    <tr>
      <td BGcolor="#000035">
      <font face="Impact" color="White"> <xsl:value-of
            select='name'/></font>
      </td>
    </tr>
    <xsl:apply-templates select='item' mode='leftbar'/>
  </table>
</xsl:template>
```

Each item is generated separately, and each item is a row in the table.

```
<xsl:template match='item' mode='leftbar'>
  <tr valign='top'>
    <td valign='top' width="120">
      <font face="Impact" size="-2" color="#000035" >
        <a href="{@link}"><xsl:value-of select='.'/></a>
      </font>
    </td>
  </tr>
</xsl:template>
```

12.4.9   *Poll*

As with advertisements, the placement of polls should be as dynamic as possible. However, since a lineup file is used for a summary page, the name of the file containing the poll will be included in the lineup file. First, let us look at the main template for generating the form for a poll.

```
<xsl:template match='poll' mode='poll'>
  <table border="0" width="100%">
    <tr>
      <td width="100%">
        <form method="{method}" action="{action}">
          <table  border='0' cellpadding='0' cellspacing='0'
                  bgcolor='#BEC8B9' width="100%>
            <tr>
              <td bgcolor="#000035" width='125' valign='top'>
```

```
        <font face="Impact" color="white"> 
          <xsl:value-of select='@name'/></font>
          </td>
        </tr>
        <tr>
          <td width='125'>
            <font face="ARIAL" size='-2'>
              <b><br/><xsl:value-of select='question'/></b>
            </font>
          </td>
        </tr>
        <xsl:apply-templates select='response' mode='poll'/>
        <tr>
          <td><br/>
            <center>
              <font size='-1'>
                <input name='{@name}' type='submit'
                       value='{button}'/>
              </font>
            </center>
          </td>
        </tr>
        <tr><td> </td></tr>
      </table>
    </form>
  </td>
 </tr>
</table>
</xsl:template>
```

The information about a poll is all in the poll XML file. Each possible response is generated by the template like this.

```
<xsl:template match='response' mode='poll'>
  <tr>
    <td><br/>
      <input name='{position()}'
        type='radio' value='{@value}'/><!--
      --><font size='-1'><xsl:value-of select='.'/></font>
    </td>
  </tr>
</xsl:template>
```

To test the templates, we can have this template.

```
<xsl:template match='/'>
  <html>
    <xsl:apply-templates
        select='document(/lineup/poll/@url)/poll' mode='poll'/>
  </html>
</xsl:template>
```

Notice how the URL for the poll XML file is obtained from the lineup file. This is another way of handling information from an external XML file.

12.4.10   *Left Side Bar for the Summary Page*

The left side bar for a summary page has more items than the left side bar of a detail page. However, the principle for the template that generates the left side bars is the same.

```
<xsl:template name='generateLeft' mode='left'>
  <table border='0' cellspacing='0' cellpadding='0' bgcolor="silver"
         width='130' height='100%' bordercolor="#000035">
    <tr>
      <td>
        <xsl:apply-templates select='/lineup/leftbar' mode='leftbar'/>
      </td>
    </tr>
    <tr><td> </td></tr>
    <tr>
      <td>
        <xsl:apply-templates
            select='document(/lineup/poll/@url)/poll' mode='poll'/>
      </td>
    </tr>
    <tr><td> </td></tr>
    <tr>
      <td>
        <xsl:call-template name='generateAd'>
          <xsl:with-param name='fileName' select='$adFile'/>
        </xsl:call-template>
      </td>
    </tr>
  </table>
</xsl:template>
```

The same templates for generating the advertisements are used in both sets of templates.

12.4.11 *Stories*

The templates for generating the main story and the secondary stories in a summary page use features that have been discussed before. First, here are the templates for generating the main story.

```
<xsl:template name='generateMainStory' mode='mainStory'>
  <xsl:param name='fileName'/>
  <table width="100%" border='0' cellspacing='0' cellpadding='0' >
    <tr>
      <td colspan='2' align="right" bgcolor="#BEC8B9">
        <font face="Impact" size="6" color="white">
          <xsl:value-of select='/lineup/department'/> 
        </font>
      </td>
    </tr>
    <xsl:apply-templates
        select='document($fileName)' mode='mainStory'/>
  </table>
</xsl:template>


<xsl:template match='story' mode='mainStory'>
  <xsl:apply-templates select='images/@main' mode='mainStory'/>
  <xsl:apply-templates select='title' mode='mainStory'/>
  <tr>
    <td width="100%" align='top'>
      <xsl:call-template name='byLine' mode='mainStory'>
        <xsl:with-param name='date' select='date'/>
        <xsl:with-param name='source' select='source'/>
        <xsl:with-param name='writer' select='writer'/>
      </xsl:call-template>
      <xsl:apply-templates select='body' mode='mainStory'/>
    </td>
  </tr>
</xsl:template>


<xsl:template match='title' mode='mainStory'>
  <tr>
    <td width="100%"  >
```

```
              <font face="impact" color="#000035" size="5">
                <b><center><xsl:value-of select='.'/></center></b>
              </font>
            </td>
          </tr>
          <tr><td> </td></tr>
        </xsl:template>


        <xsl:template match='images/@main' mode='mainStory'>
          <tr><td width="100%"> </td></tr>
          <tr>
            <td width="100%" align='top'>
              <center>
                <img src="{.}" width="260" height="125"/>
              </center>
            </td>
          </tr>
          <tr><td width="100%"> </td></tr>
        </xsl:template>


        <xsl:template name='byLine' mode='mainStory'>
          <xsl:param name='date'/>
          <xsl:param name='source'/>
          <xsl:param name='writer'/>
          <font size="-2">
             Date: <xsl:value-of select='$date'/><br/>
             Source: <xsl:value-of select='$source'/><br/>
             Posted By: <xsl:value-of select='$writer'/><br/><br/>
          </font>
        </xsl:template>


        <xsl:template match='body' mode='mainStory'>
          <font size="-1" face="Arial">
            <xsl:apply-templates select='summary' mode='mainStory'/>
          </font>
          <tr><td height='10' width="100%"> </td></tr>
        </xsl:template>


        <xsl:template match='summary' mode='mainStory'>
          <i><xsl:value-of select='.'/></i><a href='.html'>Full Story</a><br/><br/>
        </xsl:template>
```

```
<xsl:template match='link' mode='mainStory'>
  <a href='{@url}'><xsl:value-of select='.'/></a>
</xsl:template>

<xsl:template match='break' mode='mainStory'>
  <br/><br/>
</xsl:template>
```

New templates that look the same as those that generate the full story on a detail page are declared for maintenance purposes. The formatting of the stories may look identical right now, but in general, the formatting will be different when new features are needed. Using different modes (for full stories and main stories), these elements are separated from each other. Now the templates for the secondary stories look like this.

```
<xsl:template match='story' mode='secondary'>
  <xsl:param name='fileName'/>
  <table width="461" border='0' cellspacing='0' cellpadding='0' >
    <tr>
      <td colspan='2' bgcolor="#000035" width="459" >
        <font face="impact" color="WHITE" size="3">
           <xsl:apply-templates select='title'/>
        </font>
      </td>
    </tr>
    <tr><td><font size="-5"> </font></td></tr>
    <tr valign='top'>
      <td align='top' width='51' height='50'>
        <xsl:apply-templates select='images/@side' mode='secondary'/>
      </td>
      <td align='top' width="406">
        <font size="-2" face="Arial">
          <xsl:call-template name='byLine' mode='secondary'>
            <xsl:with-param name='date' select='date'/>
            <xsl:with-param name='source' select='source'/>
            <xsl:with-param name='writer' select='writer'/>
          </xsl:call-template>
        </font>
        <xsl:apply-templates select='body/summary' mode='secondary'/>
        <font size="-1" face="Arial">
          <a href='{$fileName}.html'>Full Story</a>
```

```
        </font>
      </td>
    </tr>
  </table >
</xsl:template>

<xsl:template match='title' mode='secondary'>
  <tr>
    <td width="100%">
      <font face="impact" color="#000035" size="5">
        <b><center><xsl:value-of select='.'/></center></b>
      </font>
    </td>
  </tr>
  <tr><td> </td></tr>
</xsl:template>

<xsl:template match='images/@side' mode='secondary'>
  <center>
    <img src="{.}" width="50" height="51"/>
  </center>
</xsl:template>

<xsl:template name='byLine' mode='secondary'>
  <xsl:param name='date'/>
  <xsl:param name='source'/>
  <xsl:param name='writer'/>
  <font size="-2">
     Date: <xsl:value-of select='$date'/><br/>
     Source: <xsl:value-of select='$source'/><br/>
     Posted By: <xsl:value-of select='$writer'/><br/><br/>
  </font>
</xsl:template>

<xsl:template match='summary' mode='secondary'>
  <font size="-1" face="Arial">
    <i><xsl:value-of select='.'/></i><br/><br/>
  </font>
</xsl:template>

<xsl:template match='link' mode='secondary'>
  <a href='{@url}'><xsl:value-of select='.'/></a>
```

```
</xsl:template>

<xsl:template match='break' mode='secondary'>
  <br/><br/>
</xsl:template>
```

12.4.12   *Summary Page*

Finally, let's look at the templates for generating a summary page. We can use many of the templates used by a detail page.

```
<?xml version='1.0'?>
<xsl:stylesheet
 xmlns:xsl='http://www.w3.org/1999/XSL/Transform'
 version='1.0'>
  <xsl:output method='html'/>

  <xsl:import href='ad.xsl'/>
  <xsl:import href='detail_left.xsl'/>
  <xsl:import href='footer.xsl'/>
  <xsl:import href='header.xsl'/>
  <xsl:import href='full.xsl'/>
  <xsl:import href='htmlhead.xsl'/>
  <xsl:import href='left.xsl'/>
  <xsl:import href='main_story.xsl'/>
  <xsl:import href='secondary_story.xsl'/>

  <xsl:param name='adFile'/>

  <!-- The Templates -->

</xsl:stylesheet>
```

We have also decided to follow the template for a detail page by having one template generate the whole summary page.

```
<xsl:template match='/'>
  <html>
    <xsl:call-template name='generateHtml'/>
    <body text="#000035" bgcolor="#dddddd" link="#000035"
          vlink="#000035"
          alink="#000035">
      <table bgcolor="#dddddd">
        <tr>
```

```
                       <td>
                          <font face='Impact'>
             <script LANGUAGE="Javascript">displayDate(getToday());</script>
                          </font><br/>
                       </td>
                    </tr>
                    <tr>
                      <td>
                        <xsl:call-template name='generateHeader'/>
                        <table border='0' cellspacing='6' cellpadding='6'
                               width="630"
                               bgcolor="#dddddd" bordercolor="#000066" >
                          <tr valign='top'>
                            <td BGcolor="silver">
                              <xsl:call-template name='generateLeft' mode='left'/>
                            </td>
                            <td colspan='2' align='top'>
                              <xsl:call-template name='generateMainStory'
                                    mode='mainStory'>
                                <xsl:with-param name='fileName'
                                     select='/lineup/news[1]'/>
                              </xsl:call-template>
                              <xsl:apply-templates
                        select='document(/lineup/news[position() != 1])/story'
                                    mode='secondary'/>
                            </td>
                          </tr>
                        </table>
                        <xsl:call-template name='generateFooter'/>
                      </td>
                    </tr>
                 </table>
               </body>
             </html>
           </xsl:template>
```

12.5   Summary

This has been a long chapter. It is packed with details you will need when you are constructing a Web site. As a developer, you are probably resigned to the

fact that real-world problems usually require solutions that are not as elegant as you'd like. This is especially true when the schedule is tight.

Still, XSLT is more sophisticated than most other methods because XML and HTML look similar, so you do not have to switch "presentation contexts" too much when you write XSLT documents.

12.6   Looking Ahead

This is the end of the discussion on transforming XML to HTML documents. The next chapter will provide a few examples for using XSLT to transform XML documents to other XML documents or text.

PART IV

⟨13⟩

Transforming to XML and Text

Come!
Let me tell you.
The transformation of all things does not end;
but people think it has a beginning and an end.
—*Zhuang Zi*

So far we have only seen transformations from XML to HTML. Of course, this is not the only transformation performed by XSLT. On the contrary, XSLT's primary design goal is to provide a transformation language for XSL (Extensible Stylesheet Language), an XML vocabulary. The transformation to HTML is only a side goal.

Transforming an XML document to another XML document sounds rather mundane and uninteresting. In fact, this is a very rewarding activity when you realize that XML vocabularies and applications for presentation, vector graphics, hyperlinks, and so on are being developed as we speak. Even the mundane, simple transformation of an XML document to a slightly different XML document provides the interoperability that is so critical for Internet commerce and business.

In this chapter, we will look at producing non-HTML documents: XML documents and text documents. We will talk about a few useful XML technologies and how to generate documents for them. We will also see a simple example of how to produce a text document in XSLT. The purpose of this chapter is to present examples of the technologies, but in-depth discussions of these technologies are best left to other books.

13.1 XHTML

One way to use XML on the World Wide Web is to "reproduce, subset, and extend"[1] HTML in XML. XHTML has all the benefits of XML, and, because it comes from HTML, it will be familiar to HTML developers.

One benefit of using XSLT to transform XML to HTML is that whether XHTML is used or not, the XSLT documents will work because the HTML in them is already well-formed XML.

XHTML also facilitates XML to HTML transformation, especially for Web site generation. Incorporating HTML fragments into an XML-based publishing system is one of the biggest headaches because HTML is not XML. Somehow, the HTML fragments must be transformed (not by XSLT) into XML before they can be put into XML documents and handled by the publishing pipeline.

13.1.1 *An XHTML Document*

Here is a simple XHTML document.

```
<?xml version='1.0'?>
<html xmlns='http://www.w3.org/1999/xhtml' xml:lang='en'>
  <head><title>An example in XHTML</title></head>
  <body>
    <h1>Example</h1>
    <p>A simple XHTML example to show that it is
       really not very different from HTML except everything
       must be well-formed in the sense of XML.</p>
  </body>
</html>
```

Notice that in XHTML, all elements are in lower case. As XHTML is a special class of XML documents, all XHTML documents must also be well-formed XML documents. This means you must have end-tags for all elements, all attributes must quote their values, and so forth.

---

1. From "XHTML 1.0: The Extensible HyperText Markup Language, A Reformulation of HTML 4.0 in XML 1.0," A W3C recommendation, dated January 26, 2000.

13.2   XSL

An XSL document contains information to instruct a "rendering engine" how a document looks on a presentation device. The information is given in elements called formatting objects. For instance, the amount for the left margin is represented by a formatting object. By specifying formatting objects for the concepts used for formatting a document for a screen, book, or whatever, XSL allows the maximum flexibility in describing the presentation of a document without going into the placement of inks on the devices.

The role of XSLT is the same as in the transformation of XML documents to HTML: the language used to transform an XML document to a presentation language. In this case, the presentation language is XSL.

13.2.1   *A Simple Example*

XSL is in the process of being standardized. At the time of this writing, the specification is in the candidate recommendation stage. The specification will change. However, the basics of our discussion should be the same.

We will use the story document from the case study chapter. Let's see how the XML document can be converted into XSL format objects. The steps are very similar to the transformation of the same document to HTML, but in this case, XSL elements are used.

The XSLT document for the transformation has different attributes for the `xsl:stylesheet` and the `xsl:output` elements. They look like this.

```
<?xml version='1.0'?>
<xsl:stylesheet
 xmlns:xsl='http://www.w3.org/1999/XSL/Transform'
 version='1.0'
 xmlns:fo='http://www.w3.org/1999/XSL/Format'
 result-ns='fo'>

  <xsl:output method='xml' indent='yes'/>

  <!-- The templates -->

</xsl:stylesheet>
```

XSL documents are a special class of XML documents, so the output method should be set to `xml`. The resulting namespace prefix is `fo`. All elements with this namespace are considered literal elements by XSLT.

We will use the bottom-up approach. The simplest element in the XML document is the `break` element. We need something equivalent to a line break to simulate a paragraph break. To do this, we can use an empty block object followed by a space.

```
<xsl:template match='break' mode='fullStory'>
 <fo:block space-after.optimum='10pt'/>
</xsl:template>
```

The break will be 10 points.[2]

Next, we can handle the summary part of the story. We'll use the italicized version of whatever font is in effect, just like in the HTML version.

```
<xsl:template match='summary' mode='fullStory'>
  <fo:block font-style='italic' space-after.optimum='10pt'>
    <xsl:value-of select='.'/>
  </fo:block>
</xsl:template>
```

The template for the link will also be in italics. The difference is that a link is an inline object rather than a block.

```
<xsl:template match='link' mode='fullStory'>
  <fo:inline-sequence font-style='italic'>
    <xsl:value-of select='.'/>
  </fo:inline-sequence>
</xsl:template>
```

In XSL, links can be specified, just like in HTML. But we will omit that feature in this example. The next element that we can tackle is the body of the story.

```
<xsl:template match='body' mode='fullStory'>
  <fo:block
      font-size="10pt"
      face="serif"
      space-after.optimum='10pt'>
    <xsl:apply-templates mode='fullStory'/>
  </fo:block>
</xsl:template>
```

2. One inch is about 72 points. The exact number depends on where you look.

We will omit showing images for now. The template for the main image is therefore empty.

```
<xsl:template match='images/@main' mode='fullStory'>
</xsl:template>
```

We want to center the title of the story and make the letters much bigger than the story text.

```
<xsl:template match='title' mode='fullStory'>
  <fo:block
      text-align='centered'
      font-family='serif'
      font-size='15pt'
      space-after.optimum='30pt'>
    <xsl:value-of select='.'/>
  </fo:block>
</xsl:template>
```

The main template to handle all the elements in a story is also quite straightforward.

```
<xsl:template match='story' mode='fullStory'>
  <xsl:apply-templates select='images/@main' mode='fullStory'/>
  <xsl:apply-templates select='title' mode='fullStory'/>
  <fo:block>
      <xsl:call-template name='byLine' mode='fullStory'>
        <xsl:with-param name='date' select='date'/>
        <xsl:with-param name='source' select='source'/>
        <xsl:with-param name='writer' select='writer'/>
      </xsl:call-template>
      <xsl:apply-templates select='body' mode='fullStory'/>
  </fo:block>
</xsl:template>
```

We have not defined the template for the byline yet. We will make it look very similar to the version for HTML.

```
<xsl:template name='byLine' mode='fullStory'>
  <xsl:param name='date'/>
  <xsl:param name='source'/>
  <xsl:param name='writer'/>
  <fo:block space-after.optimum='15pt' font-size='8pt'>
    <fo:block> Date: <xsl:value-of select='$date'/>
```

```
            </fo:block>
            <fo:block> Source: <xsl:value-of select='$source'/>
            </fo:block>
            <fo:block> Writer: <xsl:value-of select='$writer'/>
            </fo:block>
          </fo:block>
        </xsl:template>
```

Since we know that we will be generating one document for each story,
the named template for generating one story does not need to take a file name
anymore.

```
        <xsl:template name='generateFullStory' mode='fullStory'>
          <fo:block
            font-size='18pt'
            font-family='sans-serif'
            text-align='end'>Story</fo:block>
          <xsl:apply-templates select='/story' mode='fullStory'/>
        </xsl:template>
```

So far, everything is quite straightforward, with HTML elements replaced by
XSL elements.

The next thing we want to specify is a master page.

```
        <xsl:template name='generateMasters'>
          <fo:layout-master-set>
            <fo:simple-page-master
                page-master-name='all'
                height='11in' width='8in'
                margin-top='1in' margin-bottom='1in'
                margin-left='0.5in' margin-right='0.5in'>
              <fo:region-before extent="2in"/>
              <fo:region-body margin-top="2in"/>
              <fo:region-after extent="1in"/>
            </fo:simple-page-master>
          </fo:layout-master-set>
        </xsl:template>

        <xsl:template name='generateSequence'>
          <fo:sequence-specification>
            <fo:sequence-specifier-repeating
                page-master-first='all'
```

```
                page-master-repeating='all'/>
        </fo:sequence-specification>
    </xsl:template>
```

Finally, we can put together everything in the template that matches the root.

```
<xsl:template match='/'>
  <fo:root xmlns:fo='http://www.w3.org/1999/XSL/Format'>
    <xsl:call-template name='generateMasters'/>
    <fo:page-sequence>
      <xsl:call-template name='generateSequence'/>
      <fo:static-content flow-name='xsl-after'>
        <fo:block
            text-align='centered'
            font-size='12pt'
            font-family='sans-serif'>
          <fo:page-number/>
        </fo:block>
      </fo:static-content>
      <fo:flow flow-name='xsl-body'>
        <xsl:call-template
            name='generateFullStory'
            mode='fullStory'/>
      </fo:flow>
    </fo:page-sequence>
  </fo:root>
</xsl:template>
```

The page has two main components: a footer that is centered on the page that shows the page number and the body of the page.

13.2.2   *Rendering Formatting Objects*

After an XML document has been transformed to an XSL document, the next step is to render the output document. The application that does the rendering is called a rendering engine or a formatting engine. The format of the output presumably is whatever the Web browser (or any XSL rendering engine that you may want to use) uses internally.

13.3   SVG

SVG (scalable vector graphics) is a markup language for describing two-dimensional graphics, with optional sophisticated effects and animation, in XML.

XSLT can be used with SVG the same as with XSL: as a transformation language to convert an XML document into a SVG document. The process is very similar to XSL with one difference: too much bandwidth is needed to generate XSL documents on the server side and then send to the client for rendering. For SVG, however, it is probably much better to generate SVG documents on the server side, convert the SVG document into the final format like GIF or JPEG, and then send the GIF or JPEG file to the client for rendering.

This process should sound familiar by now. A graphics designer designs a sample image. Using a conversion tool, the image is converted to an SVG document. Just as with HTML mockups, the SVG document is then carved up and parts of it are embedded in an XSLT document. The XSLT document then takes parameters from the input XML document to generate SVG documents.

A simple example is the generation of artistic numbers found in many Web sites. The current practice is to design each of them beforehand. If the numbers from 1 to 100 are needed, then the images for all 100 of them are designed before they are used.

Using SVG, any number in the same style can be generated when it is needed. For example, the following is a simple SVG file for showing a number.

```
<?xml version="1.0"?>
<svg width="40pt" height="40pt">

 <g style='fill:#000035'>
    <path d='M0,0v20h50v-20z'/>
 </g>

 <!-- the attribute value for the {style} must be
      on the same line. It is broken off here to fit
      on the page -->
 <g style='fill:#ffffff; font-size:15;
           font-family: ariel; stroke-width:5'>
    <text x='0' y='15'
         style='text-anchor:start'>10000</text>
 </g>
</svg>
```

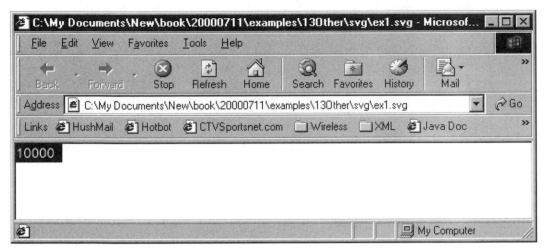

FIGURE

13.1   An SVG example

The result of rendering the SVG file is shown in Figure 13.1. Converting this into an XSLT template that generates a SVG file is straightforward.

```
<?xml version="1.0"?>

<xsl:stylesheet
 xmlns:xsl='http://www.w3.org/1999/XSL/Transform'>

  <xsl:output method='xml'/>

  <xsl:param name='number'/>

  <xsl:template match='/'>
    <svg width="40pt" height="40pt">
      <g style='fill:#000035'>
        <path d='M0,0v20h50v-20z'/>
      </g>

      <!-- the attribute value for the {style} must be
           on the same line. It is broken off here to fit
           on the page -->
      <g style='fill:#ffffff; font-size:15;
             font-family: ariel; stroke-width:5'>
        <text x='0' y='15'
```

```
                style='text-anchor:start'><xsl:value-of select='$number'/></text>
        </g>
      </svg>
    </xsl:template>
</xsl:stylesheet>
```

Note that we assume we will pass in the number to be generated via an `xsl:param` element. Of course, the SVG files can be as complicated as necessary. This is just a taste of how SVG can be used, even if it is used only on the server side.

13.4   Transforming an XML Document to Text

Finally, let us look at a simple example of transforming an XML document to a text document. We will use PDF as the output format. The basic PDF document format is shown in Figure 13.2. Basically, there are five parts in a PDF document.

1. The header contains the string `%PDF-1.0`, `%PDF-1.1`, `%PDF-1.2`, or `%PDF-1.3`, depending on the version of the PDF document format used. We will use `%PDF-1.0`.

2. The body is a list of objects. For our purpose, we have to know that there is always a `Catalog` object that is really the root of the document. We will also use an `outlines` object to represent the outlines of a document; a `pages` object used to group a list of `page` objects together; and `page` objects to contain the actual content of the pages.

3. After the body is a cross-reference section that contains pointers into each of the objects in the document.

4. After the cross-reference section is the trailer section that points to the root of the document and also the start of the cross-reference section.

5. Finally, the string `%EOF` signals the end of the document.

This is the most basic PDF document that shows only the string `Hello World! Success! Free at last!`[3]

```
%PDF-1.0
1 0 obj
```

---

3. This example document is generated by the XSLT document, but the model document is taken from *The Portable Document Format Reference Manual*, Version 1.3, by Adobe Systems Incorporated.

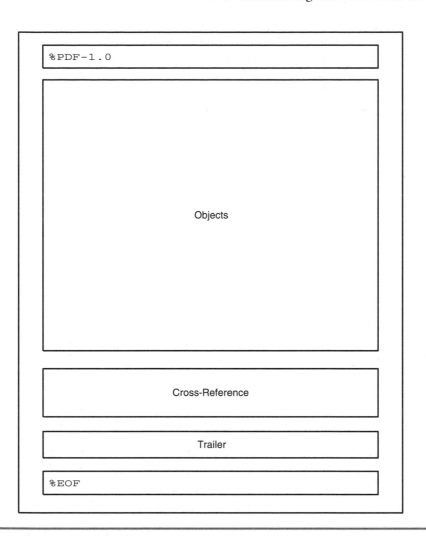

13.2   The basic structure of a PDF document

```
<<
/Type /Catalog
/Pages 3 0 R
/Outlines 2 0 R
>>
endobj
2 0 obj
<<
/Type /Outlines
```

```
/Count 0
>>
endobj
3 0 obj
<<
/Type /Pages
/Count 1
/Kids [4 0 R]
>>
endobj
4 0 obj
<<
/Type /Page
/Parent 3 0 R
/Resources << /Font << /F1 7 0 R >> /ProcSet 6 0 R
>>
/MediaBox [0 0 612 792]
/Contents 5 0 R
>>
endobj
5 0 obj
<< /Length 68 >>
stream
BT
/F1 24 Tf
100 100 Td (Hello World! Success! Free at last!) Tj
ET

endstream
endobj
6 0 obj
[/PDF /Text]
endobj
7 0 obj
<<
/Type /Font
/Subtype /Type1
/Name /F1
/BaseFont /Helvetica
/Encoding /MacRomanEncoding
>>
```

```
endobj
xref
0 8
0000000000 65535 f
0000000009 00000 n
0000000074 00000 n
0000000120 00000 n
0000000177 00000 n
0000000318 00000 n
0000000436 00000 n
0000000464 00000 n
trailer
<<
/Size 8
/Root 1 0 R
>>
startxref
572
%%EOF
```

Each object in a PDF file contains the object number, the generation number, and the word `obj` in the beginning of the object. Then the object specifies its properties in a dictionary. The dictionary is delimited by << and >>. For instance, the first object in the PDF file we have shown has three properties in the dictionary.

```
/Type /Catalog
/Pages 3 0 R
/Outlines 2 0 R
```

The first property says that the type of the object is a catalog; the pages of the PDF starts with object number 3; and the outlines object is object number 2. The character `R` means reference. An object ends with the word `endobj`.

Other objects in the PDF file shown have other properties in their dictionaries. Object number 3 has the property `count` with the value 1: the object indexes only one page. Object number 3 also has the property `Kids`, which specifies the child objects of the object. There is only one child object for object number 3: object number 4.

Object number 4 specifies its parent object as object 3; it also specifies where it obtains information about fonts.

Object number 5 is the most interesting object because it contains the actual information to be shown on a page. We will not go into details about the instructions used in the object.

The cross-reference section of a PDF file contains the number of objects in the file, the starting location of the objects counting from the first byte of the file, and whether an object is active. For instance, from the cross-reference section of the PDF file we showed this.

```
0 8
0000000000 65535 f
0000000009 00000 n
0000000074 00000 n
0000000120 00000 n
0000000177 00000 n
0000000318 00000 n
0000000436 00000 n
0000000464 00000 n
```

Ignore the first entry. The first object starts from byte number 9 from the beginning of the file. The second object starts from byte number 74 from the beginning of the file. The last object starts from byte 464 from the beginning of the file.

Finally, the `trailer` section specifies how many objects are in the file (there are eight for our PDF file), the root object of the PDF file (object number 1 in our case), and the starting byte of the cross-reference section of the file. The trailer is used to find the cross-reference section and the first object by the viewer of a PDF file.

As for the case study in the previous chapter, the basic document is cut up and put into different templates. Let's look at the templates that are more or less static first.

```
<?xml version='1.0'?>
<xsl:stylesheet
 xmlns:xsl='http://www.w3.org/1999/XSL/Transform'
 version='1.0'>
  <xsl:output method='text'/>

  <xsl:template name='catalog'>
    <xsl:variable name='catalog'>%PDF-1.0
1 0 obj
&lt;&lt;
```

```
/Type /Catalog
/Pages 3 0 R
/Outlines 2 0 R
>>
endobj
</xsl:variable>
    <xsl:value-of select='$catalog'/>
  </xsl:template>

  <xsl:template name='outlines'>
    <xsl:variable name='outlines'>2 0 obj
&lt;&lt;
/Type /Outlines
/Count 0
>>
endobj
</xsl:variable>
    <xsl:value-of select='$outlines'/>
  </xsl:template>

  <xsl:template name='pages'>
    <xsl:variable name='pages'>3 0 obj
&lt;&lt;
/Type /Pages
/Count 1
/Kids [4 0 R]
>>
endobj
</xsl:variable>
    <xsl:value-of select='$pages'/>
  </xsl:template>

  <xsl:template name='page'>
    <xsl:variable name='page'>4 0 obj
&lt;&lt;
/Type /Page
/Parent 3 0 R
/Resources &lt;&lt; /Font &lt;&lt; /F1 7 0 R >> /ProcSet 6 0 R
>>
/MediaBox [0 0 612 792]
/Contents 5 0 R
```

```
        >>
        endobj
        </xsl:variable>
            <xsl:value-of select='$page'/>
          </xsl:template>

          <xsl:template name='procset'>
            <xsl:variable name='procset'>6 0 obj
        [/PDF /Text]
        endobj
        </xsl:variable>
            <xsl:value-of select='$procset'/>
          </xsl:template>

          <xsl:template name='resource'>
            <xsl:variable name='resource'>7 0 obj
        &lt;&lt;
        /Type /Font
        /Subtype /Type1
        /Name /F1
        /BaseFont /Helvetica
        /Encoding /MacRomanEncoding
        >>
        endobj
        </xsl:variable>
              <xsl:value-of select='$resource'/>
            </xsl:template>
```

We use a template for each of the objects here for ease of modification. For instance, when a different font is desired, the template for defining the font used in the document can be modified easily to use the desired font.

Strings in PDF (and Postscript as well) are in parentheses. That is, the string "This is a test" will be presented in PDF as (This is a test). If a string has the parentheses characters, they must be escaped by prefixing a backslash. The backslash character must be escaped as well. This is the template that escapes all the characters.

```
<xsl:template name='escape'>
  <xsl:param name='text'/>
  <xsl:param name='character'/>
  <xsl:choose>
```

```
    <xsl:when test='contains($text, $character)'>
      <xsl:variable name='first'
        select='substring-before($text, $character)'/>
      <xsl:variable name='last'>
        <xsl:call-template name='escape'>
          <xsl:with-param name='text'
            select='substring-after($text, $character)'/>
          <xsl:with-param name='character' select='$character'/>
        </xsl:call-template></xsl:variable>
      <xsl:value-of
        select='concat($first, "\", $character, $last)'/>
    </xsl:when>
    <xsl:otherwise>
      <xsl:value-of select='$text'/>
    </xsl:otherwise>
  </xsl:choose>
</xsl:template>
```

Finally, the **stream**[4] object in the PDF file must be constructed. We will use the template matching the root to get the content of an XML file and pretend that it will fit on one line in the PDF file.

Our biggest problem is to find out the byte numbers of the objects from the start of the document for the cross-reference section. The simplest solution is to store all the objects before they are output. Then we write all the objects to the output. When we have to generate cross-references, we compute the lengths of the objects using the `string-length` function. The format of an entry in the cross-reference is fixed, with the first number being a 10-digit number (with leading zeroes when necessary); the second number (the generation number) being a 5-digit number, again with leading zeroes when necessary; and then last character being "n" if the object is defined in the document. The convention is that the first object always has the pointer number as zero, the generation number as 65535, and the last character "f." Here is the root template for the text to PDF XSLT document.

```
  <xsl:template match='/'>
    <xsl:variable name='catalog'>
      <xsl:call-template name='catalog'/></xsl:variable>
    <xsl:variable name='outlines'>
```

---

4. In PDF, this means whatever is on the page.

305

```
      <xsl:call-template name='outlines'/></xsl:variable>
   <xsl:variable name='pages'>
     <xsl:call-template name='pages'/></xsl:variable>
   <xsl:variable name='page'>
     <xsl:call-template name='page'/></xsl:variable>
   <xsl:variable name='thePage'>BT
/F1 24 Tf
100 100 Td (<xsl:call-template name='escape'>
  <xsl:with-param name='text'><xsl:call-template name='escape'>
          <xsl:with-param name='text'><xsl:call-template name='escape'>
                   <xsl:with-param name='text'>
<xsl:value-of select='/'/></xsl:with-param>
                   <xsl:with-param name='character'>
</xsl:with-param>
               </xsl:call-template></xsl:with-param>
         <xsl:with-param name='character'>(</xsl:with-param>
     </xsl:call-template></xsl:with-param>
  <xsl:with-param name='character'>)</xsl:with-param>
</xsl:call-template>) Tj
ET
</xsl:variable>
   <xsl:variable name='stream'>5 0 obj
&lt;&lt; /Length <xsl:value-of select='string-length($thePage)'/> >>
stream
<xsl:value-of select='$thePage'/>
endstream
endobj
</xsl:variable>
   <xsl:variable name='resource'>
<xsl:call-template name='resource'/></xsl:variable>
   <xsl:variable name='procset'>
<xsl:call-template name='procset'/></xsl:variable>
<xsl:value-of select='$catalog'/>
<xsl:value-of select='$outlines'/>
<xsl:value-of select='$pages'/>
<xsl:value-of select='$page'/>
<xsl:value-of select='$stream'/>
<xsl:value-of select='$procset'/>
<xsl:value-of select='$resource'/>
   <xsl:text>xref
```

```
0 8
0000000000 65535 f &#x0D;0000000009 00000 n &#x0D;</xsl:text>
<xsl:variable name='l1' select='string-length($catalog)'/>
<xsl:variable name='l2' select='$l1+string-length($outlines)'/>
<xsl:variable name='l3' select='$l2+string-length($pages)'/>
<xsl:variable name='l4' select='$l3+string-length($page)'/>
<xsl:variable name='l5' select='$l4+string-length($stream)'/>
<xsl:variable name='l6' select='$l5+string-length($procset)'/>
<xsl:variable name='l7' select='$l6+string-length($resource)'/>
<xsl:value-of select='format-number($l1, "0000000000")'/>
<xsl:text> 00000 n &#x0D;</xsl:text>
<xsl:value-of select='format-number($l2, "0000000000")'/>
<xsl:text> 00000 n &#x0D;</xsl:text>
<xsl:value-of select='format-number($l3, "0000000000")'/>
<xsl:text> 00000 n &#x0D;</xsl:text>
<xsl:value-of select='format-number($l4, "0000000000")'/>
<xsl:text> 00000 n &#x0D;</xsl:text>
<xsl:value-of select='format-number($l5, "0000000000")'/>
<xsl:text> 00000 n &#x0D;</xsl:text>
<xsl:value-of select='format-number($l6, "0000000000")'/>
<xsl:text> 00000 n &#x0D;</xsl:text>
<xsl:text>
trailer
&lt;&lt;
/Size 8
/Root 1 0 R
>>
startxref
</xsl:text>
<xsl:value-of select='$l7'/>
<xsl:text>
%%EOF
</xsl:text>
  </xsl:template>
```

We are taking a shortcut with respect to the number of objects in the PDF file. It should be a variable reference, just like the starting byte numbers for the objects in the cross-reference section. The PDF containing the string "Hello World! (Good?) (Good!)" is shown in Figure 13.3. It shows that the parentheses are handled properly.

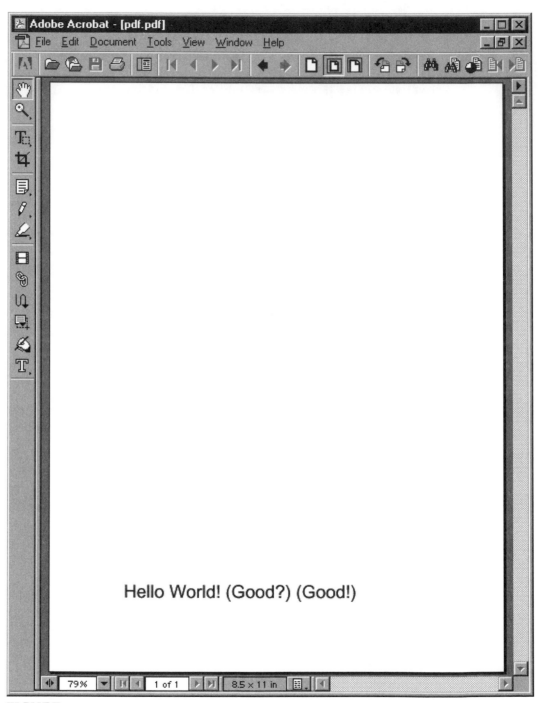

FIGURE

13.3   Screen shot of a file generated by the XSLT document

13.4.1   *Enhancements*

To make the XSLT document more useful, metrics for fonts can be stored in XML files. In this way, the XSLT document can handle basic pagination. With the metric information, it is also possible to do basic formatting of the paragraphs into lines.[5] Inclusion of images can be achieved if SVG is the source for the HTML (or XHTML) version and also for the PDF documents.

When all of these capabilities have been achieved, it is possible to build a Web site that will allow the user to surf using a Web browser and to print out interesting stories.

13.5   Summary

This chapter has shown you some examples of using XSLT to transform XML documents to other XML documents and text. It really cannot do justice to these topics, since each of the document types described here deserves a book of its own. However, the chapter should have given you a taste of the power of XSLT used for purposes other than producing HTML Web pages.

---

5. An interesting exercise would be to implement Knuth's algorithm for breaking paragraphs into lines in XSLT. Or use an extension function or element to perform the task.

Appendixes

Tools and Resources

Since September 1999, I have seen many projects that used XML and XSLT, ranging from 3 XSLT documents to as many as 50. Not surprisingly, the smaller projects share a lot of common characteristics. The tools they use and the problems they face are also quite similar. Besides the XSLT documents, these projects required little programming other than the odd Perl scripts. The big project, on the other hand, was a full-fledged software development project with database, application servers, and so on. The tools it used were more varied, and the problems it faced were much more difficult to solve.

This appendix provides you with the tools that are actually used in the projects and supplies the names of the tools used in this book. However, this should not be considered an endorsement of these products. Some tools have already been eclipsed by newer versions, but this will give you an idea of the kinds of tools you might need for a project using XSLT.

The second part of the appendix lists links to some of the major sites where you can find the more up-to-date tools for XML and XSLT.

A.1 XML Tools

XSLT must be used in conjunction with XML because the input of an XSLT document has to be an XML document. Creating XML documents is one of the most important activities. The large project I mentioned faced the most difficulty in the creation of the XML documents from data from external sources (a database, loose XML document fragments, external data feed). Basically, after the XML documents have been created, the transformation process using XSLT documents was relatively straightforward.

A.1.1 *XML Editors*

In most cases, XML document fragments are created by writers. To prevent ill-formed or invalid XML document fragments, the writers used an XML editor called XML Pro in the big project. They also wrote XML documents, which is especially common for smaller projects. Most HTML authoring tools can be configured to accept XML as well. Many of the developers prefer HomeSite and use it to write their XSLT documents.

Finally, some of the programmers had to write some XML and XSLT documents. The various flavors of Emacs and vi are the common choices of the programmers.

A.1.2 *XML Databases*

The big project required storage for the XML fragments. To avoid using a relational database, because of the mismatch in paradigms (XML data is usually hierarchical and reliable databases tend to be relational), we considered eXchelon from eXchelonCorp. However, it did not have Java support at that time, and it did not support Solaris. We finally wrote our own database-to-XML mapping framework, which used URI extensively.

A.1.3 *XSLT Processors*

We use many of the available XSLT processors: IBM's XML4J XML parser, the Lotus XSL processor, James Clark's XT XSLT processor, and Microsoft's MSXML XML/XSLT processor. Some of us also used Xalan and Xerces for the smaller projects. We will probably investigate Oracle's XML and XSLT tools soon as well.

A.1.4 *DOM and SAX APIs*

Only one project so far used the XML DOM and SAX APIs. We also called the LotusXSL processor from inside a Java program because we needed to integrate the creation of XML documents from databases and the conversion of the XML documents to HTML. The XML document creation process used DOM extensively.

A.2 Resources

This section contains some of the more popular links that have up-to-date listings of XML and XSLT tools. As new tools come out quite frequently now, it is very difficult to provide a comprehensive list here. Check out the links to find out tools that suit your needs.

A.2.1 *W3C Specifications*

These are the URLs for the W3C specifications mentioned in this book.

XML   http://www.w3.org/TR/REC-xml

XSLT   http://www.w3.org/TR/xslt

SVG   http://www.w3.org/TR/SVG

XSL   http://www.w3.org/TR/xsl

XPath   http://www.w3.org/TR/xpath

Namespace   http://www.w3.org/TR/REC-xml-names

XHTML   http://www.w3.org/TR/xhtml1

A.2.2 *XSLT Processors*

There are quite a few free XSLT processors available on the Internet. This is not meant to be an exhaustive list.

Xalan   http://xml.apache.org

Lotus XSL   http://www.alphaworks.ibm.com

SAXON   http://users.iclway.co.uk/mhkay/saxon.

Oracle   http://technet.oracle.com

XT   http://www.jclark.com

XSL:P   http://www.clc-marketing.com/xslp

Microsoft   Go to http://www.msdn.microsoft.com/xml and follow the link.

You can check the following sites for listings of XSLT tools.

> `http://www.xslt.com/xslt_tools.htm`

> `http://www.xml.com/pub/Guide/XSLT`

A.3   XSLT Web Sites and Mailing Lists

There are a few good places to find XSLT resources. The first place I always go to is the OASIS Web site (`http://www.oasis-open.org/cover`) maintained by Robin Cover.

The URL for the XSL mailing list is `http://www.mulberrytech` `.com/xsl/xsl-list/index.html`. The main topics on this mailing list are XSL and XSLT.

Of course, the main XML development mailing list is invaluable as well. This is where you go to find out what is going in the XML development world. Its URL is `http://www.xml.org/xml-dev/index.shtml`.

A.4   Where to Find the Examples

The examples in this book are on both the CD accompanying the book and on `http://www.awl.com/cseng/titles/0-201-71103-6`. I will also provide errata and updates on that site.

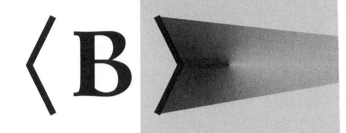

Character Sets and Encoding Schemes

Many people remember having to deal with ASCII and EBCDIC and how much hassle it can be to handle two character sets at one time. Fortunately, those days are gone. Now instead of one alphabet we must handle many if the programs are to be useful to people in other countries.

Characters have always been visual markings. The best thing to do is select the markings needed to exchange documents, put them in a table, and assign a number to each. The ordering of the markings should be logical—for example, the letter B's number would be one greater than A's.

The set of markings is called a **character set**. The set of numbers assigned to the markings is called an **encoding scheme**. There is a character set that enumerates many of the world's alphabets, characters, ideographs, symbols, glyths, and so on. This character set is called the **Universal Character Set (UCS)**. It has all the markings that we use in daily life.

The character set allocates four bytes to number the characters within it. This may seem rather expensive, especially when you usually need only one byte for a character, such as in English. It is difficult to justify using four times as much storage for character data.

There are two ways to reduce the number of bytes: (1) pick only the characters that are used in a document and (2) use a variable number of bytes to encode the characters, with more frequently used characters using fewer bytes than less frequently used characters.

Picking only certain characters limits a document to only those characters. For most Western text documents, this is acceptable. For example, the encoding scheme ISO-8859-1 can be used for most Web pages in Canada because it covers both English and French, the official languages.

The advantage in using the fewest bytes for the most frequently used characters is that most documents will use the minimum amount of storage. The disadvantages are that the number of bytes for each character is not fixed, and sometimes more than four bytes are needed. The default encoding scheme for XML documents, **UTF-8**, is such an encoding scheme. ASCII characters still need only seven bits, and that satisfies most North Americans.

Unlike ISO-8859-1, UTF-8 encodes all UCS characters. A document using this encoding scheme can contain multiple languages as long as only UCS characters are needed.

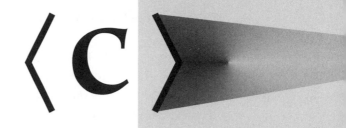

XSLT and XPath Reference

Not all XSLT elements are created equal. The same applies to XSLT functions and attributes. I know of only one project in which 23 different XSLT elements were used. Among these elements, the `xsl:value-of` element was used the most. The element used second most was the `xsl:template` element—quite a surprise for me. The third most used element was the `xsl:when` element. After that, in decreasing popularity were the `xsl:variable`, `xsl:call-template`, `xsl:apply-templates`, `xsl:if`, `xsl:choose`, and `xsl:text` elements.

This sample is too small for any meaningful analysis. However, this much is certain: The XML to HTML transformation is dominated by the copying of content from the instruction tree to the result tree, which means that templates dominate the landscape.

With this in mind, we will look at all the XSLT elements, attributes, and functions in this appendix.

A note on the notation: The superscript (0 or 1) of a parameter means the you can omit the parameter. The superscript (0 or more) of a parameter means you can have zero or more of the parameter.[1]

C.1   XSLT Elements

Table C.1 shows all the top-level elements and instruction elements in XSLT.

The two elements `xsl:stylesheet` and `xsl:transform` are the two document elements that you can use. Only one of them can be used in one XSLT document. The `xsl:when` and `xsl:otherwise` elements can only be inside an `xsl:choose` element.

The `xsl:sort` can only be inside an `xsl:apply-templates` element or an `xsl:for-each` element. When it is inside an `xsl:apply-templates`, `xsl:sort` must come before other elements, except `xsl:with-param` elements. It must be the first element inside an `xsl:for-each`.

The `xsl:param` element, when it is not a top-level element, must be the first element in an `xsl:template` element.

Finally, the `xsl:with-param` element can only be the first element of an `xsl:call-template`. It must come before any other element except the `xsl:sort` element if inside an `xsl:apply-templates` element.

We will present the syntax of an XSLT element like this.

```
<!-- either top-level or instruction Element -->
<xsl:name-of-the-element
  optional-attribute = type-of-attribute-value
  mandatory-attribute = type-of-attribute-value>
  attribute-allowing-AVT = { type-of-attribute-value }>
  <!-- Content: ordering of specific elements -->
<xsl:name-of-the-element>
```

The syntax block always starts with a comment specifying whether the element is a top-level element, an instruction element, or neither.

---

1. In the specifications, (0 or 1) is represented by the ? character, and (0 or more) is represented by the * character.

Top-Level Elements	Instruction Elements
attribute-set	apply-imports
decimal-format	apply-templates
import	attribute
include	call-template
key	choose
namespace-alias	comment
output	copy
param	copy-of
preserve-space	element
strip-space	fallback
template	for-each
variable	if
	message
	number
	processing-instruction
	text
	value-of
	variable

**TABLE
C.1**   XSLT elements in the categories

After that comes the name of the element, always with the `xsl` prefix. Attributes of the elements are listed inside the element. Mandatory attributes are in bold. The other attributes are optional. Each attribute is listed with the data type of its value. Most data types are self-explanatory. These are the less familiar data types.

`node-set expression`   An XPath expression that results in a node-set.

`qname`   The qualified name of an element, attribute, namespace, or processing instruction, depending on the context. The qualified name is the local-name and namespace URI pair. If the element (or attribute, or namespace, or processing instruction) does not have a namespace, then the qualified name is simply the local-name.

`ncname`   A name with no namespace prefix.

`uri-reference`   A URI reference.

pattern   A location path, but with the restrictions explained in Section 6.5.

nmtoken   A string that could be used as a name in an XML document. See Section 2.3 for details.

nmtokens   A list of nmtokens separated by space characters.

If there is a pair of braces ({ and }) surrounding the value of an attribute, it means the attribute value can be specified by an attribute-value-template (see Section 8.2.1 for details).

If it is not an empty element, after the begin-tag comes the description of the content of the element. If there is a specific order for some XSLT elements in the content, the specific order will be given here. The symbol | is also used to mean *or*. The XSLT elements are listed here in alphabetical order.

C.1.1   xsl:apply-imports

When you want to wrap a template imported from another document rather than to override it, you can define a new template. You define the new template to match the same nodes as the imported template. You can then incorporate the functionality of the imported template by using the xsl:apply-imports element.

Syntax

```
<!-- Instruction Element -->
<xsl:apply-imports/>
```

When this element is encountered, the processor applies the template with the next highest import precedence for the node matched by the template this xsl:apply-imports is in.

Examples

Suppose we have the following template in a document.

```
<xsl:template match='top'>
  <b><xsl:value-of select='.'/></b>
</xsl:template>
```

And we decide that the top element should be doubly highlighted with italic and boldfaced text. Furthermore, we want to add a comment after the element. We can do this.

```
<xsl:template match='top'>
  <i><xsl:apply-imports/></i>
```

```
  <xsl:comment>The top template has been used.</xsl:comment>
</xsl:template>
```

Suppose the input is this.

```
<?xml version='1.0'?>
<top>This is a text node in the top element.</top>
```

Then the first template would transform it into

```
<b>This is a text node in the top element.</b>
```

and the second template would transform it into

```
<i><b>This is a text node in the top element.</b></i>
<!-- The top template has been used. -->
```

NESTING `xsl:apply-imports` ELEMENTS. You can nest `xsl:apply-imports` inside the template applied by another `xsl:apply-imports` element. For example, suppose we have the following XML document.

```
<top>
   The content of the first apply-imports example.
</top>
```

And we first define a simple template to simply get the string of the **top** element.

```
<?xml version='1.0'?>
<xsl:stylesheet version='1.0'
    xmlns:xsl='http://www.w3.org/1999/XSL/Transform'>

  <xsl:output method='html' indent='no'/>

  <xsl:template match='top'>
    <xsl:value-of select='.'/>
  </xsl:template>
</xsl:stylesheet>
```

Let's call this document *ex1-import2.xsl*.

Then we decide to use the boldface style for the value. However, we do not know whether other XSLT documents are using this template or not. If we go ahead and modify *ex1-import2.xsl*, these other documents will also be changed, and we probably do not know what these documents are or even where they are. If we use `xsl:apply-imports`, these other documents will behave as before. The newly created template looks like this.

```
<?xml version='1.0'?>
<xsl:stylesheet version='1.0'
    xmlns:xsl='http://www.w3.org/1999/XSL/Transform'>

  <xsl:import href='ex1-import2.xsl'/>

  <xsl:output method='html' indent='no'/>

  <xsl:template match='top'>
    <B><xsl:apply-imports/></B>
  </xsl:template>
</xsl:stylesheet>
```

Let's call this document *ex1-import1.xsl*. You can see the xsl:import element that imports the *ex1-import2.xsl* document.

If we decide to italicize the top element again, we can use another xsl:apply-imports element like this.

```
<?xml version='1.0'?>
<xsl:stylesheet version='1.0'
    xmlns:xsl='http://www.w3.org/1999/XSL/Transform'>

  <xsl:import href='ex1-import1.xsl'/>

  <xsl:output method='html' indent='no'/>

  <xsl:template match='/'>
    <HTML>
      <HEAD>
        <TITLE>The First apply-imports Example</TITLE>
      </HEAD>
      <BODY><xsl:apply-templates/></BODY>
    </HTML>
  </xsl:template>

  <xsl:template match='top'>
    <I><xsl:apply-imports/></I>
  </xsl:template>
</xsl:stylesheet>
```

From these examples, you can see that the `xsl:apply-imports` element is very useful in not modifying existing templates, even when these existing templates are being reused.

A PITFALL. To use the `xsl:apply-imports` element effectively, you want to make sure the templates with `xsl:apply-imports` have very high template priority. So, if you want to italicize all elements and you define a template like this

```
<xsl:template match='*'>
  <I><xsl:apply-imports/></I>
</xsl:template>
```

chances are high that you will get more than you bargain for. It will even cause a problem if you happen to have a template like this.

```
<xsl:template match='table'>
  <TABLE><TR><xsl:apply-templates/></TR></TABLE>
</xsl:template>
<xsl:template match='cell'>
  <TD><xsl:value-of select='.'/></TD>
</xsl:template>
```

If the source XML document is

```
<table><cell>Cell 1</cell><cell>Cell 2</cell></table>
```

the output will look like the following if you apply the XSLT document.

```
<I>
  <TABLE>
    <TR>
      <I>
        <TD>Cell 1</TD>
      </I>
      <I>
        <TD>Cell 2</TD>
      </I>
    </TR>
  </TABLE>
</I>
```

This is not what you want.

My rule of thumb for using the `xsl:apply-imports` element is to use the exact same `match` attribute as the template I want to wrap around. In this way, there are no surprises.

C.1.2   xsl:apply-templates

To copy the content of templates from the instruction tree to the result tree, first select the nodes in the source trees that you want to match and then find the templates that match them. Finally, copy the content of the templates that match the nodes selected to the result tree.

Syntax

```
<!-- Instruction Element -->
<xsl:apply-templates
  select = node-set-expression
  mode = qname>
  <!-- Content: (xsl:sort | xsl:with-param)(0 or more) -->
</xsl:apply-templates>
```

The `select` attribute is optional. When it is absent, all children of the current node are selected. Otherwise, the nodes matched are determined by the value of the XPath expression in the `select` attribute.

In the body of the element, parameters can be passed to the templates. Additionally, the elements selected can be sorted as well.

The `mode` attribute of the element is optional. It is used to provide modularity for templates so that you can group templates together by sharing the same value for the `mode` attribute.

Examples

To match templates to each of the children of the current node in turn, use the basic form of this element.

```
<xsl:apply-templates/>
```

Remember that by not specifying a `select` attribute you will be matching all the child nodes of an element. Elements, comments, and processing instructions will all be selected. Since the context position depends on the position of the current node in the current node list, you may mistake the position of the elements you select. Suppose we have the following XML document.

```
<document>
  <title-page>XSLT Processors Comparison</title-page>
```

```
    <chapter>Introduction</chapter>
    <chapter>Outline of Methodology</chapter>
    <chapter>Speed</chapter>
    <chapter>Space</chapter>
    <chapter>Conformance</chapter>
    <chapter>Conclusion</chapter>
</document>
```

Suppose you want to output something simple like this.

```
<HTML>
  <HEAD><TITLE>XSLT Processors Comparison</TITLE></HEAD>
  <BODY>
    <H1>XSLT Processors Comparison</H1>
    <H2>Chapter 1. Introduction</H2>
    <H2>Chapter 2. Outline of Methodology</H2>
    <H2>Chapter 3. Speed</H2>
    <H2>Chapter 4. Space</H2>
    <H2>Chapter 5. Conformance</H2>
    <H2>Chapter 6. Conclusion</H2>
  </BODY>
</HTML>
```

So you have the following templates in your XSLT document.

```
<xsl:template match='/'>
<HTML>
  <HEAD>
    <TITLE><xsl:value-of select='document/title-page'/></TITLE>
  </HEAD>
  <BODY><xsl:apply-templates/></BODY>
</HTML>
</xsl:template>

<xsl:template match='title-page'>
  <H1><xsl:value-of select='.'/></H1>
</xsl:template>

<xsl:template match='chapter'>
  <H2>Chapter <xsl:value-of
      select='position()'/>. <xsl:value-of select='.'/></H2>
</xsl:template>
```

But the output turns out to be this.

```
<HTML>
  <HEAD><TITLE>XSLT Processors Comparison</TITLE></HEAD>
  <BODY>
    <H1>XSLT Processors Comparison</H1>
    <H2>Chapter 4. Introduction</H2>
    <H2>Chapter 6. Outline of Methodology</H2>
    <H2>Chapter 8. Speed</H2>
    <H2>Chapter 10. Space</H2>
    <H2>Chapter 12. Conformance</H2>
    <H2>Chapter 14. Conclusion</H2>
  </BODY>
</HTML>
```

How did the numbers get so wrong? The culprit is the way the nodes are selected for the `xsl:apply-templates` element in the root template. If you modify the root template to

```
<xsl:template match='/'>
<HTML>
  <HEAD>
    <TITLE><xsl:value-of select='document/title-page'/></TITLE>
  </HEAD>
  <BODY><xsl:apply-templates select='document/title-page'/>
        <xsl:apply-templates select='document/chapter'/></BODY>
</HTML>
</xsl:template>
```

then the output is more or less (other than the whitespaces) what you expect.

CHOOSING MORE THAN YOU EXPECTED.   This problem can also happen in a very unexpected way. Suppose the source XML document looks like this.

```
<shopping-list>
  <item>Peanut-butter</item>
  <item>Shampoo</item>
  <item>Ground beef</item>
  <!-- This is optional -->
  <item>Pork</item>
</shopping-list>
```

Now that we know what whitespace-only text nodes did in the previous example, we use the following XSLT document.

```
<?xml version='1.0'?>
<xsl:stylesheet version='1.0'
    xmlns:xsl='http://www.w3.org/1999/XSL/Transform'>

  <xsl:output method='html' indent='yes'/>
  <xsl:strip-space elements='shopping-list item'/>

  <xsl:template match='/'>
  <HTML>
    <HEAD><TITLE>Shopping List</TITLE></HEAD>
    <BODY><xsl:apply-templates/></BODY>
  </HTML>
  </xsl:template>

  <xsl:template match='item'>
    <H2>
      <xsl:value-of select='position()'/>. <xsl:value-of
          select='.'/>
    </H2>
  </xsl:template>

</xsl:stylesheet>
```

Are you sure that this time the positions will be correct? Here is the output.

```
<HTML>
<HEAD>
<TITLE>Shopping List</TITLE>
</HEAD>
<BODY>
<H2>1. Peanut-butter</H2>
<H2>2. Shampoo</H2>
<H2>3. Ground beef</H2>
<H2>5. Pork</H2>
</BODY>
</HTML>
```

Of course, the comment has been selected as well as all the item elements.

The size of the node-set selected by an xsl:apply-templates is also not obvious. You must be careful when you need the size of the node-set selected by the xsl:apply-templates element as well.

Here is a rule of thumb for not specifying the **select** attribute. Use an **xsl:apply-templates** element without the **select** attribute if the positions of the nodes or the size of the node-set selected is not important.

SELECTING NODES FROM AN EXTERNAL DOCUMENT.   It is also possible to select nodes from a different document.

```
<xsl:apply-templates
 select='document("http://www.jmedium.com/external")/top'/>
```

The nodes selected will be from the document referred to in the **document()** function. The source tree is switched to the external document.

The value used by the **mode** attribute must be a name. To choose the **mode** attribute according to a value obtained in the source document, **xsl:if** elements or **xsl:choose** can be used, for example,

```
<xsl:choose>
  <xsl:when test='$var = sports'>
    <xsl:apply-templates mode='sports'/>
  </xsl:when>
  <xsl:otherwise>
    <xsl:apply-templates mode='news'/>
  </xsl:otherwise>
</xsl:choose>
```

You are not allowed to use something like this

```
<xsl:apply-templates mode='{$var}'/>
```

because the value of the **mode** attribute cannot be an attribute-value-template.

PASSING PARAMETERS.   You can pass parameter values to templates using the **xsl:with-param** elements. Simply include them inside your **xsl:apply-templates** element.

Suppose on your Web pages that there is a button for the user to vote on the usefulness of the page. Obviously you want to transmit the identification of the Web page each time a user presses the button, but you want only one template to generate the button because you want all of them to look the same. The Web page identification is, of course, the perfect information to pass to the template that generates the button. The **xsl:apply-templates** element will look something like this.

```
<xsl:apply-templates select='button'>
  <xsl:with-param name='page-id' select='@id'/>
</xsl:apply-templates>
```

Because you never know for sure exactly which template will be applied for the nodes when you use an `xsl:apply-templates`, you want to make sure that the templates that match the nodes selected do not use the same name for their parameters for different purposes. To prevent this problem, choose your parameter names carefully for all your templates.

C.1.3   xsl:attribute

The `xsl:attribute` element is used inside a template. It must be inside an `xsl:element` element or a literal element. You can have more than one `xsl:attribute` element for the same element for multiple attributes.

Syntax

```
<!-- Instruction Element -->
<xsl:attribute
  name = { qname }
  namespace = { uri-reference }>
  <!-- Content: instruction elements -->
</xsl:attribute>
```

The effect of the element is to add an attribute to the nonXSLT parent of the element in the result tree.

Examples

Here is a simple example for constructing an attribute.

```
<xsl:attribute
  name='href'>http://www.jmedium.com/image.img</xsl:attribute>
```

If the attribute needs a namespace declaration, then the `namespace` attribute is used. For instance, if the namespace of the `href` attribute shown above is `html`, then the `xsl:attribute` may look like this.

```
<xsl:attribute
  namespace='http://www.w3.org/TR/xhtml1/strict'
  name='html:href'>http://www.jmedium.com/image.img</xsl:attribute>
```

Suppose the containing element is `a`. Then the output looks like this.

```
<a html:href='http://www.jmedium.com/image.img'
 xmlns:html='http://www.w3.org/TR/xhtml1/strict'></a>
```

Of course, this does not make a lot of sense in XML to HTML transformations because HTML does not have XML namespaces.

GENERATING A NAME ON THE FLY. You can use information from the source tree to create the name of the attribute. You do that by using an attribute value template for the name. Suppose you have this source XML document.

```
<link label='Museum of Civilization'>
 <href>http://www.civilmuseum.org</href>
</link>
```

You can have this template

```
<xsl:template match='link'>
  <a>
    <xsl:for-each select='*'>
      <xsl:attribute name='{name()}'><xsl:value-of select='.'/>
      </xsl:attribute>
    </xsl:for-each>
    <xsl:value-of select='.'/>
  </a>
</xsl:template>
```

and this is the result.

```
<a href="http://www.civilmuseum.org">Museum of Civilization</a>
```

Some Web applications, for whatever reason, cannot handle the character entity reference & or even the character reference & in a URL reference. They insist on asking for the literal & character. When you encounter such a Web server, you can either ask the application developers to fix the bug or you will have to perform some postprocessing after you have generated the HTML documents.

C.1.4   xsl:attribute-set

You use an xsl:attribute-set element to group attributes together and assign a name to the group so that they can be referenced from multiple places. You can include another attribute-set in your attribute group as well.

Syntax

```
<!-- Category: top-level-element -->
<xsl:attribute-set
  name = qname
  use-attribute-sets = qnames>
  <!-- Content: xsl:attribute(0 or more) -->
</xsl:attribute-set>
```

You must supply the name of the attribute-set. The `xsl:attribute-set` element can then contain all the `xsl:attribute` elements you want to group together.

To include attributes in your other attribute groups in the new group, use the `use-attribute-sets` attribute. The names in its value should be separated by a space character in the attribute. All the attributes in the current attribute sets will be included in the new attribute-set.

Examples

This is a simple example of using the `xsl:attribute-set` element.

```
<xsl:attribute-set name="header">
  <xsl:attribute name="face">verdana,geneva,arial</xsl:attribute>
  <xsl:attribute name="size">1</xsl:attribute>
  <xsl:attribute name="color">#ffffff</xsl:attribute>
</xsl:attribute-set>
```

A more complicated example is to include the preceding attribute-set in another attribute-set.

```
<xsl:attribute-set name="moreheader" use-attribute-sets="header">
  <xsl:attribute name="bgcolor">#336699</xsl:attribute>
</xsl:attribute-set>
```

C.1.5   `xsl:call-template`

The `xsl:call-template` is used for invoking a template by its name.

Syntax

```
<!-- Instruction Element -->
<xsl:call-template
  name = qname>
  <!-- Content: xsl:with-param(0 or more) -->
</xsl:call-template>
```

You must specify the `name` of the template you want to call.

Examples

Suppose there is a named template named `tax` that computes the tax for an item in an invoice, given the amount and the tax rate. Suppose the parameter for the tax rate is called `tax-rate`, and the parameter name for the amount of money is `amount`. In this case the element to call the template to compute the tax that should be charged is as follows.

```
<xsl:call-template name='tax'>
  <xsl:with-param name='tax-rate' select='7'/>
  <xsl:with-param name='amount' select='1000'/>
</xsl:call-template>
```

This is assuming that the tax rate is in percentage form. Also, if the name of a parameter in the `xsl:with-param` is not one of the parameters of the named template, then it is ignored. If a parameter of the template called is not given a value by the `call-template` element (that is, there is a missing parameter), and the named template does not define a default value for the parameter, then it is assumed to be an empty string.

You do not need to have parameters for the template. If you only use the template to avoid having the same piece of code in many places of your XSLT document, then you can simply factor out the code and put it in a template.

NESTING `xsl:call-template` ELEMENTS.   You can also have another `xsl:call-template` element inside a template that is calling itself. When you have such a template, check it carefully to make sure that the chain of `xsl:call-template` elements will stop.

In most cases, the terminating condition is supplied by an `xsl:if` element. Inside the `xsl:if` element is the `xsl:call-template` element that calls the template again.

Let's look at an example. Usually, we look at a source tree from the top down. As we have more and more branches we use `xsl:apply-templates` elements to go down the source tree, branching as we go. Going up the tree is much easier because we already know that a node can have at most one parent. Therefore, we can use `xsl:call-template` elements instead. The following XSLT document generates an HTML document that shows all the elements in the source XML document that have text nodes.

```
<?xml version='1.0'?>
<xsl:stylesheet version='1.0'
    xmlns:xsl='http://www.w3.org/1999/XSL/Transform'>

  <xsl:output method='html' indent='no'/>

  <xsl:template match='/'>
    <HTML><HEAD><TITLE>Elements with Text Nodes</TITLE></HEAD>
      <BODY><xsl:for-each select='//*/text()/..'>
        <H3>Path to element:<xsl:call-template name='upTheTree'/>
        </H3>
      </xsl:for-each></BODY>
    </HTML>
```

```
    </xsl:template>

    <xsl:template name='upTheTree'>
       <xsl:if test='..'>
         <xsl:for-each select='..'>
           <xsl:call-template name='upTheTree'/>
         </xsl:for-each>/<xsl:value-of select='name()'/>
       </xsl:if>
    </xsl:template>
</xsl:stylesheet>
```

Suppose the source document looks like this

```
<document>
  <title>The Purple Book</title>
  <chapter><title>Introduction</title>Some text here. <section>
    <title>Purpose</title><bookmark>Purpose Section</bookmark>...
    </section>
  </chapter>
  .
  .
  .
  <chapter><title>Speed</title><bookmark>Speed chapter</bookmark>...
  </chapter>
</document>
```

and the output looks like this.

```
<HTML>
<HEAD>
<TITLE>Elements with Text Nodes</TITLE>
</HEAD>
<BODY>
<H3>Path to element:/document</H3>
<H3>Path to element:/document/title</H3>
<H3>Path to element:/document/chapter</H3>
<H3>Path to element:/document/chapter/title</H3>
<H3>Path to element:/document/chapter/section</H3>
<H3>Path to element:/document/chapter/section/title</H3>
<H3>Path to element:/document/chapter/section/bookmark</H3>
<H3>Path to element:/document/chapter</H3>
<H3>Path to element:/document/chapter/title</H3>
<H3>Path to element:/document/chapter/bookmark</H3>
</BODY>
</HTML>
```

C.1.6   xsl:choose

The xsl:choose element allows you to specify alternative subtrees to put in the result tree—in other words, to select from two or more alternatives.

Syntax

```
<!-- Instruction Element -->
<xsl:choose>
  <!-- Content: (xsl:when^(1 or more), xsl:otherwise^(0 or 1)) -->
</xsl:choose>
```

There must be at least one xsl:when element, and there can be an xsl: otherwise element.

Examples

Sometimes you want to find out the node type of the current node. This XSLT document takes all the nodes in the XML source document and then calls a template that determine the node type of each node in the source document.

```
<?xml version='1.0'?>
<xsl:stylesheet version='1.0'
    xmlns:xsl='http://www.w3.org/1999/XSL/Transform'>

  <xsl:output method='html' indent='yes'/>

  <xsl:template match='/'>
    <HTML><HEAD><TITLE>Node Types</TITLE></HEAD>
    <BODY>
    <xsl:for-each select='//node() | //*/@*'>
      <xsl:call-template name='nodeType'/>
    </xsl:for-each>
    </BODY>
    </HTML>
  </xsl:template>

  <xsl:template name='nodeType'>
    <H3>A Node</H3>
    <xsl:choose>
      <xsl:when test='name()'>
        <P>The name of the current node is: '<xsl:value-of
            select='name()'/>'</P>
```

```
      </xsl:when>
      <xsl:otherwise>
        <P>The string value of the current node is:
           '<xsl:value-of select='.'/>'</P>
      </xsl:otherwise>
    </xsl:choose>

    <xsl:choose>
      <xsl:when test='../comment() = current()'>
        <P>The current node is a comment.</P>
      </xsl:when>
      <xsl:when test='../processing-instruction() = current()'>
        <P>The current node is a processing-instruction.</P>
      </xsl:when>
      <xsl:when test='../text() = current()'>
        <P>The current node is a text node.</P>
      </xsl:when>
      <xsl:when test='../* = current()'>
        <P>The current node is an element.</P>
      </xsl:when>
      <xsl:when test='../@* = current()'>
        <P>The current node is an attribute.</P>
      </xsl:when>
      <xsl:otherwise>
        <P>Don't know what the current node is.</P>
      </xsl:otherwise>
    </xsl:choose>
  </xsl:template>

</xsl:stylesheet>
```

The expression `../comment() = current()` evaluates to true whenever there is a node in the node-set returned by `../comment()` that is the same as the current node—that is, when the current node is a comment. This is also true for processing instructions, elements, text nodes, and attributes.

This template is not very accurate, however. It is possible that the string value of one of the comment nodes is the same as the string value of the current node, even though the current node is not a comment. An accurate template is quite elaborate and long. In any case, it is highly unlikely that the string value of one of the comment nodes is the same as the string value of the current node.

C.1.7   xsl:comment

The xsl:comment element creates a comment in the result tree.

Syntax

```
<!-- Instruction Element -->
<xsl:comment>
  <!-- Content: template -->
</xsl:comment>
```

An xsl:comment element can contain only character data and instructions that create character data. The character data cannot contain the sequence --, and the last character cannot be -. Nested comments are not allowed in XML.

Examples

To generate a simple comment that says This is a comment, use

```
<xsl:comment>This is a comment</xsl:comment>
```

and the result looks like this.

```
<!-- This is a comment -->
```

C.1.8   xsl:copy

The xsl:copy element copies the current node to the result tree. What is actually copied depends on the type of current node. If the current node is an element, then the element node is copied to the result tree. If it is an attribute, an attribute is copied to the current element in the result tree.

Syntax

```
<!-- Instruction Element -->
<xsl:copy
  use-attribute-sets = qnames>
  <!-- Content: template -->
</xsl:copy>
```

If the current node is an element, attribute sets can be selected using the use-attribute-sets attribute. The attributes in the attribute sets will be included in the element.

Examples

Suppose we have this document

```
<?xml version='1.0'?>
<top>
␣␣<element a='attribute'>
␣␣␣␣<child/>
␣␣␣␣<!-- a comment here -->
␣␣␣␣<?java processing instruction ?>
␣␣␣␣Text here and there.
␣␣</element>
</top>
```

and this XSLT document

```
<?xml version='1.0'?>
<xsl:stylesheet version='1.0'
    xmlns:xsl='http://www.w3.org/1999/XSL/Transform'>

<xsl:template match='/'>
<xsl:apply-templates select='//node()'/>
</xsl:template>

<xsl:template match='comment()'>
comment:'<xsl:copy/>'
</xsl:template>

<xsl:template match='processing-instruction()'>
processing instruction:'<xsl:copy/>'
</xsl:template>

<xsl:template match='*'>
Element:'<xsl:copy/>'
</xsl:template>

<xsl:template match='@*'>
<element><xsl:copy/></element>
</xsl:template>

<xsl:template match='text()'>
text:'<xsl:copy/>'
</xsl:template>

</xsl:stylesheet>
```

This is the result.

```
Element:'<top></top>'

text:'
␣␣'

Element:'<element></element>'

text:'
␣␣␣␣'

Element:'<child></child>'

text:'
␣␣␣␣'

comment:'<!--␣a␣comment␣here␣-->'

text:'
␣␣␣␣'

processing instruction:'<?java␣processing␣instruction >'

text:'
␣␣␣␣Text here and there.
␣␣'

text:'
'
```

PROCESSING THE CHILDREN. To process the children in an element, use `xsl:apply-templates` elements or `xsl:for-each` elements. Suppose you have an element like this in the source tree

```
<link href='http://www.w3.org'>W3C</link>
```

and you want to transform it to an HTML A element.

```
<A href='http://www.w3.org'>W3C</A>
```

You can use this template.

```
<xsl:template match='link'>
  <A>
    <xsl:for-each select='text()|@*'>
      <xsl:copy/>
    </xsl:for-each>
  </A>
</xsl:template>
```

Actually, this template can be simplified like this.

```
<xsl:template match='link'>
  <A>
    <xsl:copy-of select='node()|@*'/>
  </A>
</xsl:template>
```

So why do we need the `xsl:copy` element?

FILTERING THE SOURCE DOCUMENT. The `xsl:copy` is most useful when
you want to filter the source tree to remove some nodes. If you want to remove
all the comments in the source tree, you can use the following document

```
<?xml version='1.0'?>
<xsl:stylesheet version='1.0'
    xmlns:xsl='http://www.w3.org/1999/XSL/Transform'>

  <xsl:output method='xml' indent='no'/>

  <xsl:template match='/'>
    <xsl:apply-templates
        select='node()|@*|processing-instruction()'/>
  </xsl:template>

  <xsl:template match='comment()'/>

  <xsl:template match='*|@*'>
    <xsl:copy>
      <xsl:apply-templates
          select='node()|@*|processing-instruction()'/>
    </xsl:copy>
  </xsl:template>
```

```
<xsl:template match='text()|processing-instruction()'>
  <xsl:copy/>
</xsl:template>

</xsl:stylesheet>
```

Use an `xsl:copy-of` element if you simply copy everything contained in a node. Otherwise, use `xsl:copy`.

It is not often that you will ever use `xsl:copy` elements to transform to HTML. You will sometimes use `xsl:copy-of` to copy HTML (in well-formed XML format, of course) content in your source document.

C.1.9   xsl:copy-of

With `xsl:copy-of`, you select some nodes and then copy all of them and their descendants to the result tree.

Syntax

```
<!-- Instruction Element -->
<xsl:copy-of
  select = expression />
```

Use the `select` attribute to select the nodes you want to copy to the result tree. If it is an XPath expression returning a node-set, then for each of the nodes in the node-set, copy the node and its descendants to the result tree. If it returns anything else, the result is converted to a string before the string is copied to the result tree.

The difference between this element and the `xsl:value-of` element is that the `xsl:value-of` element always converts the result to a string before copying it to the result tree. Because of that, the only way to copy a result tree fragment assigned to a variable is to use an `xsl:copy-of` element.

Examples

Suppose you have the following fragment.

```
<top>
<xsl:variable name='var'><second>Text here</second></xsl:variable>
<xsl:copy-of select='$var'/>
</top>
```

When the first element is processed, the variable named `var` is set to the result tree fragment.

```
<second>Text here</second>
```

When the `xsl:copy-of` element is encountered, it evaluates the XPath expression in its `select` attribute. The data type is the result tree fragment. The `xsl:copy-of` element is replaced by the result tree fragment. The result tree now looks like this.

```
<top>
<second>Text here</second>
</top>
```

PASSING ELEMENTS TO A TEMPLATE.   The `xsl:copy-of` element is handy when you want to pass result tree fragments as well as nodes from the source trees. For instance, you can define a template to format a hyperlink that is either an anchor or an image. You don't want to write two templates to format one or the other, and you don't particularly care to look at the anchor or image element when the template receives it. And later on, using the same format, you may have to handle more than simply an anchor or an image. You define the following template.

```
<xsl:template match='linkButton'>
  <xsl:param name='link'/>
  <TABLE><xsl:attribute use-attribute-sets='buttonLandF'/>
    <TR><TD><xsl:copy-of select='$link'/></TD></TR>
  </TABLE>
</xsl:template>
```

This template can be used like this

```
<xsl:apply-templates>
  <xsl:with-param name='link'>
    <A HREF='http://www.w3.org/TR'>W3C Technical Reports</A>
  </xsl:with-param>
</xsl:apply-templates>
```

and later like this.

```
<xsl:apply-templates>
  <xsl:with-param name='link'><A HREF='http://www.w3.org/TR'>
      <img width="67"
           src="/images/technical_report.jpg"
           height="20" border="0"
           alt="W3C Technical Reports"/>
    </A>
  </xsl:with-param>
</xsl:apply-templates>
```

C.1.10   `xsl:decimal-format`

You assign a name to a decimal-format by using the `xsl:decimal-format` element. You can then refer to the decimal format in a `format-number()` function to format a number.

Syntax

```
<!-- Top-Level Element -->
<xsl:decimal-format
  name = qname
  decimal-separator = char
  grouping-separator = char
  infinity = string
  minus-sign = char
  NaN = string
  percent = char
  per-mille = char
  zero-digit = char
  digit = char
  pattern-separator = char />
```

A name is assigned to a decimal format by using the `name` attribute. If the attribute is absent, then the default decimal-format is assumed.

The `decimal-separator` attribute contains the decimal point character. The default character is ..

The `grouping-separator` attribute contains the character separating groups of digits in a number. The default character is ,.

The `infinity` attribute defines what string to use to represent infinity. The default string is `Infinity`.

The `minus-sign` attribute defines the character used to represent the minus sign of a negative number. The default character is -.

The `NaN` attribute defines the string that is used to represent the `not a number` value. The default string is `NaN`.

The `percent` attribute defines the percentage character. The default is the % character.

The `per-mille` attribute defines the character used to represent the per-mille (per thousandth, whereas percent is per hundredth) character. The default is ‰.

The `zero-digit` attribute is used to define the character to represent the digit zero in a number. The default is 0.

344

The `digit` attribute is the character used to represent a digit in the format specified in the `format-number()` function. (See Section C.2.11 for more details.)

The `pattern-separator` attribute defines the character used for separating subpatterns in the format. (See Section C.2.11 for more details.)

Examples

Suppose we are defining European numbers for which the decimal point should be a comma and the grouping-separator should be the period. The decimal format element is this.

```
<xsl:decimal-format decimal-separator=',' grouping-separator='.'/>
```

Once this element has been defined, we can use the `format-number()` function to apply this format.

```
<xsl:value-of select='format-number(12345.66, "#,##0.0#")'/>
```

The output looks like this.

```
12.345,66
```

Please see Section C.2.11 for an explanation on how to specify the format of a number.

C.1.11   xsl:element

An `xsl:element` constructs an element in the result tree.

Syntax

```
<!-- Instruction Element -->
<xsl:element
  name = { qname }
  namespace = { uri-reference }
  use-attribute-sets = qnames>
  <!-- Content: template -->
</xsl:element>
```

The mandatory attribute is the `name` attribute, which specifies the name of the element to be generated. If the element contains elements that use a different namespace, or the element itself is from another namespace, then the attribute `namespace` can be used to specify the URI of the namespace.

An attribute value template can be used to find the qualified name for the `name` attribute. The result should be a valid name in XML. An attribute value template can also be used in the `namespace` attribute. The result of the expression should be a URI. You can use the `use-attribute-sets` attribute to include attributes defined in attribute-groups. Separate the names of the attribute sets with the space character.

In the body of the element, other elements can be used to construct the rest of the element, including attributes of the element that are not in one of the named attribute-sets.

Examples

A simple example showing the use of the `xsl:element` element is the anchor element in HTML.

```
<xsl:element name='a'><xsl:apply-templates/></xsl:element>
```

This example does not show the power of the `xsl:element` element because it can also be written as

```
<a><xsl:apply-templates/></a>
```

If the name of the element is known when the XSLT document is designed, this element is generally not necessary. However, it is possible that the name of an element is the value of an XPath expression. When that is the case, then this element can be used to construct the element at runtime.

Suppose you want to use the same template to format a component on a Web page, either in italic or boldface. You can use this pattern to define a template.

```
<xsl:template match='link'>
  <xsl:param name='fontStyle' select='"I"'/>
  <xsl:element name='$fontStyle'>
    <!-- whatever you want to do with a link -->
  </xsl:element>
</xsl:template>
```

You can then apply a template as follows.

```
<xsl:apply-templates>
  <xsl:with-param name='fontStyle' select='"B"'/>
</xsl:apply-templates>
```

And the default is I, in italic. Templates defined this way are easier to reuse.

C.1.12   xsl:fallback

The `xsl:fallback` element is processed whenever its parent element is not available in the XSLT processor. If the element is available then the `xsl:fallback` element is simply ignored by the XSLT processor. This is typically used for extension elements.

Syntax

```
<!-- Instruction Element -->
<xsl:fallback>
  <!-- Content: template -->
</xsl:fallback>
```

Examples

Suppose the XSLT processor does not implement the `os:ps` element and it is used in a template.

```
<os:ps><xsl:fallback>ps is not available</xsl:fallback></os:ps>
```

Then the text node `ps is not available` is inserted in the result tree. Otherwise, the result of the `os:ps` is inserted instead. Caution: Some processors do not support this element.

C.1.13   xsl:for-each

An `xsl:for-each` element replicates its contents for each of the nodes selected by its `select` attribute.

Syntax

```
<!-- Instruction Element -->
<xsl:for-each
  select = node-set-expression>
  <!-- Content: (xsl:sort(0 or more), template) -->
</xsl:for-each>
```

The mandatory attribute is the `select` attribute, which selects the nodes.

Sorting is allowed for the nodes in the node-set returned by the `select` attribute. The `xsl:sort` elements must occur before other elements inside the `xsl:for-each` element.

Examples

Suppose we have the following fragment of an XML document

```
<element>
  <child>1</child>
  <child>2</child>
  <child>3</child>
  <child>4</child>
</element>
```

and the XSLT document is

```
<?xml version='1.0'?>
<xsl:stylesheet
 version='1.0'
 xmlns:xsl='http://www.w3.org/1999/XSL/Transform'>
<xsl:output method='html' media-type='text/html'/>

<xsl:template match='/'>
  <xsl:apply-templates/>
</xsl:template>

<xsl:template match='element'>
  <xsl:for-each select='child'>
    <xsl:value-of select='.'/>
  </xsl:for-each>
</xsl:template>

</xsl:stylesheet>
```

then the output looks like

```
1234
```

SEPARATE PROCESSING. The `xsl:for-each` element has a local scope; it replicates only its descendants for the nodes it selects. This local scope is very useful when the task at hand need not be flexible.

A good example of this local scope is the generation of a document on a Web page. If you want a table of contents and an index along with the document body, you can have this root template.

```
<xsl:template match='/'>
  <HTML>
```

```
      <HEAD>
        <TITLE><xsl:value-of select='title'/></TITLE>
      </HEAD>
      <BODY>
        <H1><xsl:value-of select='title'/></H1>
        <H3>Table of Contents</H3>
        <xsl:call-template name='TOC'/>
        <xsl:apply-templates/>
        <xsl:call-template name='index'/>
      </BODY>
    </HTML>
  </xsl:template>
```

This can be the template to generate the table of contents.

```
  <xsl:template name='TOC'>
    <xsl:for-each select='chapter'>
      <!-- format the chapter entry -->
      <xsl:for-each select='section'>
        <!-- format the section entry -->
        <xsl:for-each select='subsection'>
          <!-- format the subsection entry -->
          <xsl:for-each select='subsubsection'>
            <!-- format the subsubsection entry -->
            <xsl:for-each select='paragraph'>
              <!-- format the paragraph entry -->
            </xsl:for-each>
          </xsl:for-each>
        </xsl:for-each>
      </xsl:for-each>
    </xsl:for-each>
  </xsl:template>
```

Meanwhile, you can define templates to handle the body of the chapters, sections, subsections, subsubsections, and paragraphs. Using the xsl:for-each element won't interfere with that.

C.1.14   xsl:if

The xsl:if element is the conditional element in XSLT. If the expression specified for the element is evaluated to true, the descendants of the element are inserted in the result tree. Otherwise, the descendants are ignored.

Syntax

```
<!-- Instruction Element -->
<xsl:if
  test = Boolean-expression>
  <!-- Content: template -->
</xsl:if>
```

The mandatory attribute is the `test` attribute. If the XPath expression in this attribute evaluates to true, then the content of the `xsl:if` element is kept in the result tree. If the expression evaluates to false, then the whole `xsl:if` element is discarded.

Examples

You can use an `xsl:if` element to decide whether to include an image element, depending on the value of a variable called `imageallowed`.

```
<xsl:if test='$imageallowed'> <img src='http://www.jmedium.com'/>
  </xsl:if>
```

The `xsl:if` element is also very useful for specifying the terminating condition for templates that call themselves.

C.1.15   xsl:import

The `xsl:import` element is used to import templates that have been defined in a different file.

Syntax

```
<xsl:import
  href = uri-reference />
```

The mandatory attribute is the `href` attribute, which specifies the URL of the XSLT file to be imported. When the patterns of an imported template and a templated declared directly in an XSLT document match the same node, the imported template always has the lower priority.

Examples

Here is an example using the `xsl:import` element.

```
<xsl:import href='www.jmedium.com/templates'/>
```

An imported template always has a lower precedence than a template in the importing document.

C.1.16   xsl:include

The XSLT document that is referenced is included where the xsl:include element is located. The import priorities of the templates in the included document are assumed to be the same as the including document.

Syntax

```
<!-- Top-Level Element -->
<xsl:include href = uri-reference />
```

The mandatory attribute is the href attribute, which specifies where the included document is located.

Examples

Here is an example of xsl:include.

```
<xsl:include href='http://www.jmedium.com/templates'/>
```

C.1.17   xsl:key

In XSLT, you can specify a name for a group of nodes selected by a pattern. You also specify how the nodes should be differentiated when they are needed.

After such a group, called a **key**, has been defined, you can refer to some of the nodes in a key by using the key() function. Keys are useful for replacing IDs.

Syntax

```
<!-- Top-Level Element -->
<xsl:key
  name = qname
  match = pattern
  use = node-set-expression />
```

All attributes are mandatory for the element xsl:key. This top-level element can only be declared as a child of the xsl:stylesheet element.

Examples

Let's say we have a key called k that contains only the elements named **second** in the source tree. We'll use the value of the text node contained in a **second** element as the way to differentiate the members of the key. The declaration looks like this.

```
<xsl:key name='k' match='second' use='text()'/>
```

What the element means is this: There is a key called k, which contains the set of nodes matched by the pattern second, whose members can be discriminated using the node-set expression text(). In other words, they can be differentiated by their text content. If we use the key function with the key's name and value, we are interested in all the nodes with the key that have a text node with a string value of 1.

```
<xsl:value-of select='key("k", "1")'/>
```

Suppose the source document is

```
<?xml version='1.0'?>
<top>
  <second name='abc'>1</second>
  <second name='d'>1</second>
  <second name='e'>1</second>
  <second name='f'>2</second>
  <second name='g'>1</second>
  <second name='h'>2</second>
  <second name='1'>100</second>
</top>
```

Then the output is

```
<second name="abc">1</second>
<second name="d">1</second>
<second name="e">1</second>
<second name="g">1</second>
```

All the second elements in the document are members of the key named k. However, because we only want nodes with text node 1, only four nodes qualify.

The use attribute can be as broad as you like. Use the | (union) operator to specify whatever criteria you want. For instance, for the input XML file

```
<?xml version='1.0'?>
<top>
  <second name='abc'>1</second>
  <second name='d'>1</second>
  <second name='e'>1</second>
  <second name='f'>2</second>
  <second name='g'>1</second>
  <second name='h'>2</second>
  <second name='1'>100</second>
  <second name='1'>1</second>
</top>
```

if the `xsl:key` element is given as

```
<?xml version='1.0'?>
<xsl:stylesheet
 xmlns:xsl='http://www.w3.org/1999/XSL/Transform'
 version='1.0'>

<xsl:output method='html'/>
<xsl:key name='k' match='second' use='text()|@name'/>

<xsl:template match='/'>
  <xsl:for-each select='key("k", "1")'>
    <xsl:copy-of select='.'/>
  </xsl:for-each>
</xsl:template>

</xsl:stylesheet>
```

then the output looks like this.

```
<second name="abc">1</second>
<second name="d">1</second>
<second name="e">1</second>
<second name="g">1</second>
<second name="1">100</second>
<second name="1">1</second>
<second name="1">1</second>
```

The last element is output twice because the node has a key value of 1 for both the text and the `name` attribute.

MULTIPLE MEMBERSHIPS.   There is no limit to how many keys to which a node can belong.

C.1.18   `xsl:message`

If you want to log a message to the console, you can use the `xsl:message` element. The result tree will not have the message. When a fatal error occurs, you can also use it to stop the processing of the XSLT document.

Syntax

```
<!-- Instruction Element -->
<xsl:message
  terminate = ( "yes" | "no" ) >
```

```
    <!-- Content: template -->
</xsl:message>
```

The attribute `terminate` determines whether processing should stop after this element has been processed by the XSLT processor. If the value is `yes`, then the processing should stop. If the value is `no`, then the processing should continue after the message has been written to the console.

Examples

Here is an example of the `xsl:message`.

```
<xsl:message>This is a warning message.</xsl:message>
```

To stop processing after output of the message, an `xsl:message` may look like this.

```
<xsl:message terminating='yes'>A fatal error occurs. Stopping.
    </xsl:message>
```

C.1.19   xsl:namespace-alias

The `xsl:namespace-alias` is used to specify an alias for the namespace prefixes in the XSLT document and in the result tree. This is necessary mainly because you may want to transform an XSLT document. If you only have to transform XML documents to HTML documents, you will never need to use this element.

The following template tries to match an `xsl:stylesheet` element in the source tree and then puts it to the result tree.

```
<xsl:template match='xsl:stylesheet'>
  <xsl:stylesheet><xsl:attribute name='version'>
  <xsl:value-of select='@version'/></xsl:attribute></xsl:stylesheet>
</xsl:template>
```

Of course, the `xsl:stylesheet` element is not allowed inside a template. So this template will be rejected.

One way to avoid this problem is to use different namespace prefixes for the input, the instruction, and the output XSLT documents. The `xsl:namespace-alias` element is the way to specify the namespace prefix of XSLT fragments to be included in the XSLT processing document and the actual namespace prefix that should be written to the output.

Syntax

```
<!-- Top-Level Element -->
<xsl:namespace-alias
   stylesheet-prefix = ( prefix | "#default" )
   result-prefix = ( prefix | "#default" )  />
```

Both attributes `stylesheet-prefix` and `result-prefix` are mandatory. The `stylesheet-prefix` attribute specifies the namespace that will be used in the processing XSLT document, while the `result-prefix` specifies the namespace that will be used in the output document.

Examples

Here is a simple example to eliminate this confusion.

```
<?xml version='1.0'?>
<xsl:stylesheet
   xmlns:xsl='http://www.w3.org/1999/XSL/Transform'
   xmlns:oxsl='http://www.w3.org/1999/XSL/TransformAlias'
   version='1.0'>

<xsl:namespace-alias stylesheet-prefix='oxsl'
    result-prefix='xsl'/>

<xsl:output method='xml' omit-xml-declaration='no'/>

<xsl:template match='/'>
  <oxsl:stylesheet version='1.0'>
  </oxsl:stylesheet>
</xsl:template>

</xsl:stylesheet>
```

Given an XSLT document, the result is going to look like this.

```
<?xml version='1.0'?>
<xsl:stylesheet version='1.0'
xmlns:xsl='http://www.w3.org/1999/XSL/Transform'>
</xsl:stylesheet>
```

C.1.20   `xsl:number`

The `xsl:number` element is used to number nodes in the source tree. It allows you to count nodes in sophisticated ways.

Syntax

```
<!-- Instruction Element -->
<xsl:number
  level = ( "single" | "multiple" | "any" )
  count = pattern
  from = pattern
  value = number-expression
  format = { string }
  lang = { nmtoken }
  letter-value = ( "alphabetic" | "traditional" )
  grouping-separator = { char }
  grouping-size = { number } />
```

Examples

Using the *bookings.xml* file from Chapter 3, you can use this template to number all the meetings with their titles only.

```
<xsl:template match='/'>
  <HTML>
    <HEAD>
      <TITLE>Example 1 for &lt;xsl:number&gt;</TITLE>
    </HEAD>
    <BODY>
      <H1>Example 1 for  &lt;xsl:number&gt;</H1>
      <xsl:for-each select='//meeting'>
        <P>
          <xsl:number value='position()' format='(1) '/>
          <xsl:value-of select='meetingTitle'/>
        </P>
      </xsl:for-each>
    </BODY>
  </HTML>
</xsl:template>
```

The result looks something like:

```
<HTML>
<HEAD>
<TITLE>Example 1 for &lt;xsl:number&gt;</TITLE>
</HEAD>
<BODY>
<H1>Example 1 for  &lt;xsl:number&gt;</H1>
```

```
<P>(1) Project Status</P>
<P>(2) Javascript Code Review</P>
<P>(3) Breakfast Meeting for Future
        Projects</P>
<P>(4) Conference Selection Meeting</P>
<P>(5) XML Editor Evaluation</P>
<P>(6) Co-op Interviews Debriefing</P>
<P>(7) Baseball League Kickoff</P>
<P>(8) Labor Day BBQ Planning</P>
<P>(9) Interview Strategy Meeting</P>
.
.
.
</BODY>
</HTML>
```

You do not have to specify the `value` attribute; the default value is `position()`. The default value for the `format` attribute is 1. In most cases, you will keep the default `value` attribute, but you will modify the `format` attribute.

NUMBERING FOR DIFFERENT LEVELS. We can number the elements in multiple levels. For instance, we can number the meeting rooms in *bookings.xml* like this.

```
<xsl:template match='/'>
  <HTML>
    <HEAD><TITLE>Example 2 for &lt;xsl:number&gt;</TITLE>
    </HEAD>
  <BODY>
  <H1>Example 2 for &lt;xsl:number&gt;</H1>
  <H3>Rooms</H3>
  <xsl:for-each select='//room'>
    <P>Room:<xsl:number count='room' level='single'
                format='1 '/>
      <xsl:value-of select='@name'/></P>
  </xsl:for-each>
  </BODY>
  </HTML>
</xsl:template>
```

You can number the dates within the meeting rooms in multiple levels. The first date in the first meeting room has the number 1.1, the second 1.2, the first date in the second meeting room 2.1, and so on.

```
<xsl:template match='/'>
  <HTML>
    <HEAD><TITLE>Example 2 for &lt;xsl:number&gt;</TITLE>
    </HEAD>
    <BODY>
    <H1>Example 2 for &lt;xsl:number&gt;</H1>
    <H3>Rooms</H3>
    <xsl:for-each select='//room'>
      <P>Room:<xsl:number count='room'
                  level='single' format='1 '/>
        <xsl:value-of select='@name'/></P>
    </xsl:for-each>

    <H3>Dates</H3>
    <xsl:for-each select='//date'>
      <P>Date:<xsl:number count='room|date'
                  level='multiple' format='1.1 '/>
        <xsl:value-of select='year'/> 
        <xsl:value-of select='month'/> 
        <xsl:value-of select='day'/></P>
    </xsl:for-each>
    </BODY>
    </HTML>
</xsl:template>
```

And the output looks like this.

```
<HTML>
<HEAD>
<TITLE>Example 2 for &lt;xsl:number&gt;</TITLE>
</HEAD>
<BODY>
<H1>Example 2 for &lt;xsl:number&gt;</H1>
<H3>Rooms</H3>
<P>Room:1 Red</P>
<P>Room:2 Green</P>
<P>Room:3 Blue</P>
<P>Room:4 White</P>
<P>Room:5 Silver</P>
<H3>Dates</H3>
<P>Date:1.1 2000 
        June 
```

```
        23</P>
<P>Date:1.2 2000 
        July 
        10</P>
<P>Date:2.1 2000 
        June 
        23</P>
<P>Date:2.2 2000 
        July 
        13</P>
<P>Date:2.3 2000 
        August 
        02</P>
<P>Date:3.1 2000 
        June 
        23</P>
<P>Date:3.2 2000 
        June 
        26</P>
<P>Date:3.3 2000 
        July 
        03</P>
<P>Date:3.4 2000 
        July 
        10</P>
<P>Date:3.5 2000 
        July 
        17</P>
    .
    .
    .
</BODY>
</HTML>
```

Finally, if you want to number the meeting rooms, the dates, and the meetings in a multiple level numbering scheme, like this

```
<HTML>
<HEAD>
<TITLE>Example 2 for &lt;xsl:number&gt;</TITLE>
</HEAD>
<BODY>
<H1>Example 2 for &lt;xsl:number&gt;</H1>
```

```
<H3>Rooms</H3>
<P>Room:1 Red</P>
<P>Room:2 Green</P>
<P>Room:3 Blue</P>
<P>Room:4 White</P>
<P>Room:5 Silver</P>
<H3>Dates</H3>
<P>Date:1.1 2000 
        June 
        23</P>
<P>Date:1.2 2000 
        July 
        10</P>
<P>Date:2.1 2000 
        June 
        23</P>
<P>Date:2.2 2000 
        July 
        13</P>
   .
   .
   .
<H3>Meetings</H3>
<P>Meeting: 1.1.1 Project Status</P>
<P>Meeting: 1.1.2 Javascript Code Review</P>
<P>Meeting: 1.2.1 Breakfast Meeting for Future
        Projects</P>
<P>Meeting: 2.1.1 Conference Selection Meeting</P>
<P>Meeting: 2.1.2 XML Editor Evaluation</P>
<P>Meeting: 2.1.3 Co-op Interviews Debriefing</P>
<P>Meeting: 2.2.1 Baseball League Kickoff</P>
<P>Meeting: 2.3.1 Labor Day BBQ Planning</P>
<P>Meeting: 3.1.1 Interview Strategy Meeting</P>
<P>Meeting: 3.1.2 Sell to the World!</P>
   .
   .
   .
</BODY>
</HTML>
```

this template would generate that output.

```
<xsl:template match='/'>
  <HTML>
```

```
    <HEAD><TITLE>Example 2 for &lt;xsl:number&gt;</TITLE>
    </HEAD>
  <H1>Example 2 for &lt;xsl:number&gt;</H1>
  <H3>Rooms</H3>
  <xsl:for-each select='//room'>
    <P>Room:<xsl:number count='room'
                level='single' format='1 '/>
      <xsl:value-of select='@name'/></P>
  </xsl:for-each>

  <H3>Dates</H3>
  <xsl:for-each select='//date'>
    <P>Date:<xsl:number count='room|date'
                level='multiple' format='1.1 '/>
      <xsl:value-of select='year'/> 
      <xsl:value-of select='month'/> 
      <xsl:value-of select='day'/></P>
  </xsl:for-each>

  <H3>Meetings</H3>
  <xsl:for-each select='//meeting'>
    <P>Meeting: <xsl:number count='room|date|meeting'
        level='multiple' format='1.1 '/>
      <xsl:value-of select='meetingTitle'/></P>
  </xsl:for-each>
  </HTML>
</xsl:template>
```

Finally, if you want the meeting rooms, dates, and meetings to look like this

```
<HTML>
<HEAD>
<TITLE>Example 2 for &lt;xsl:number&gt;</TITLE>
</HEAD>
<BODY>
<H1>Example 2 for &lt;xsl:number&gt;</H1>
<H3>Rooms</H3>
<P>Room:1 Red</P>
<P>Date:1.1 2000 
     June 
     23</P>
<P>Meeting: 1.1.1 Project Status</P>
```

```
<P>Meeting: 1.1.2 Javascript Code Review</P>
<P>Date:1.2 2000 
      July 
      10</P>
<P>Meeting: 1.2.1 Breakfast Meeting for Future
        Projects</P>
<P>Room:2 Green</P>
<P>Date:2.1 2000 
      June 
      23</P>
<P>Meeting: 2.1.1 Conference Selection Meeting</P>
<P>Meeting: 2.1.2 XML Editor Evaluation</P>
<P>Meeting: 2.1.3 Co-op Interviews Debriefing</P>
<P>Date:2.2 2000 
      July 
      13</P>
<P>Meeting: 2.2.1 Baseball League Kickoff</P>
<P>Date:2.3 2000 
      August 
      02</P>
<P>Meeting: 2.3.1 Labor Day BBQ Planning</P>
<P>Room:3 Blue</P>
<P>Date:3.1 2000 
      June 
      23</P>
<P>Meeting: 3.1.1 Interview Strategy Meeting</P>
<P>Meeting: 3.1.2 Sell to the World!</P>
<P>Meeting: 3.1.3 Hotrod Kickoff Meeting</P>
<P>Meeting: 3.1.4 HR Meeting</P>
      .
      .
      .
</BODY>
</HTML>
```

then use these templates to do that.

```
<xsl:template match='/'>
  <HTML>
    <HEAD><TITLE>Example 2 for &lt;xsl:number&gt;</TITLE>
    </HEAD>
  <BODY>
  <H1>Example 2 for &lt;xsl:number&gt;</H1>
```

```
      <H3>Rooms</H3>
      <xsl:apply-templates select='bookings/room'/>
      </BODY>
      </HTML>
</xsl:template>

<xsl:template match='room'>
   <P>Room:<xsl:number count='room' level='single' format='1 '/>
      <xsl:value-of select='@name'/></P>
   <xsl:apply-templates select='date'/>
</xsl:template>

<xsl:template match='date'>
   <P>Date:<xsl:number count='room|date'
               level='multiple' format='1.1 '/>
      <xsl:value-of select='year'/> 
      <xsl:value-of select='month'/> 
      <xsl:value-of select='day'/></P>
   <xsl:apply-templates select='meeting'/>
</xsl:template>

<xsl:template match='meeting'>
   <P>Meeting: <xsl:number count='room|date|meeting'
      level='multiple' format='1.1 '/>
      <xsl:value-of select='meetingTitle'/></P>
</xsl:template>
```

NUMBERING GLOBALLY. Suppose you want to number the rooms and dates in multiple levels, but you want to number the meetings starting from one, independent of the rooms and dates—in other words, to generate output like this.

```
<HTML>
<HEAD>
<TITLE>Example 2 for &lt;xsl:number&gt;</TITLE>
</HEAD>
<BODY>
<H1>Example 2 for &lt;xsl:number&gt;</H1>
<H3>Rooms</H3>
<P>Room:1 Red</P>
<P>Date:1.1 2000 
```

```
          June 
          23</P>
<P>Meeting: (1) Project Status</P>
<P>Meeting: (2) Javascript Code Review</P>
<P>Date:1.2 2000 
          July 
          10</P>
<P>Meeting: (3) Breakfast Meeting for Future
          Projects</P>
<P>Room:2 Green</P>
<P>Date:2.1 2000 
          June 
          23</P>
<P>Meeting: (4) Conference Selection Meeting</P>
<P>Meeting: (5) XML Editor Evaluation</P>
<P>Meeting: (6) Co-op Interviews Debriefing</P>
<P>Date:2.2 2000 
          July 
          13</P>
<P>Meeting: (7) Baseball League Kickoff</P>
     .
     .
     .
</BODY>
</HTML>
```

You only have to change the template for the meeting element.

```
<xsl:template match='meeting'>
  <P>Meeting: <xsl:number count='meeting'
      level='any' format='(1) '/>
    <xsl:value-of select='meetingTitle'/></P>
</xsl:template>
```

SETTING THE STARTING ELEMENT.   Suppose you want to number the meetings not globally but only within the same meeting room. This is what you want.

```
<HTML>
<HEAD>
<TITLE>Example 2 for &lt;xsl:number&gt;</TITLE>
</HEAD>
<BODY>
<H1>Example 2 for &lt;xsl:number&gt;</H1>
```

```
<H3>Rooms</H3>
<P>Room:1 Red</P>
<P>Date:1.1 2000 
      June 
      23</P>
<P>Meeting: (1) Project Status</P>
<P>Meeting: (2) Javascript Code Review</P>
<P>Date:1.2 2000 
      July 
      10</P>
<P>Meeting: (3) Breakfast Meeting for Future
        Projects</P>
<P>Room:2 Green</P>
<P>Date:2.1 2000 
      June 
      23</P>
<P>Meeting: (1) Conference Selection Meeting</P>
<P>Meeting: (2) XML Editor Evaluation</P>
<P>Meeting: (3) Co-op Interviews Debriefing</P>
<P>Date:2.2 2000 
      July 
      13</P>
<P>Meeting: (4) Baseball League Kickoff</P>
<P>Date:2.3 2000 
      August 
      02</P>
<P>Meeting: (5) Labor Day BBQ Planning</P>
<P>Room:3 Blue</P>
<P>Date:3.1 2000 
      June 
      23</P>
<P>Meeting: (1) Interview Strategy Meeting</P>
<P>Meeting: (2) Sell to the World!</P>
<P>Meeting: (3) Hotrod Kickoff Meeting</P>
<P>Meeting: (4) HR Meeting</P>
<P>Date:3.2 2000 
      June 
      26</P>
<P>Meeting: (5) Weekly Meeting</P>
</BODY>
</HTML>
```

Again, the template matching the `meeting` element is the only place that you need to modify.

```
<xsl:template match='meeting'>
  <P>Meeting: <xsl:number count='meeting' from='room'
      level='any' format='(1) '/>
    <xsl:value-of select='meetingTitle'/></P>
</xsl:template>
```

The `from` attribute of the `xsl:number` element says that the numbering is global but local within the ancestor `room` element.

CHOOSING ELEMENTS FOR NUMBERING.   Suppose you want to number the date and meetings only, not the rooms. The two templates modified are as follows.

```
<xsl:template match='room'>
  <P>Room: <xsl:value-of select='@name'/></P>
  <xsl:apply-templates select='date'/>
</xsl:template>

<xsl:template match='date'>
  <P>Date:<xsl:number count='date'
                 level='multiple' format='1.1 '/>
    <xsl:value-of select='year'/> 
    <xsl:value-of select='month'/> 
    <xsl:value-of select='day'/></P>
  <xsl:apply-templates select='meeting'/>
</xsl:template>
```

And the result looks like this.

```
<HTML>
<HEAD>
<TITLE>Example 2 for &lt;xsl:number&gt;</TITLE>
</HEAD>
<BODY>
<H1>Example 2 for &lt;xsl:number&gt;</H1>
<H3>Rooms</H3>
<P>Room: Red</P>
<P>Date:1 2000 
      June 
      23</P>
```

```
<P>Meeting: (1) Project Status</P>
<P>Meeting: (2) Javascript Code Review</P>
<P>Date:2 2000 
     July 
     10</P>
<P>Meeting: (3) Breakfast Meeting for Future
        Projects</P>
<P>Room: Green</P>
<P>Date:1 2000 
     June 
     23</P>
<P>Meeting: (1) Conference Selection Meeting</P>
<P>Meeting: (2) XML Editor Evaluation</P>
<P>Meeting: (3) Co-op Interviews Debriefing</P>
<P>Date:2 2000 
     July 
     13</P>
<P>Meeting: (4) Baseball League Kickoff</P>
<P>Date:3 2000 
     August 
     02</P>
<P>Meeting: (5) Labor Day BBQ Planning</P>
```

THE NUMBERING LETTERS.   Normally elements are numbered with Arabic numerals, but outline letters—I, i, A, a—are common. The numbering format is specified using the `format` attribute of the `xsl:number` element. Numbers are specified by `format='1'`. Multiple-level numbers are specified as `format='1.1'`. Two levels of numbers are sufficient even though there may be more than two levels of elements. The XSLT processor is intelligent enough to pick up the other letters. To specify something like A.1, use `format='A.1'`.

The XSLT processor reads the format string like this.

1. Find all non-alphanumeric characters (such as whitespace characters or punctuation) from the beginning of the format string. This is the starting token for all the numbers where every number will start.

2. Find all non-alphanumeric characters from the end of the format string. This is the ending token for all the numbers, and every number will end with this token.

3. Any non-alphanumeric characters in the middle of the string are considered separators for the numbering letters.

4. If a number is found, this is the numbering scheme.

   a. If the number ends with 1 and has leading zeros, then the numbering has at least the length of the number. For instance, `01` means that any number less than 100 has a leading zero. If the number is `00001`, then any number less than 100000 will have leading zeros.

   b. Otherwise, the numbering scheme is a number. For instance, `9999` means that the numbers start from `1`, `2`, and so on.

5. If the character is A, a, i, or I, then the numbering scheme follows the numbering character. The first two will start with A and a respectively. The third and the fourth will follow the Roman numerals: i, ii, and so on, and I, II, and so on.

6. How other characters are handled depends on the language used. The XSLT processor may or may not implement the numbering scheme. Read the documentation from the XSLT processor to find out what other numbering schemes are supported by the XSLT processor. This is a processor-dependent issue.

Although extensive, this scheme is not exhaustive. For instance, it is not possible to have an alphanumeric character as a separator.

NUMBER GROUPING.   Different languages have different ways of grouping digits. For instance, in North America, outside Quebec, the number 100000000 is usually written 100,000,000. In Quebec, this number is written 100.000.000. The separators and the grouping size (3 in North America) are specified using the `grouping-separator` attribute and `grouping-size`. Both attributes must be present at the same time, or the only attribute present will be ignored.

C.1.21   xsl:otherwise

The `xsl:otherwise` element does not exist alone; it must be contained inside an `xsl:choose` element. It acts as the default case when the `test` attribute of all the `xsl:when` elements inside the `xsl:choose` element do not evaluate to true.

Syntax

```
<xsl:otherwise>
  <!-- Content: template -->
</xsl:otherwise>
```

Examples

See Section C.1.6 for examples.

C.1.22   xsl:output

The `xsl:output` element contains hints to the XSLT processor to write the output in a certain way. There may be more than one `xsl:output` element in an XSLT document.

Syntax

```
<!-- Top-Level Element -->
<xsl:output
   method = ( "xml" | "html" | "text" | qname-but-not-ncname )
   version = nmtoken
   encoding = string
   omit-xml-declaration = ( "yes" | "no" )
   standalone = ( "yes" | "no" )
   doctype-public = string
   doctype-system = string
   cdata-section-elements = qnames
   indent = ( "yes" | "no" )
   media-type = string />
```

The word `qnames` means that the value is a string with qualified names separated by whitespaces.

The `method` attribute defines the output format of the XSLT document. There are three values that must be supported: `html`, `text`, and `xml`. The default value is `xml`. Furthermore, an XSLT processor may choose to support more than these three output methods.

The `version` attribute provides the version of the output method. Different versions of the output methods may be supported by different XSLT processors. Consult the documentation of the XSLT processors to find out which versions of the output methods are supported.[2]

The `encoding` attribute specifies the character encoding scheme of the output.

The `omit-xml-declaration` attribute hints at whether the `<?xml` line is output as the first line of the output. A value of `no` means it is output (this is the default). A value of `yes` means it is not output.

---

2. For XML right now, the version is 1.0. For HTML, the default version is 4.0.

The standalone attribute specifies that the output document is not a standalone XML document. This attribute is not used if the output is an HTML document.

The doctype-public attribute hints at outputting a public doctype element. And the string in the doctype element is provided as the value of the attribute.

The doctype-system attribute hints at outputting a system doctype element. And the string in the doctype element is provided as the value of the attribute.

The cdata-section-elements attribute specifies which elements in the output XML document should use the <![CDATA[construct. For the HTML output method, this attribute should probably not be used.

The indent attribute specifies whether the output elements should be indented. If the value is yes, then the output is indented. If the value is no, then the output is not indented (this is the default).

Finally, the media-type attribute presents the media-type of the output document. For the HTML output method, the media-type should be text/html.

Examples

Your xsl:output element for an XSLT document transforming an XML document to an HTML document is almost always this.

```
<xsl:output method='html'/>
```

If the version of HTML is desired, then the element looks like this.

```
<xsl:output method='html' version='4.0'/>
```

A more elaborate xsl:output element for HTML is probably this.

```
<xsl:output method='html'
  doctype-public="-//W3C//DTD HTML 4.0//EN"
  doctype-system="http://www.w3.org/TR/REC-html40/strict.dtd"
  encoding='ISO-8859-1'
  indent='no'
  media-type='text/html'
  version='4.0'
/>
```

C.1.23   xsl:param

The xsl:param element is used in two different roles, depending on its location in the document. In one role, it specifies the parameters of a template. In the other, it specifies the parameters of the XSLT document itself.

A parameter defined in a template declares the name of a parameter and optionally the default value of the parameter if the calling template does not set the value for the parameter.

A parameter that is a child of the xsl:stylesheet element has a different meaning. It specifies a parameter whose value can be set outside the document. The XSLT processor sets the values of the xsl:param elements that are children of the xsl:stylesheet element. However, the XSLT specification does not specify how this should be done. It is up to the individual XSLT processors to decide how the parameters can be set. This is often accomplished by the command line, although it does not have to be.

Syntax

```
<!-- Top-Level Element -->
<xsl:param
  name = qname
  select = expression>
  <!-- Content: template -->
</xsl:param>
```

The name attribute is mandatory and it specifies the name of the parameter.

The attribute select sets the value of the parameter. The value of the parameter can also be set by the result of the elements contained in the element.

For xsl:param elements that are children of the xsl:stylesheet, the values are set by a processor-dependent method.

If the select attribute is present, its value is treated as the default value for that parameter. At the time the template is invoked (called or applied), if the parameter is assigned a value in an xsl:with-param element, the default value of the parameter is ignored. If the parameter is not given a value, on the other hand, the default value of the parameter will then be used as the value of the parameter.

Examples

The first role of xsl:param requires it to be inside a template. Suppose the name of the parameter is length.

```
<xsl:template name='month'>
  <xsl:param name='length'/>
```

```
        <!-- something else in the template -->
      </xsl:template>
```

The second role of the `xsl:param` element is that it has to be a child of the `xsl:stylesheet` element.

```
<xsl:stylesheet
 xmlns:xsl='http://www.w3.org/1999/XSL/Transform'
 version='1.0'>

  <xsl:param name='sport'/>
  <!-- template(s) -->

</xsl:stylesheet>
```

We'll call this document *sport.xsl*. The parameter `sport` will receive its value when the XSLT document is processed. For XT, for instance, you can specify

```
xt sport.xml sport.xsl sport='basketball'
```

on the command line. The parameter will receive its value.

C.1.24   xsl:preserve-space

The `xsl:preserve-space` element can be used to list all the elements in the source trees that should not have text nodes with only whitespaces stripped in the source document. In the beginning, all elements in the source trees preserve their whitespace-only text nodes.

Syntax

```
<!-- Top-Level Element -->
<xsl:preserve-space
  elements = tokens />
```

The mandatory attribute is the `elements` attribute. It contains a list of names separated by whitespaces for elements that preserve their whitespace-only text nodes.

Examples

Suppose the output element `top` should preserve its whitespace-only text nodes. Declare it like this.

```
<xsl:preserve-space elements='top'/>
<xsl:strip-space elements='second'/>
```

Then if there is an element in the source document that looks like this

```
<top>
  <second>
  </second>
</top>
```

then the element effectively becomes

```
<top>
  <second/></top>
```

C.1.25   xsl:processing-instruction

The `xsl:processing-instruction` element is used to output a processing instruction.

Syntax

```
<!-- Instruction Element -->
<xsl:processing-instruction
  name = { ncname }>
  <!-- Content: template -->
</xsl:processing-instruction>
```

The mandatory attribute is the `name` attribute. This is the target of the processing instruction.

The elements contained in the `xsl:processing-instruction` should produce a text node.

Examples

An example of outputting a processing instruction with the name (or the target) `java` and with the instruction (it is also called the data or the value of the processing instruction) `java.io` is

```
<xsl:processing-instruction
    name='java'>java.io</xsl:processing-instruction>
```

C.1.26   xsl:sort

The `xsl:sort` element is always used inside the `for-each` element or the `apply-templates` element. It sorts the current node list according to some criteria that can be set using the attributes of the element.

Syntax

```
<xsl:sort
  select = string-expression
  lang = { nmtoken }
  data-type = { ( "text" | "number" ) }
  order = { ( "ascending" | "descending" ) }
  case-order = { ( "upper-first" | "lower-first" ) } />
```

Examples

Sorting can be done using one criterion or more. Suppose the input XML document is

```
<?xml version='1.0'?>
<top>
  <element name='second'>
    <child attr='Tom'/>
    <child attr='Conny'/>
    <child attr='Vinny'/>
    <child attr='Ginny'/>
  </element>
  <element name='first'>
    <child attr='James'/>
    <child attr='John'/>
    <child attr='Ann'/>
    <child attr='Guy'/>
  </element>
</top>
```

To sort only the `child` elements regardless of the parent, the following element can be used.

```
<xsl:for-each select='element/child'>
  <xsl:sort select='@attr'/>
  <xsl:copy-of select='.'/>
</xsl:for-each>
```

The output looks like this.

```
<child attr="Ann"></child><child attr="Conny"></child>
<child attr="Ginny"></child><child attr="Guy"></child>
<child attr="James"></child><child attr="John"></child>
<child attr="Tom"></child><child attr="Vinny"></child>
```

To sort the elements first by `element` and then by `child`, this element can be used.

```
<xsl:for-each select='element'>
  <xsl:sort select='@name'/>
  <element name='{@name}'>
  <xsl:for-each select='child'>
  <xsl:sort select='@attr'/>
    <xsl:copy-of select='.'/>
  </xsl:for-each>
  </element>
</xsl:for-each>
```

The output looks like this.[3]

```
<element name="first">
<child attr="Ann"></child><child attr="Guy"></child>
<child attr="James"></child><child attr="John"></child>
</element>
<element name="second">
<child attr="Conny"></child><child attr="Ginny"></child>
<child attr="Tom"></child><child attr="Vinny"></child>
</element>
```

Notice that whitespaces have been added to the output to make them easier to read.

DEFINING YOUR OWN ORDER. Sometimes you want an order that is not based on ascending or descending order of the letters. For instance, maybe the order is highest to lowest in the following way:

```
Professional League
Junior League
Senior League
```

Suppose you have this XML source document.

```
<games>
  <game league='Junior League'>
    <date year='2000' month='2' day='12'/>
```

---

3. Notice the end-tags are specified separately. Some processors always output empty elements this way.

```
    </game>
    <game league='Professional League'>
      <date year='2000' month='3' day='2'/></game>
    <game league='Senior League'>
      <date year='2000' month='1' day='8'/>
    </game>
    <game league='Professional League'>
      <date year='2000' month='2' day='28'/>
    </game>
    <game league='Junior League'>
      <date year='2000' month='3' day='3'/>
    </game>
    <game league='Professional League'>
      <date year='2000' month='4' day='6'/>
    </game>
    <game league='Junior League'>
      <date year='2000' month='2' day='16'/>
    </game>
  </games>
```

Suppose you want to output the following.

```
<HTML><HEAD><TITLE>League Game Dates</TITLE></HEAD>
  <BODY><H1>Game Dates</H1>
    <P>Professional League Year: 2000 Month: February Day: 28</P>
    <P>Professional League Year: 2000 Month: March Day: 2</P>
    <P>Professional League Year: 2000 Month: April Day: 6</P>
    <P>Junior League Year: 2000 Month: February Day: 12</P>
    <P>Junior League Year: 2000 Month: February Day: 16</P>
    <P>Junior League Year: 2000 Month: March Day: 3</P>
    <P>Senior League Year: 2000 Month: January Day: 8</P>
  </BODY>
</HTML>
```

How do we design the XSLT document? Let's design the other aspects of the document first. Define a document like this.

```
<months>
  <month number='1' name='January'/>
  <month number='2' name='February'/>
  <month number='3' name='March'/>
  <month number='4' name='April'/>
  <month number='5' name='May'/>
```

```
    <month number='6' name='June'/>
    <month number='7' name='July'/>
    <month number='8' name='August'/>
    <month number='9' name='September'/>
    <month number='10' name='October'/>
    <month number='11' name='November'/>
    <month number='12' name='December'/>
  </months>
```

Let's call this document *months.xml*. The main XSLT document so far looks like this.

```
<?xml version='1.0'?>
<xsl:stylesheet version='1.0'
    xmlns:xsl='http://www.w3.org/1999/XSL/Transform'>

  <xsl:output method='html' indent='yes'/>

  <xsl:variable name='months' select='document("months.xml")/months'/>

  <xsl:template match='/'>
    <HTML><HEAD><TITLE>League Game Dates</TITLE></HEAD>
      <BODY><H1>Game Dates</H1>
        <xsl:apply-templates select='games/game'>
          <xsl:sort select='@league'/>
          <xsl:sort select='date/@year'/>
          <xsl:sort select='date/@month'/>
          <xsl:sort select='date/@day'/>
        </xsl:apply-templates>
      </BODY>
    </HTML>
  </xsl:template>

  <xsl:template match='game'>
    <xsl:variable name='current' select='current()'/>
    <P><xsl:value-of select='@league'/> Year: <xsl:value-of
    select='date/@year'/> Month: <xsl:value-of
    select='$months/month[@number = $current/date/@month]/@name'/> Day:
    <xsl:value-of select='date/@day'/></P>
  </xsl:template>

</xsl:stylesheet>
```

The output looks like this.

```
<HTML>
<HEAD>
<TITLE>League Game Dates</TITLE>
</HEAD>
<BODY>
<H1>Game Dates</H1>
<P>Junior League Year: 2000 Month: February Day: 12</P>
<P>Junior League Year: 2000 Month: February Day: 16</P>
<P>Junior League Year: 2000 Month: March Day: 3</P>
<P>Professional League Year: 2000 Month: February Day: 28</P>
<P>Professional League Year: 2000 Month: March Day: 2</P>
<P>Professional League Year: 2000 Month: April Day: 6</P>
<P>Senior League Year: 2000 Month: January Day: 8</P>
</BODY>
</HTML>
```

The ordering of the leagues can also be put into a file, just like the names of the months.

```
<order>
  <league order='1' name='Professional League'/>
  <league order='2' name='Junior League'/>
  <league order='3' name='Senior League'/>
</order>
```

Let's call it *order.xml*. We can now write the templates to sort the games in our order. First, we'll declare a global variable.

```
<xsl:variable name='order' select='document("order.xml")/order'/>
```

We change the first `xsl:sort` element to

```
<xsl:sort select='$order/league[@name = (current())/@league]/@order'/>
```

and the desired result is finally obtained.

Pay attention to the step `(current())`. It is the filtering step of an XPath location path. Without the parentheses, the expression would not be considered as a filter.

This way of sorting according to your own ordering system can be customized to any style.

C.1.27   `xsl:strip-space`

The `xsl:strip-space` element lists all the elements in the source document that should have their whitespace-only text nodes stripped.

Syntax

```
<!-- Top-Level Element -->
<xsl:strip-space
  elements = tokens />
```

The mandatory attribute is the **elements** attribute. It is a list of names delimited by whitespace characters. All elements listed in this element will have their whitespace-only text nodes stripped before being processed by the XSLT processor.

Examples

Suppose the **top** element should have its whitespace-only text nodes stripped. Then the element

```
<top>
  <second/>
</top>
```

is equivalent to

```
<top><second/></top>
```

Suppose there is an XSLT document that looks like this.

```
<?xml version='1.0'?>
<xsl:stylesheet
 xmlns:xsl='http://www.w3.org/1999/XSL/Transform'
 version='1.0'>

<xsl:template match='/'>
  <xsl:copy-of select='.'/>
</xsl:template>

</xsl:stylesheet>
```

And the source document looks like this.

```
<?xml version='1.0'?>
<top>
  <second/>
</top>
```

The output looks like this.

```
<top>
  <second></second>
</top>
```

On the other hand, if we have this.

```
<?xml version='1.0'?>
<xsl:stylesheet
 xmlns:xsl='http://www.w3.org/1999/XSL/Transform'
 version='1.0'>

<xsl:strip-space elements='top'/>

<xsl:template match='/'>
  <xsl:copy-of select='.'/>
</xsl:template>

</xsl:stylesheet>
```

Then the output looks like this.

```
<top><second></second></top>
```

All the whitespace-only text nodes are stripped.

C.1.28   xsl:stylesheet

The xsl:stylesheet element is the document element in an XSLT document. It defines the namespace used by the XSLT elements. It also declares the version of the XSLT being used in the document.

Syntax

```
<xsl:stylesheet
  id = id
  extension-element-prefixes = tokens
  exclude-result-prefixes = tokens
  version = number>
  <!-- Content: (xsl:import(0 or more), statics) -->
</xsl:stylesheet>
```

The mandatory attribute is the version attribute. This attribute declares the version of the XSLT being used. So far, the only value allowed is 1.0.

The id attribute is used to declare an ID for the element.

The extension-element-prefixes attribute defines all the extension namespaces that can be used as the prefix of an extension element or an extension function. All the namespaces are separated by a space character.

The `exclude-result-prefixes` attribute defines all the namespaces whose elements should not have their namespaces written to the output document. Again, all the namespaces are separated by a white space.

Although not included as an attribute, the namespace declaration is necessary to ensure that the XSLT document can be parsed properly. This namespace declaration is almost always like this.

```
xmlns:xsl='http://www.w3.org/1999/XSL/Transform'
```

Notice that the namespace prefix does not have to be `xsl`. It can be any name. Once the namespace prefix has been chosen, all XSLT elements should use this prefix.

Examples

Most XSLT documents for the HTML output method will probably use the following `xsl:stylesheet` element.

```
<xsl:stylesheet
 version='1.0'
 xmlns:xsl='http://www.w3.org/1999/XSL/Transform'>
```

If a prefix other than `xsl` is desired, the preferred prefix can be declared using this element as well.

```
<x:stylesheet
 version='1.0'
 xmlns:x='http://www.w3.org/1999/XSL/transform'>
```

All the elements in the document, including the `stylesheet` itself, should then use the prefix `x`.

C.1.29   xsl:template

The `xsl:template` element is the most important element in XSLT. It is the basis for matching patterns to perform transformation. This is also the way to declare subroutines.

Syntax

```
<!-- Top-Level Element -->
<xsl:template
  match = pattern
  name = qname
  priority = number
```

```
mode = qname>
<!-- Content: (xsl:param(0 or more), template) -->
</xsl:template>
```

At least one of the attributes `match` and `name` should be present. However, both can be present for the same template.

The `match` attribute is used to match a pattern. The template will be invoked when it matches a node selected by an `xsl:apply-templates` element.

The `name` attribute is used to give a name to a template. A named template can then be called by using `xsl:call-template` elements.

The `priority` attribute is used to assign a priority to the template. This priority is used to select one template out of all the templates that match the pattern used in an `xsl:apply-templates` element.

The `mode` attribute is used to partition templates into different categories.

Examples

To show that the XSLT processor conforms to the priorities defined by the XSLT developer, let's define two templates with the same values for their `match` attributes. The priority of one template is higher than the other. Here are the templates defined in an XSLT document.

```
<xsl:template match='/'>
  <xsl:apply-templates/>
</xsl:template>

<xsl:template match='top' priority='20'>
  <output>This should be chosen.</output>
</xsl:template>

<xsl:template match='top' priority='10'>
  <output>This should not be chosen.</output>
</xsl:template>
```

Suppose the source document looks like this.

```
<?xml version='1.0'?>
<top/>
```

Applying the XSLT document to this source document, the output document is

```
<output>This should be chosen.</output>
```

Without specifying the `priority` attribute, the XSLT processor would complain that there are two templates matching the same element. Or, as allowed by the specification, the processor could choose to apply the last matching template.

C.1.30   xsl:text

The `xsl:text` element is used to write text nodes to the output. Whitespaces are always preserved inside the element. However, if the output method is HTML, then the whitespace characters should not be considered to be "hard space" as the ` ` entity reference in HTML. To write that entity to the output, use the character entity reference ` ` instead. The XSLT processor should convert that into the ` ` entity reference when this character is encountered.

Syntax

```
<!-- Instruction Element -->
<xsl:text disable-output-escaping = ("yes" | "no" ) >
  <!-- Content: #PCDATA -->
</xsl:text>
```

The content of an `xsl:text` element must be character data only. You can use the `disable-output-escaping` attribute to disable escaping for special characters like < and &.

Examples

Suppose you want to output < as is and then use the `xsl:text` this way.

```
<xsl:text disable-output-escaping='yes'>&lt;</xsl:text>
```

The entity reference `&lt;` must still be used in the XSLT document because an XSLT document must be well formed. But the output will be < instead of `&lt;`. If you do not set the `disable-output-escaping` attribute to `yes`, then you will get `&lt;` instead.

C.1.31   xsl:transform

The `xsl:transform` is a synonym for the `xsl:stylesheet` element. See Section C.1.28 for details.

C.1.32   `xsl:value-of`

The `value-of` element returns the string value of the expression given in the `select` attribute.

Syntax

```
<!-- Instruction Element -->
<xsl:value-of
  select = string-expression
  disable-output-escaping = ( "yes" | "no" ) />
```

The mandatory attribute is `select`. This attribute sets the value to evaluate. The result is always converted to a string first.

Examples

The examples will be based on the expression of the `select` attribute.

VARIABLES.   The value of a variable can be obtained by using the `$` prefix. Suppose this is the declaration of a variable.

```
<xsl:variable name='var' select='123'/>
```

Then the XSLT element

```
<xsl:value-of select='$var'/>
```

returns

```
123
```

If the variable is a result tree fragment like this

```
<xsl:variable name='var'><top>text1<second/>text2</top></xsl:variable>
```

the same `xsl:value-of` element will convert it to a string first. The result looks like this.

```
text1text2
```

PROCESSING INSTRUCTIONS, COMMENTS, TEXT NODES.   When using an `xsl:value-of` on a processing instruction, suppose the input XML file is like this

```
<element>
<?java processing instruction for Java ?>
</element>
```

and the XSLT element

```
<xsl:value-of select='element/processing-instruction()'/>
```

the output looks like this.

```
processing instruction for Java
```

Comments and text nodes are similar to processing instructions when their string values are obtained.

NODE-SETS.   If the `select` attribute selects a node-set, the node-set is first converted to a string. For example, the following XML document

```
<?xml version='1.0'?>
<element>abc
<?java processing instruction for Java ?>def
</element>
```

is processed by the following XSLT document.

```
<?xml version='1.0'?>

<xsl:stylesheet
 version='1.0'
 xmlns:xsl='http://www.w3.org/1999/XSL/Transform'>

<xsl:template match='/'>
<xsl:value-of select='element'/>
</xsl:template>

</xsl:stylesheet>
```

produces

```
abc
def
```

The processing instruction is ignored because it is part of the markup rather than the element node.

RESULT TREE FRAGMENTS.   If you use an `xsl:value-of` element to get the string value of a result tree fragment, the same operation is carried for the result tree fragment as that for a node-set. That is, all the nodes will be converted to strings, and the strings will be concatenated.

C.1.33   xsl:variable

The `xsl:variable` element in XSLT is used to store information so that it can be referred to by name.

The scope of a variable depends on where it is declared. A variable can be declared as a child of the `xsl:stylesheet` or it can be declared inside a template. The visibility of a variable—we'll call it `var`—is as follows.

The variable `var` is visible to its following siblings and their descendants. It is an error to declare another variable with the name `var` if there is a `var` visible at the point for the declaration unless the `var` variable that is visible is a child of the `xsl:stylesheet` element.

No two variables with the same name can be declared as the children of the `xsl:stylesheet` element.

A variable declared as a child node of `xsl:stylesheet` is visible everywhere in the XSLT document. However, it is possible to have two declarations with the same names in two XSLT documents as child nodes of their respective `xsl:stylesheet`. The declaration with the highest import precedence will be used.

The visibility rule applies to both `xsl:param` and `xsl:variable`. So if a parameter with the name `var` is visible when `xsl:variable` is used to declare a variable called `var`, it is still an error.

Syntax

```
<!-- Top-Level Element -->
<!-- Instruction Element -->
<xsl:variable
  name = qname
  select = expression>
  <!-- Content: template -->
</xsl:variable>
```

The mandatory attribute is the **name** attribute. It is the name of the variable.

The value of a variable can be empty when the `xsl:variable` element is an empty element, or it can be specified using the `select` attribute. The initial value can also be set using the execution of elements contained in the `xsl:variable` element. However, the descendants of the `xsl:variable` can be literal result elements. In this case, the descendants are called a result tree fragment.

Examples

Suppose we have XSLT document 1:

```
<?xml version='1.0'?>
<xsl:stylesheet version='1.0'
    xmlns:xsl='http://www.w3.org/1999/XSL/Transform'>

  <xsl:import href='document2.xsl'/>

  <xsl:output method='text'/>

  <xsl:variable name='var' select='1'/>

  <xsl:template match='/'>
    <xsl:value-of select='$var'/>
  </xsl:template>

</xsl:stylesheet>
```

And XSLT document 2 contains

```
<?xml version='1.0'?>
<xsl:stylesheet version='1.0'
    xmlns:xsl='http://www.w3.org/1999/XSL/Transform'>

  <xsl:variable name='var' select='2'/>
</xsl:stylesheet>
```

Let's see what the result is.

```
1
```

So the variable declaration in document 1 is used because the importing document has higher precedence than the one that is imported.

If you change the `xsl:import` element to an `xsl:include` element, you will see an error message.[4]

RESULT TREE FRAGMENTS.   You can store a result tree fragment in a variable. For instance, this example is perfectly reasonable.

```
<xsl:variable name='rtf'><A
    HREF='http://www.w3.org'>W3C</A></xsl:variable>
```

---

4. Your XSLT processor may not report the error.

However, we have said that result tree fragments are not the same as node-sets. Therefore, if we then use the variable

```
<xsl:value-of select='$rtf/A/@HREF'/>
```

an error will occur.

However, you can copy the whole result tree fragment to the result tree with an `xsl:copy-of` element:

```
<xsl:copy-of select='$rtf'/>
```

C.1.34   xsl:when

The `xsl:when` element is always contained in an `xsl:choose` element.

Syntax

```
<xsl:when
  test = Boolean-expression>
  <!-- Content: template -->
</xsl:when>
```

The mandatory attribute of `xsl:when` is `test`. The value of the attribute is an expression in XPath. If the expression evaluates to true, then the descendants of the `xsl:when` element are processed; otherwise, the element is skipped.

Inside an `xsl:choose` element, the `xsl:when` elements are evaluated in the document order. Whenever the XPath expression of the `test` attribute in an `xsl:when` element evaluates to true, that `xsl:when` element is selected.

If none of the XPath expressions of the `test` attribute in the `xsl:when` elements in an `xsl:choose` element evaluates to true, then the descendants of the `xsl:otherwise` element in the `xsl:choose` element are processed. If the `xsl:choose` element does not have an `xsl:otherwise` child element, then the whole `xsl:choose` element is skipped.

Examples

See Section C.1.6 for examples.

C.1.35   xsl:with-param

The `xsl:with-param` element is used to pass parameters to a template.

Syntax

```
<xsl:with-param
  name = qname
```

```
select = expression>
<!-- Content: template -->
</xsl:with-param>
```

The mandatory attribute is the `name` attribute. It is the name of the parameter.

If the select attribute is present, then it is evaluated and its result assigned to the parameter.

When a template is applied, the parameter list of the template is examined. If there is a parameter with the same name as the `name` attribute of the `xsl:with-param` element, the value of the `xsl:with-element` element is assigned to the parameter in the template.

Examples

Here is an example of using the `select` attribute to assign a value to the parameter.

```
<xsl:apply-templates>
  <xsl:with-param name='length' select='123'/>
</xsl:apply-templates>
```

The template that is chosen for the `xsl:apply-templates` element will take the value of the parameter called `length`. If the template does not have a parameter called `length`, the `length` parameter is ignored.

It is also possible to set the value using element content.

```
<xsl:apply-templates>
  <xsl:with-param name='length'>123</xsl:with-param>
</xsl:apply-templates>
```

In this case, the value of the parameter is a result tree fragment with one text node containing the string `123`.

C.2   XSLT and XPath Functions

The XSLT and XPath specifications define functions that can be used to manipulate numbers, strings, Boolean values, and node-sets.

These functions can be used within an XPath expression or as parts of a predicate of a step in the location path.

The name of each function is in the section head. The name, return type, and the parameter list of a function are then given, followed by a table containing descriptions of the parameters (or arguments) and return value. Their data types will also be provided. This table is an example.

Argument Position	Number of Occurrences	Type	Description
1	1	*Argument date type*	The description of the first argument
Return Value		*Return value type*	The description of the return value

C.2.1   *boolean*

Function: *Boolean* boolean(*object*)

Argument Position	Number of Occurrences	Type	Description
1	1	*Object*	This is the object to be converted. It can be any type (number, Boolean, string, or node-set).
Return Value		*Boolean*	The Boolean value of the argument

DESCRIPTIONS AND EXAMPLES.   The boolean() function converts an object to a Boolean value. If the object is a number, then the result is **true** unless the number is negative zero, positive zero, or NaN; otherwise, it returns false. If the object is a string and the string is not empty, then the function returns true; otherwise, it returns false. If the object is a node-set, then the function returns true if the node-set is not empty, otherwise, it returns false.

C.2.2   *ceiling*

Function: *number* ceiling(*number*)

Argument Position	Number of Occurrences	Type	Description
1	1	*number*	The number to find the ceiling of
Return Value		*number*	The ceiling of the argument

DESCRIPTIONS AND EXAMPLES.   The ceiling function returns the **ceiling** of a number. The ceiling of a number is the smallest integer that is larger than or equal to the number. For instance, the ceiling of 1.2 is 2. The ceiling of an integer is itself. The same definition applies to negative numbers as well.

C.2.3   *concat*

Function: *string* concat(*string*, *string*, *string*^(0 or more))

Argument Position	Number of Occurrences	Type	Description
1	1	*string*	The first string to concatenate
2	1	*string*	The second string to concatenate
3 ...	0 or more	*string*	Optional strings to concatenate
Return Value		*string*	The concatenated string of all the arguments

DESCRIPTIONS AND EXAMPLES. The concat() function concatenates strings together and requires at least two parameters. The result is a string that concatenates all the parameters—converted to strings as necessary—together. For example,

```
concat('abc', 'def')
```

produces

```
abcdef
```

as the result. If one of the arguments is not a string, it will be converted to a string first before the function is applied.

C.2.4   *contains*

Function: *Boolean* contains(*string*, *string*)

Argument Position	Number of Occurrences	Type	Description
1	1	*string*	The string to find the occurrences of the second string
2	1	*string*	The string you want to find in the first argument
Return Value		*Boolean*	True if the first string contains the second string. False otherwise.

DESCRIPTIONS AND EXAMPLES. The contains function checks if the first parameter contains the second parameter—in other words, if the second parameter is a substring of the first parameter. If so, the function returns true, otherwise, it returns false. For example,

```
contains('abcd', 'bc')
```

returns `true`; but

```
contains('abcd', 'de')
```

returns `false`.

C.2.5   *count*

Function: *number* `count(`*node-set*`)`

Argument Position	Number of Occurrences	Type	Description
1	1	*node-set*	The node-set to count the number of nodes
Return Value		*number*	The number of nodes in the node-set

DESCRIPTIONS AND EXAMPLES.   The `count()` function returns the number of nodes in a node-set. For instance, the number of elements in an XML document can be obtained by

```
<xsl:value-of select='count(//*)'/>
```

This takes a long time even for a moderate-sized document. Do not use it unless you have no other alternative.

C.2.6   *current*

Function: *node-set* `current()`

Argument Position	Number of Occurrences	Type	Description
Return Value		*node-set*	The node-set containing the current node.

DESCRIPTIONS AND EXAMPLES.   The `current()` returns the current node in a node-set. The current node does not change in an XPath expression.

For instance, you can specify

```
<xsl:for-each select='../*[name() = name(current())]'>
  <!-- all the siblings of the current node
       with the same name -->
</xsl:for-each>
```

to process all the siblings of the current node with the same name as the current node. Here is a different way.

```
<!-- the value of the select attribute must be
     on the same line. I break it up to show
     it here. -->
<xsl:for-each
   select='preceding-sibling::*[name() = name(current())] |
           following-sibling::*[name() = name(current())]'>
  <!-- all the siblings of the current node
       with the same name -->
</xsl:for-each>
```

The expression name() = name(current()) means "if the name of the context node is the same as the name of the current node."

C.2.7   *document*

Function: *node-set* document(*object*, *node-set*$^{(0\ or\ 1)}$)

Argument Position	Number of Occurrences	Type	Description
1	0 or 1	*object*	If it is absent then it is the root of the current XSLT document. Otherwise, it is the object containing the URI to the document to be referred to.
2	0 or 1	*node-set*	Must be absent if the first argument is absent. Otherwise, it contains nodes to infer the base URI of the documents to be referred.
Return Value		*node-set*	The node-set contains the root of the document referred.

DESCRIPTIONS AND EXAMPLES.   The document() function is used to incorporate additional source trees. This function takes up to two parameters.

If the first parameter is not a node-set, then the parameter is converted to a string first. The string is treated as a URI. The resource associated with the URI is incorporated as one additional source tree. You can handle the additional source tree just like the initial source document you specify when the XSLT processor is first invoked.

For instance, suppose you want to find out the import hierarchy of an XSLT document you have

```
<xsl:stylesheet version='1.0'
    xmlns:xsl='http://www.w3.org/1999/XSL/Transform'>

  <xsl:output method='html' indent='yes'/>

  <xsl:template match='/'>
    <HTML><HEAD><TITLE>Import Hierarchy</TITLE></HEAD>
    <BODY><H1>Import Hierarchy</H1>
    <P>The initial source document</P>
    <xsl:call-template name='import'>
      <xsl:with-param name='root' select='/'/>
      <xsl:with-param name='indent' select='"-->"'/>
    </xsl:call-template>
    </BODY>
    </HTML>
  </xsl:template>

  <xsl:template name='import'>
    <xsl:param name='root'/>
    <xsl:param name='indent'/>
    <!-- the value for the test should be on the same line.
         I break it up to show it
         here -->
    <xsl:if
      test='local-name($root/*) = "stylesheet" and
         namespace-uri($root/*) =
            "http://www.w3.org/1999/XSL/Transform"'>
      <!-- the value of the select attribute should
           be on the same line. I break it up to show
           it here. -->
      <xsl:for-each
        select='$root/*/*[local-name() = "import" and
          namespace-uri() = "http://www.w3.org/1999/XSL/Transform"]/@href'>
        <P>
          <xsl:value-of select='$indent'/>File
            <xsl:value-of select='.'/>
        </P>
        <xsl:call-template name='import'>
```

```
        <xsl:with-param name='root' select='document(.)'/>
        <xsl:with-param name='indent'
            select='concat($indent, "-->")'/>
      </xsl:call-template>
      </xsl:for-each>
    </xsl:if>
  </xsl:template>

</xsl:stylesheet>
```

Suppose *a.xsl* imports *b.xsl* and *c.xsl*; *b.xsl* imports *d.xsl* and *f.xsl*; *c.xsl* imports *e.xsl*. This is the HTML document generated.

```
<HTML>
<HEAD>
<TITLE>Import Hierarchy</TITLE>
</HEAD>
<BODY>
<H1>Import Hierarchy</H1>
<P>The initial source document</P>
<P>--&gt;File b.xsl</P>
<P>--&gt;--&gt;File d.xsl</P>
<P>--&gt;--&gt;File f.xsl</P>
<P>--&gt;File c.xsl</P>
<P>--&gt;--&gt;File e.xsl</P>
</BODY>
</HTML>
```

BASE URI. The second parameter, if it exists, specifies the base URI to retrieve the documents specified in the first parameter. The second parameter must be a node-set, and its first node in the document order is used as the reference node for the base URI. Its base URI is the base URI for the documents in the first parameter.

MULTIPLE DOCUMENTS. The document function can be used to incorporate more than one document at a time. To incorporate more than one source document, use a node-set as the first parameter. The string value of each node represents one document.

If the second parameter is present, then the base URI of the first node in the node-set is used as the base URI for the documents.

If the second parameter is absent, then the base URI of each node in the node-set is the base URI of the node.

THE CURRENT STYLESHEET.   If you need to refer to the current stylesheet, use the expression `document("")`.

C.2.8   *element-available*

Function: *Boolean* `element-available(string)`

Argument Position	Number of Occurrences	Type	Description
1	1	*string*	The name of the element you want to check the availability for
Return Value		*Boolean*	True if the element is available in the current processor

DESCRIPTIONS AND EXAMPLES.   The `element-available()` function returns true if the string given is the name of an available element.

To find out whether the `xsl:key` element is available, you can use the following.

```
<xsl:template match='/'>
  <xsl:choose>
    <xsl:when test='element-available("xsl:key")'>
      <P>The <I>xsl:key</I> element is available</P>
    </xsl:when>
    <xsl:otherwise>
      <P>The <I>xsl:key</I> element is not available</P>
    </xsl:otherwise>
  </xsl:choose>
</xsl:template>
```

C.2.9   *false*

Function: *Boolean* `false()`

Argument Position	Number of Occurrences	Type	Description
Return Value		*Boolean*	False

DESCRIPTIONS AND EXAMPLES. The `false` function returns the Boolean false value. This function is seldom used other than to force the conversion of expressions in other areas where the expression is found.

See C.2.35 for an example for `true()`, which is used the same way as `false()`.

C.2.10   *floor*

Function: *number* `floor(`*number*`)`

Argument Position	Number of Occurrences	Type	Description
1	1	*number*	The number to find the floor
Return Value		*number*	The floor of the argument

DESCRIPTIONS AND EXAMPLES.   The `floor()` function returns the floor of a number, which is the largest integer that is smaller than or equal to the number. For instance, if the number passed in is `1.2`, then the floor of the number is `1`. If the number itself is an integer, then the floor of the number is itself.

Notice that the floor of the number `1.8` is `1`. The same definition is used for negative numbers, too. For instance, the floor of `-1.2` is `-2`.

C.2.11   *format-number*

Function: *string* `format-number(`*number*`, `*string*`, `*string*$^{(0\ or\ 1)}$`)`

Argument Position	Number of Occurrences	Type	Description
1	1	*number*	The number to format
2	1	*string*	The formatting string
3	0 or 1	*string*	The name of the decimal-format declared. See C.1.10.
Return Value		*string*	The formatted number in a string

DESCRIPTIONS AND EXAMPLES.   The `format-number()` function is used to format a number for output. The first parameter is the number to be formatted, the second parameter is the format string for the number, and the third parameter is the name of the decimal-format. If the third parameter is absent, then the default decimal-format is used.

A decimal-format is defined using the `xsl:decimal-format` element. See Section C.1.10 for details on how a decimal-format can be declared.

The default format string has these special characters.

0   Represents a digit. For example,

```
<xsl:value-of select='format-number(1234, "00000")'/>
```

has the result 01234. The leading zero is there because the format string specifies five digits. If the number to be formatted is negative, for instance,

```
<xsl:value-of select='format-number(-1234, "00000")'/>
```

the result is -01234 because the negative sign does not take up a digit. If you fail to provide enough digits for the number, such as

```
<xsl:value-of select='format-number(1234, "00")'/>
```

the result will still be 1234. However, the format-number() function is used when the format is important. Not providing enough digits is usually an oversight.

If you do not want leading zeros, you can use the # character to specify a digit. For example,

```
<xsl:value-of select='format-number(1234, "#####")'/>
```

results in 1234 with no leading zero.

.   This character represents the decimal point. You can format a floating point number by specifying the number of digits in front of and after the decimal point. For example,

```
<xsl:value-of select='format-number(1 div 3, "#####.####")'/>
```

prints only 4 digits after the decimal point: .3333. There is no leading zero in front of the decimal point because the # character means absent leading zero. To output 0.3333, use

```
<xsl:value-of select='format-number(1 div 3, "####0.####")'/>
```

The format string ####0.#### does not give you trailing zeros if the number to be formatted is a whole number. To output something like 3.0, use the format string '####0.0###' instead.

,   The comma character represents the digit grouping character. For instance, if you want to output 1,000.00 for the number 1000, use the format string #,##0.00.

There is no reason to group digits by thousands. You can certainly group digits by hundreds (not that I would ever need to do that). To do that, use the format string ##,#0.00##. The output of

```
<xsl:value-of select='format-number(1000, "#,##,#0.00##")'/>
```

is 10,00.00.

E   For whatever reason, if you want to use the scientific notation to format a number, you can use the E character to represent the delimiter between the mantissa and the exponent. The following

```
<xsl:value-of select='format-number(100000, "#,###.0E0###")'/>
```

outputs 10,000.0E1.

%   Format the number as a percentage. For instance,

```
<xsl:value-of select='format-number(1000, "###0%")'/>
```

outputs 100000%.

‰   Format the number a per-mille. For instance,

```
<xsl:value-of select='format-number(0.001, "###0&#x2030;")'/>
```

outputs 1‰, where ‰ is the per-mille entity reference in HTML.

If you are in the financial sector, negative numbers are usually inside parentheses. For instance, -1234 becomes (1234). You can specify a subformat for negative numbers.

```
<xsl:value-of select='format-number(-0.001, "####0.0##;(#)")'/>
```

Subformats are separated by the ; character. The first subformat is for positive numbers, and the second is for negative numbers. You do not need to specify the whole format again, just the prefix and suffix. The preceding element produces (0.001).

DECIMAL-FORMATS AND format-number(). The actual characters used in the output not only depend on the format string but on the decimal-format used. This XSLT document

```
<?xml version='1.0'?>
<xsl:stylesheet version='1.0'
   xmlns:xsl='http://www.w3.org/1999/XSL/Transform'>

  <xsl:output method='html' indent='no'/>

  <xsl:decimal-format name='my'
    decimal-separator=','
```

```
            grouping-separator='.'
            minus-sign='_'/>

  <xsl:template match='/'>
    result:<xsl:value-of
               select='format-number(1234, "00000", "my")'/>
    result:<xsl:value-of
               select='format-number(1234, "00", "my")'/>
    result:<xsl:value-of
               select='format-number(-1234, "00000", "my")'/>
    result:<xsl:value-of
               select='format-number(1234, "#####", "my")'/>
    result:<xsl:value-of
               select='format-number(1 div 3, "#####,####", "my")'/>
    result:<xsl:value-of
               select='format-number(1 div 3, "####0,####", "my")'/>
    result:<xsl:value-of
               select='format-number(3, "####0,####", "my")'/>
    result:<xsl:value-of
               select='format-number(3, "####0,0###", "my")'/>
    result:<xsl:value-of
               select='format-number(1000, "##.##0,00##", "my")'/>
    result:<xsl:value-of
               select='format-number(1000, "#.##.#0,00##", "my")'/>
    result:<xsl:value-of
               select='format-number(12345, "##0,###E0", "my")'/>
    result:<xsl:value-of
               select='format-number(1000, "###0%")'/>
    result:<xsl:value-of
               select='format-number(0.001, "###0&#x2030;", "my")'/>
    result:<xsl:value-of
               select='format-number(-0.001, "####0,0##;(#)", "my")'/>
  </xsl:template>

</xsl:stylesheet>
```

produces

```
   result:01234
   result:1234
   result:_01234
   result:1234
   result:,3333
```

```
result:0,3333
result:3
result:3,0
result:1.000,00
result:10.00,00
result:1234,5E1
result:100000%
result:1&#8240;
result:(0,001)
```

The `format-number()` is not a function that gets a lot of attention. Because of that, you may not get what is expected from the popular XSLT processors.

C.2.12   *function-available*

Function: *Boolean* `function-available(`*string*`)`

Argument Position	Number of Occurrences	Type	Description
1	1	*string*	The name of the function to find the availability for
Return Value		*Boolean*	True if the function is available

DESCRIPTIONS AND EXAMPLES. The `function-available` function returns true if the name given to the function is the name of a function available from the processor.

For instance, you can find out whether the key function is available for the XSLT processor you have.

```
<xsl:template match='/'>
  <xsl:choose>
    <xsl:when test='function-available("key")'>
      <P>The <I>key</I> function is available</P>
    </xsl:when>
    <xsl:otherwise>
      <P>The <I>key</I> function is not available</P>
    </xsl:otherwise>
  </xsl:choose>
</xsl:template>
```

Of course, it is more common to check if an extension function is available, but it is perfectly okay to check if an XSLT function is available (if, for example, your processor does not implement the key function).

C.2.13   *generate-id*

Function: *string* generate-id(*node-set*$^{(0\ or\ 1)}$)

Argument Position	Number of Occurrences	Type	Description
1	0 or 1	*node-set*	The node-set containing the node to generate an ID for
Return Value		*string*	The ID generated for the node

DESCRIPTIONS AND EXAMPLES.   The generate-id function generates a unique ID for the first node in the document order in a node-set. This ID is effective within the same invocation of the XSLT process. It is not effective in a new invocation of the XSLT processor, even of the same XSLT processor.

This function is very important for identifying nodes. For instance, if you are given one node-set and the current node, how do you know which one node in the node-set is the current node? Using this template

```
<?xml version='1.0'?>
<xsl:stylesheet version='1.0'
    xmlns:xsl='http://www.w3.org/1999/XSL/Transform'>

  <xsl:output method='html' indent='yes'/>

  <xsl:template match='/'>
    <HTML><HEAD><TITLE>Find Node</TITLE></HEAD>
    <BODY>
    <xsl:for-each select='//*/text()/..'>
      <H3>Current node is: <xsl:value-of select='name()'/> </H3>
      <xsl:call-template name='findCurrentNode'>
        <xsl:with-param name='nodeSet' select='//*'/>
      </xsl:call-template>
    </xsl:for-each>
    </BODY>
    </HTML>
  </xsl:template>
```

```
<xsl:template name='findCurrentNode'>
  <xsl:param name='nodeSet'/>
  <xsl:variable name='currentNode' select='current()'/>
  <xsl:for-each select='$nodeSet'>
    <xsl:if test='. = $currentNode'>
      <P>Found current node: <xsl:value-of select='name()'/></P>
    </xsl:if>
  </xsl:for-each>
</xsl:template>

</xsl:stylesheet>
```

and if the source document is

```
<document>
  <title>The Purple Book</title>
  <chapter><title>Introduction</title>Some text here. <section>
    <title>Purpose</title><bookmark>Bookmark here</bookmark>...
    </section>
  </chapter>
  .
  .
  .
  <chapter><title>Speed</title><bookmark>Bookmark here</bookmark>...
  </chapter>
</document>
```

then the result looks like this.

```
<HTML>
<HEAD>
<TITLE>Find Node</TITLE>
</HEAD>
<BODY>
<H3>Current node is: document</H3>
<P>Found current node: document</P>
<H3>Current node is: title</H3>
<P>Found current node: title</P>
<H3>Current node is: chapter</H3>
<P>Found current node: chapter</P>
<H3>Current node is: title</H3>
<P>Found current node: title</P>
<H3>Current node is: section</H3>
<P>Found current node: section</P>
```

```
<H3>Current node is: title</H3>
<P>Found current node: title</P>
<H3>Current node is: bookmark</H3>
<P>Found current node: bookmark</P>
<P>Found current node: bookmark</P>
<H3>Current node is: chapter</H3>
<P>Found current node: chapter</P>
<H3>Current node is: title</H3>
<P>Found current node: title</P>
<H3>Current node is: bookmark</H3>
<P>Found current node: bookmark</P>
<P>Found current node: bookmark</P>
</BODY>
</HTML>
```

You can see that for both **bookmark** elements the template cannot identify the two seemingly identical **bookmark** elements. If you cannot identify nodes that seem to be identical but are in fact not, you will find yourself in all kinds of trouble.

Of course, the **generate-id** function will help you to identify the right nodes.

```
<?xml version='1.0'?>
<xsl:stylesheet version='1.0'
    xmlns:xsl='http://www.w3.org/1999/XSL/Transform'>

  <xsl:output method='html' indent='yes'/>

  <xsl:template match='/'>
    <HTML><HEAD><TITLE>Find Node</TITLE></HEAD>
    <BODY>
    <xsl:for-each select='//*/text()/..'>
      <H3>Current node is: <xsl:value-of
          select='name()'/> with generated ID:
          <xsl:value-of select='generate-id()'/>
      </H3>
      <xsl:call-template name='findCurrentNode'>
        <xsl:with-param name='nodeSet' select='//*'/>
      </xsl:call-template>
    </xsl:for-each>
    </BODY>
```

```
    </HTML>
  </xsl:template>

  <xsl:template name='findCurrentNode'>
    <xsl:param name='nodeSet'/>
    <xsl:variable name='currentNode' select='current()'/>
    <xsl:for-each select='$nodeSet'>
      <xsl:if test='generate-id(.) = generate-id($currentNode)'>
        <P>Found current node: <xsl:value-of
         select='name()'/> with generated ID: <xsl:value-of
         select='generate-id()'/></P>
      </xsl:if>
    </xsl:for-each>
  </xsl:template>

</xsl:stylesheet>
```

With the same XML source document, the result now looks like this.

```
<HTML>
<HEAD>
<TITLE>Find Node</TITLE>
</HEAD>
<BODY>
<H3>Current node is: document with generated ID: N1</H3>
<P>Found current node: document with generated ID: N1</P>
<H3>Current node is: title with generated ID: N3</H3>
<P>Found current node: title with generated ID: N3</P>
<H3>Current node is: chapter with generated ID: N6</H3>
<P>Found current node: chapter with generated ID: N6</P>
<H3>Current node is: title with generated ID: N7</H3>
<P>Found current node: title with generated ID: N7</P>
<H3>Current node is: section with generated ID: N10</H3>
<P>Found current node: section with generated ID: N10</P>
<H3>Current node is: title with generated ID: N12</H3>
<P>Found current node: title with generated ID: N12</P>
<H3>Current node is: bookmark with generated ID: N14</H3>
<P>Found current node: bookmark with generated ID: N14</P>
<H3>Current node is: chapter with generated ID: N19</H3>
<P>Found current node: chapter with generated ID: N19</P>
<H3>Current node is: title with generated ID: N20</H3>
<P>Found current node: title with generated ID: N20</P>
```

405

```
<H3>Current node is: bookmark with generated ID: N22</H3>
<P>Found current node: bookmark with generated ID: N22</P>
</BODY>
</HTML>
```

You can clearly see the different IDs for different nodes that have the same values.

C.2.14   *id*

Function: *node-set* id(*object*)

Argument Position	Number of Occurrences	Type	Description
1	1	*object*	The ID of the nodes you want to select
Return Value		*node-set*	The node-set containing the nodes whose IDs are specified in the object in the first argument

DESCRIPTIONS AND EXAMPLES.   Given a string, the id() function returns the node having the string as its ID. If a node-set is given to the function, then apply the function to each node in the node-set. To apply the function to a node, convert the node into a string. This string is normalized (see Section C.2.21). Each space delimited substring is then taken as the ID of a node to be selected from the source tree. Combine all the nodes selected this way into a node-set. This node-set is the result of applying the id function to a node-set.

If the function is given something else, then the parameter is first converted to a string using the string() function. The string goes through the tokenization process. Each token is then taken as the ID of the node to be selected. Put the nodes selected in a node-set. Return the node-set as the result of the function.

There are two ways to use this function, just as for the key function. The first way is to use it to select the node with the object ID. For example,

```
id('abc')
```

returns only the node having the ID abc. This example

```
id('abc')/book
```

returns a node-set containing the book element whose parent has the ID abc. If there is no node with this ID, then the empty node-set is returned.

To use the id function, your XML source document must have a DTD. The elements with the ID must have the ID attribute declared as the ID datatype.

C.2.15   *key*

Function: *node-set* key(*string*, *object*)

Argument Position	Number of Occurrences	Type	Description
1	1	*string*	The key value
2	1	*object*	The criteria used to select the nodes fulfilling the key value in the first argument
Return Value		*node-set*	The node-set containing the nodes with the key specified and the criteria specified in the second argument

DESCRIPTIONS AND EXAMPLES.   The key function returns all the nodes in the key named in the first parameter fulfilling the criteria specified by the object in the second parameter. See Section C.1.17 for details on how this function can be used.

C.2.16   *lang*

Function: *Boolean* lang(*string*)

Argument Position	Number of Occurrences	Type	Description
1	1	*string*	The language code
Return Value		*Boolean*	True if the context node is in the language specified by the language code

DESCRIPTIONS AND EXAMPLES.   This function checks if the language used by the context node is the same as the parameter specified. To find the language used by the context node, search for the xml:lang attribute in the context node and all the ancestors of the context node. If there is no such node with the xml:lang attribute, the function returns false. If there is a node with this attribute, select the node closest to the context node. Compare the language with the first parameter. If they are the same, then the function returns true. Otherwise, the function returns false. The case of the language string is ignored when the comparison is done. Also, the subset of the language is ignored. Therefore, en-us is treated as en for comparison purposes.

C.2.17   *last*

Function: *number* last()

Argument Position	Number of Occurrences	Type	Description
Return Value		*Boolean*	The number of nodes in the context

DESCRIPTIONS AND EXAMPLES.   This function returns the context size. For instance, suppose this is the source document.

```
<?xml version='1.0'?>
<stories>
  <story>1</story>
  <story>2</story>
  <story>3</story>
  <story>4</story>
  <story>5</story>
  <story>6</story>
  <story>7</story>
  <story>8</story>
  <story>9</story>
</stories>
```

and suppose the XSLT document looks like this.

```
<?xml version='1.0'?>
<xsl:stylesheet
  xmlns:xsl='http://www.w3.org/1999/XSL/Transform'
  version='1.0'>

<xsl:template match='/'>
<xsl:apply-templates select='/stories/story|/stories'/>
</xsl:template>
```

```
<xsl:template match='stories|story'>
  <xsl:message>Number: <xsl:value-of select='last()'/>
</xsl:message>
</xsl:template>

</xsl:stylesheet>
```

The lines output from this XSLT document are 10 lines of `Number:` 10 because there are 10 nodes in the node-set selected by the expression `/stories/story|/stories`, nine `story` elements and one `stories` element.

C.2.18   *local-name*

Function: *string*local-name(*node-set*$^{(0 \text{ or } 1)}$)

Argument Position	Number of Occurrences	Type	Description
1	0 or 1	*node-set*	The node-set containing the node whose local-name you want to find. If it is absent, the context node is chosen.
Return Value		*string*	The local name of the node

DESCRIPTIONS AND EXAMPLES.   Given a node-set, the `local-name()` function returns the local-name of the first node in the document order. Only the local-name is returned. If the node has a namespace prefix, the prefix is removed before the name is returned.

The following template finds all the elements in the source XML document, retains only those that are in the XSLT namespace, and then sorts the elements according to their local names.

```
<?xml version='1.0'?>
<xsl:stylesheet version='1.0'
    xmlns:xsl='http://www.w3.org/1999/XSL/Transform'>

  <xsl:output method='html' indent='yes'/>

<xsl:template match='/'>
  <HTML><HEAD><TITLE>XSLT Elements</TITLE></HEAD>
    <BODY><H1>XSLT Elements</H1>
      <xsl:for-each
```

```
            select='//*[namespace-uri()="http://www.w3.org/1999/XSL/Transform"]
        <xsl:sort select='local-name()'/>
        <P><xsl:value-of select='local-name()'/></P>
      </xsl:for-each>
    </BODY>
  </HTML>
</xsl:template>

</xsl:stylesheet>
```

Using the document on itself, we have the following output:

```
<HTML>
<HEAD>
<TITLE>XSLT Elements</TITLE>
</HEAD>
<BODY>
<H1>XSLT Elements</H1>
<P>for-each</P>
<P>output</P>
<P>sort</P>
<P>stylesheet</P>
<P>template</P>
<P>value-of</P>
</BODY>
</HTML>
```

The `namespace-uri()` function uses the namespace URI to determine whether an element is in the XSLT namespace, not whether its prefix is `xsl`.

C.2.19   *name*

Function: *string* name(*node-set*$^{(0 \text{ or } 1)}$)

Argument Position	Number of Occurrences	Type	Description
1	0 or 1	*node-set*	The node-set containing the node whose name you want to find out. If it is absent, the context node is chosen.
Return Value		*string*	The name of the node

DESCRIPTIONS AND EXAMPLES.   Given a node-set, the `name()` function returns the name of the first node in the document order of the node-set.

The name returned is the qualified name of the node: If the node has a namespace prefix, the prefix will be returned as well.

An XSLT document that produces an HTML page with all the element names in the source XML document sorted in ascending order is as follows.

```
<?xml version='1.0'?>
<xsl:stylesheet version='1.0'
    xmlns:xsl='http://www.w3.org/1999/XSL/Transform'>

  <xsl:output method='html' indent='yes'/>

<xsl:template match='/'>
  <HTML><HEAD><TITLE>Element Names</TITLE></HEAD>
    <BODY><H1>Element Names</H1>
      <xsl:for-each select='//*'><xsl:sort select='name()'/>
        <P>element: '<xsl:value-of select='name()'/>'</P>
      </xsl:for-each>
    </BODY>
  </HTML>
</xsl:template>

</xsl:stylesheet>
```

Running the document against itself produces the following HTML page.

```
<HTML>
<HEAD>
<TITLE>Element Names</TITLE>
</HEAD>
<BODY>
<H1>Element Names</H1>
<P>element: 'BODY'</P>
<P>element: 'H1'</P>
<P>element: 'HEAD'</P>
<P>element: 'HTML'</P>
<P>element: 'P'</P>
<P>element: 'TITLE'</P>
<P>element: 'xsl:for-each'</P>
<P>element: 'xsl:output'</P>
<P>element: 'xsl:sort'</P>
<P>element: 'xsl:stylesheet'</P>
<P>element: 'xsl:template'</P>
```

```
<P>element: 'xsl:value-of'</P>
</BODY>
</HTML>
```

C.2.20   *namespace-uri*

Function: *string* `namespace-uri`(*node-set*$^{(0 \text{ or } 1)}$)

Argument Position	Number of Occurrences	Type	Description
1	0 or 1	*node-set*	The node-set containing the node whose namespace URI you want to find out. If it is absent, the context node is chosen.
Return Value		*string*	The namespace URI of the node

DESCRIPTIONS AND EXAMPLES.   Given a node-set, the `namespace-uri()` function returns the namespace URI of the first node of the node-set.

A simple example that uses this function is to list all the namespace URIs of all the elements and attributes of an XML document. Here is an XSLT document that does that.

```
<?xml version='1.0'?>
<xsl:stylesheet version='1.0'
    xmlns:xsl='http://www.w3.org/1999/XSL/Transform'>

  <xsl:output method='html' indent='yes'/>

<xsl:template match='/'>
  <HTML><HEAD><TITLE>Namespace URIs</TITLE></HEAD>
    <BODY><H1>Namespace URIs</H1>
      <xsl:for-each select='//*'>
        <P>element: '<xsl:value-of select='name()'/>' URI:
        <xsl:value-of select='namespace-uri()'/></P>
      </xsl:for-each>
      <xsl:for-each select='//*/@*'>
        <P>attribute: '<xsl:value-of select='name()'/>' URI:
        <xsl:value-of select='namespace-uri()'/></P>
      </xsl:for-each>
    </BODY>
  </HTML>
```

```
      </xsl:template>

      </xsl:stylesheet>
```

Using this document on itself, the result looks like this.

```
<HTML>
<HEAD>
<TITLE>Namespace URIs</TITLE>
</HEAD>
<BODY>
<H1>Namespace URIs</H1>
<P>element: 'xsl:stylesheet' URI: http://www.w3.org/1999/XSL/Transform</P>
<P>element: 'xsl:output' URI: http://www.w3.org/1999/XSL/Transform</P>
<P>element: 'xsl:template' URI: http://www.w3.org/1999/XSL/Transform</P>
<P>element: 'HTML' URI: </P>
<P>element: 'HEAD' URI: </P>
<P>element: 'TITLE' URI: </P>
<P>element: 'BODY' URI: </P>
<P>element: 'H1' URI: </P>
<P>element: 'xsl:for-each' URI: http://www.w3.org/1999/XSL/Transform</P>
<P>element: 'P' URI: </P>
<P>element: 'xsl:value-of' URI: http://www.w3.org/1999/XSL/Transform</P>
<P>element: 'xsl:value-of' URI: http://www.w3.org/1999/XSL/Transform</P>
<P>element: 'xsl:for-each' URI: http://www.w3.org/1999/XSL/Transform</P>
<P>element: 'P' URI: </P>
<P>element: 'xsl:value-of' URI: http://www.w3.org/1999/XSL/Transform</P>
<P>element: 'xsl:value-of' URI: http://www.w3.org/1999/XSL/Transform</P>
<P>attribute: 'version' URI: </P>
<P>attribute: 'method' URI: </P>
<P>attribute: 'indent' URI: </P>
<P>attribute: 'match' URI: </P>
<P>attribute: 'select' URI: </P>
<P>attribute: 'select' URI: </P>
<P>attribute: 'select' URI: </P>
<P>attribute: 'select' URI: </P>
<P>attribute: 'select' URI: </P>
<P>attribute: 'select' URI: </P>
</BODY>
</HTML>
```

Note that the attributes and some elements have no explicit namespace.

C.2.21   *normalize-space*

Function: *string* normalize-space(*string*$^{(0\ or\ 1)}$)

Argument Position	Number of Occurrences	Type	Description
1	0 or 1	*string*	The string you want to normalize. If it is absent, the string value of the context node is used.
Return Value		*string*	The normalized string

DESCRIPTIONS AND EXAMPLES.   This function normalizes the space characters in the first parameter. If the first parameter is omitted, it normalizes the context node after converting it to a string. Normalization of a string is the stripping of the leading and trailing whitespaces. It also replaces multiple consecutive occurrences of whitespace by a single space character. For instance,

```
normalize-space(' abcdef gh&#xA; ij&#xA;')
```

returns abcdef gh ij. Notice that a whitespace can be a space, a tab, or a linefeed character. The
 is the linefeed character written as an entity reference.

The following XSLT document takes an XML document, strips the markups, and then outputs every word in the document.

```
<xsl:template match='/'>
  <xsl:call-template name='words'>
    <xsl:with-param name='document' select='normalize-space(/)'/>
  </xsl:call-template>
</xsl:template>


<xsl:template name='words'>
  <xsl:param name='document'/>

  <xsl:choose>
    <xsl:when test='contains($document, " ")'>
      <xsl:value-of select='substring-before($document, " ")'/><xsl:text>
</xsl:text>
      <xsl:call-template name='words'>
        <xsl:with-param name='document'
            select='substring-after($document, " ")'/>
      </xsl:call-template>
    </xsl:when>
    <xsl:otherwise>
```

```
      <xsl:value-of select='$document'/>
    </xsl:otherwise>
  </xsl:choose>
</xsl:template>
```

Of course, this document is very ineffiecient and will overwhelm your computer when given a moderately big document. This is because the processor must first strip the markup from the document and then check for a space one word at a time.

C.2.22   *not*

Function: *Boolean* not(*Boolean*)

Argument Position	Number of Occurrences	Type	Description
1	1	*Boolean*	The Boolean expression to inverse
Return Value		*Boolean*	True if the Boolean expression is false, false otherwise

DESCRIPTIONS AND EXAMPLES.   The not function returns the Boolean true value if the parameter evaluates to false and returns the Boolean false value if the parameter evaluates to true.

Suppose you want to find out whether a node is a child of the root. You can use this element.

```
<xsl:if test='not(../..)'>
  <!-- the node is a child of the root -->
</xsl:if>
```

The expression in the xsl:if element uses the fact that the root is the only node with no parent.

C.2.23   *number*

Function: *number* number(*object*$^{(0 \text{ or } 1)}$)

Argument Position	Number of Occurrences	Type	Description
1	0 or 1	*object*	The object to convert to a number. If it is absent, the context node is converted to a number and used.
Return Value		*number*	The number converted from the object

415

DESCRIPTIONS AND EXAMPLES.   The number() function converts an object to a number. If the object is a string, the function will convert it according to the procedure specified in Section 5.4.2.

If the argument is a Boolean value, the function converts true to 1 and false to 0.

If the argument is a node-set, then the node-set is converted to a string first using the string() function, and then the string is converted to a number.

C.2.24   *position*

Function: *number* position()

Argument Position	Number of Occurrences	Type	Description
Return Value		*number*	The position of the context node in the context

DESCRIPTONS AND EXAMPLES.   The position function returns the position of the context node in the context. This is not always its position among its siblings in the source tree. For instance, for the XML document

```
<?xml version='1.0'?>
<stories>
  <story>1</story>
  <story>2</story>
  <story>3</story>
  <story>4</story>
  <story>5</story>
  <story>6</story>
  <story>7</story>
  <story>8</story>
  <story>9</story>
</stories>
```

we have the templates

```
<xsl:template match='/'>
<xsl:apply-templates select='/stories/story|/stories'/>
</xsl:template>

<xsl:template match='stories|story'>
    Node name: '<xsl:value-of select='name()'/>' Position:
```

```
    <xsl:value-of select='position()'/>
</xsl:template>
```

The result looks like this.

```
Node name: 'stories' Position: 1
Node name: 'story' Position: 2
Node name: 'story' Position: 3
Node name: 'story' Position: 4
Node name: 'story' Position: 5
Node name: 'story' Position: 6
Node name: 'story' Position: 7
Node name: 'story' Position: 8
Node name: 'story' Position: 9
Node name: 'story' Position: 10
```

THE POSITION OF THE CURRENT NODE AMONG ITS SIBLINGS.   Then how do we find the position of the current node among its siblings? Use the template below.

```
<xsl:template match='stories|story'>
    Node name: '<xsl:value-of select='name()'/>' Position:
        <xsl:value-of select='count(preceding-sibling::*) + 1'/>
</xsl:template>
```

You will get the following result.

```
Node name: 'stories' Position: 1
Node name: 'story' Position: 1
Node name: 'story' Position: 2
Node name: 'story' Position: 3
Node name: 'story' Position: 4
Node name: 'story' Position: 5
Node name: 'story' Position: 6
Node name: 'story' Position: 7
Node name: 'story' Position: 8
Node name: 'story' Position: 9
```

If the source document looks like this

```
<?xml version='1.0'?>
<stories>
  <summary>The summary of all the stories above.</summary>
  <story>1</story>
```

```
        <story>2</story>
        <story>3</story>
        <story>4</story>
        <story>5</story>
        <story>6</story>
        <story>7</story>
        <story>8</story>
        <story>9</story>
    </stories>
```

the result now looks like this.

```
Node name: 'stories' Position: 1
Node name: 'story' Position: 2
Node name: 'story' Position: 3
Node name: 'story' Position: 4
Node name: 'story' Position: 5
Node name: 'story' Position: 6
Node name: 'story' Position: 7
Node name: 'story' Position: 8
Node name: 'story' Position: 9
Node name: 'story' Position: 10
```

To choose only the siblings that have the same name as the current node, use the following template.

```
<xsl:template match='stories|story'>
    Node name: '<xsl:value-of select='name()'/>' Position:
    <xsl:value-of
        select='count(preceding-sibling::*[name() = name(current())]) +
1'/>
</xsl:template>
```

You must use the current() function to indicate the current node.

C.2.25   *round*

Function: *number* round(*number*)

Argument Position	Number of Occurrences	Type	Description
1	1	*number*	The number to round
Return Value		*number*	The rounded value of the first argument

DESCRIPTIONS AND EXAMPLES. This function rounds the argument. For instance, if the number is 1.2, then the rounded number is 1. If the number is 1.8, then the rounded number is 2.

C.2.26 *starts-with*

Function: *Boolean* `starts-with(`*string*`, `*string*`)`

Argument Position	Number of Occurrences	Type	Description
1	1	*string*	The string to match
2	1	*string*	The prefix to check the first argument
Return Value		*Boolean*	True if the first argument starts with the second argument

Given two strings, the `starts-with()` function returns true if one string is the prefix of the other one. If the first string you specify is prefixed by the second string, then you get back true. Otherwise, you get back false. For example,

```
starts-with('abc', 'def')
```

returns `false`, but

```
starts-with('abc', 'ab')
```

returns `true`. Also,

```
starts-with('abc', 'abcd')
```

return false as well.

C.2.27 *string*

Function: *string* `string(`*object*$^{(0 \text{ or } 1)}$`)`

Argument Position	Number of Occurrences	Type	Description
1	0 or 1	*string*	The object to convert to a string. If it is absent, the context node is used.
Return Value		*string*	The argument converted to string

DESCRIPTIONS AND EXAMPLES.   This function converts an object to a string. The conversion process is described in Section 5.4. Here is a summary of the process.

String.   If you specify a string as the parameter, then the string is returned with no modification.

Number.   If you want to format a number neatly, use the `format-number()` function. The `string()` function performs only rudimentary formatting.

NaN.   The string NaN.

Positive zero and negative zero.   The string 0.

Negative infinity.   The string `-Infinity`.

Positive infinity.   The string `Infinity`.

Integers.   No decimal point and no leading zeros. A minus sign if the number is negative. For instance, 123 yields `123`; −45 yields `-45`.

Floating-point numbers.   If the number is negative, the minus sign is prefixed in the string. No leading zeros. No trailing zeros for the fractional part of the number either. For instance, `string(1 div 3)` returns `0.3333333333333333`.

Boolean values.   If the value is true, then the string `true` is returned. If the value is false, then the string `false` is returned.

C.2.28   *string-length*

Function: *number* `string-length(`*string*$^{(0 \text{ or } 1)}$`)`

Argument Position	Number of Occurrences	Type	Description
1	0 or 1	*string*	The string to find the length for. If it is absent, the context node is used.
Return Value		*number*	The length of the string

DESCRIPTIONS AND EXAMPLES.   The `string-length` function returns the length of the string you specify. If you do not specify the string, then the length of the context node is returned instead.

C.2.29   *substring*

Function: *string* `substring(`*string, number, number*[0 or 1]`)`

Argument Position	Number of Occurrences	Type	Description
1	1	*string*	The string to extract the substring
2	1	*number*	The starting position of the substring
3	0 or 1	*number*	The number of characters in the substring. If it is absent, extract to the end of the string.
Return Value		*string*	The substring extracted

DESCRIPTIONS AND EXAMPLES.   The `substring()` function extracts a substring from a string. You pass to the function a string and up to two numbers. The first number you specify is the starting point of the string that you want to start extracting. The second number, if you specify it, is the number of characters you want to extract from the string. If you do not specify the second number, then the extraction will go to the end of the string. The characters in the string are counted from 1, not 0. Here is an example of the function.

```
substring('abcdefgh', 3)
```

returns `cdefgh`. And

```
substring('abcdefgh', 3, 3)
```

returns `cde` because the second number says to return 3 characters.

You should stick to integers for the two numbers you specify. But if you use numbers with decimal points, remember that they are first rounded to integers before they are used. So the starting number of `1.5` is first converted to `2`; `1.4` is converted to `1`.

There is no reason to specify a starting position to be less than one, but if you must, then the substring extracted is a prefix of the string. The length of the substring is the sum of the two numbers subtracted by 1. If the length is less than one, then the function returns an empty string. For instance, in the function

```
substring('abcdef', -2, 4)
```

the sum of the numbers is 2. Subtract 1 from the sum gives 1. The result is therefore the prefix of abcdef with the length of 1—in other words, a. If you specify the length of the substring to be less than 1, then the function always returns an empty string.

C.2.30   *substring-after*

Function: *string* substring-after(*string*, *string*)

Argument Position	Number of Occurrences	Type	Description
1	1	*string*	The string to extract the substring
2	1	*string*	The substring to match for
Return Value		*string*	The substring extracted

DESCRIPTIONS AND EXAMPLES.   The substring-after() function returns a suffix of a string. You pass two strings to this function. Suppose the first string contains the second string. This function returns the portion of the first string after the first occurrence of the second string. If the first string does not contain the second string, then an empty string is returned. For example,

```
substring-after('abcdefabcdef', 'fab')
```

returns cdef. On the other hand,

```
substring-after('abcdefabcdef', 'cd')
```

returns efabcdef. This function may return a string that still contains the second parameter.

See Section 11.2 for an example of how the substring-before, substring-after, and contains can be used to extract substrings from a string.

C.2.31   *substring-before*

Function: *string* substring-before(*string*, *string*)

Argument Position	Number of Occurrences	Type	Description
1	1	*string*	The string to extract the substring
2	1	*string*	The substring to match for
Return Value		*string*	The substring extracted

DESCRIPTIONS AND EXAMPLES. The `substring-before()` function returns a prefix of a string. You pass two strings to this function. Suppose the first string contains the second string. This function returns the portion of the first string in front of the first occurrence of the second string. If the second string is not contained in the first string, an empty string is returned. You can be sure that the string returned by this function does not contain the second string.

```
substring-before('abcdefg', 'def')
```

returns `abc`, but

```
substring-before('abcdef', 'fg')
```

returns an empty string. If the second parameter occurs more than once in the first parameter, the first occurrence is the one used. If the second parameter is a prefix of the first parameter, the function returns an empty string as well. For example,

```
substring-before('abcdef', 'abc')
```

returns an empty string, although the first parameter contains the second parameter.

C.2.32 *sum*

Function: *number* sum(*node-set*)

Argument Position	Number of Occurrences	Type	Description
1	1	*node-set*	The node-set containing the nodes whose numeric values are to be summed
Return Value		*number*	The sum of the numeric values of the nodes in the node-set

DESCRIPTIONS AND EXAMPLES. The `sum()` function takes a node-set, converts each node in the node-set to a number, then sums all the numbers.

Suppose we have the following table of expenses.

```
<expense>
  <item><name>Plane Fare</name><amount>525.00</amount></item>
  <item><name>Hotel</name><amount>275</amount></item>
  <item><name>Conference Fees</name><amount>90</amount></item>
```

```
<item><name>Transport</name><amount>100</amount></item>
<item><name>Meal</name><amount>5</amount></item>
<item><name>Meal</name><amount>5.75</amount></item>
<item><name>Meal</name><amount>45.48</amount></item>
<item><name>Meal</name><amount>5</amount></item>
<item><name>Meal</name><amount>9.35</amount></item>
<item><name>Meal</name><amount>20.54</amount></item>
<item><name>Meal</name><amount>5</amount></item>
<item><name>Meal</name><amount>4.50</amount></item>
<item><name>Meal</name><amount>37.87</amount></item>
</expense>
```

To add all the amounts together, we can use the following expression.

```
<xsl:value-of select='sum(/expense/item/amount)'/>
```

The answer is `1128.4899999999998` for the XSLT processor I use. To format the answer better, you can use the `format-number()` function (see Section C.2.11).

You want to be careful that all the nodes in the node-set can be converted into numbers. Otherwise, you will get NaN as the result. For example, if this is added to the `expense` element

```
<item><name>Toy</name><amount>$34.95</amount></item>
```

the answer is NaN. The string `$34.95` cannot be converted to a number.

C.2.33   *system-property*

Function: *object* `system-property(`*string*`)`

Argument Position	Number of Occurrences	Type	Description
1	1	*string*	The name of the system property
Return Value		*object*	The value of the system property

DESCRIPTIONS AND EXAMPLES.   The `system-property()` function returns the value associated to a string assumed to be a name for a system property.

Every XSLT processor must provide three system properties.

`xsl:version`   This property is the version number of the XSLT the processor is supporting. It is a number and must be 1.0 for now.

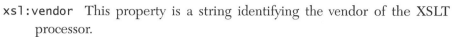

xsl:vendor   This property is a string identifying the vendor of the XSLT processor.

xsl:vendor-url   This property returns the URL of the vendor of the XSLT processor.

If a property is not available, an empty string will be returned.

C.2.34   *translate*

Function: *string* translate(*string*, *string*, *string*)

Argument Position	Number of Occurrences	Type	Description
1	1	*string*	The string to translate
2	1	*string*	The original pattern for translation
3	1	*string*	The mapping for the original pattern
Return Value		*string*	The translated string

DESCRIPTIONS AND EXAMPLES.   The translate() function takes a string, modifies its characters, and returns the modified string.

The modification is directed by two strings: the second and third parameters. The second parameter contains characters that should be modified. The third parameter specifies what the modified characters should be.

The characters in the second parameter are mapped to the characters in the third parameter by position. The first character of the second parameter is mapped to the first character of the third parameter. The second character of the second parameter is mapped to the second character of the third parameter, and so on.

If the second parameter is longer than the third parameter, each character in the second parameter without a corresponding character in the third parameter is taken to map to an empty character. If the second parameter is shorter than the third parameter, the extra characters in the third parameter are ignored.

Suppose there is a character—say, *A*—in the second parameter that maps to a character—say, *B*—in the third parameter. The translate() function finds all the occurrences of *A* in the first parameter. If there is none, then it does nothing. If the first parameter contains *A*, then each occurrence of *A* in the first

The translation scheme

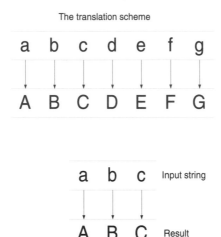

FIGURE

C.1

The translate function

parameter is replaced by B. If B is the empty character, then all occurrences of A in the first parameter are removed.

All characters in the second parameter are processed in this way simultaneously.

For example, this

```
translate('abc', 'abcdefg', 'ABCDEFG')
```

returns ABC. See Figure C.1 for a pictorial explanation of the operation. Different effects can be achieved using this function. For instance, it is possible to censor all the occurrences of the character i and use the character - instead.

```
translate('Mississippi', 'i', '-')
```

becomes M-ss-ss-pp-. Conversion to upper case or to lower case can be done with this function, too.

To remove characters in the first parameter, put the character at the end of the second parameter and make sure there is no corresponding character in the third parameter. That is, the second parameter must be longer than the third parameter. For example, to remove all instances of the vowels, use

```
translate('Mississippi', 'aeiou', '')
```

The translation scheme

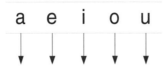

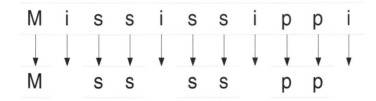

The input string

The result

FIGURE
C.2

The `translate('Mississippi', 'aeiou', '')` function

and the result is `Msssspp`. Figure C.2 shows a pictorial explanation of the translation of the example. This function can also be used to do simple mapping. Suppose we would like translate the Arabic numbers 1, 2, and 3 to Chinese characters for the numbers. Figure C.3 shows such a translation.

PARALLEL REPLACEMENT.   Because all the characters in the second parameter are all replaced at the same time, this

    translate('abc', 'abc', 'bcd')

returns `bcd`, not `ddd`.

C.2.35   *true*

Function: *Boolean* `true()`

Argument Position	Number of Occurrences	Type	Description
Return Value		*Boolean*	True

The translation scheme

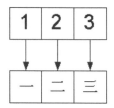

The input string

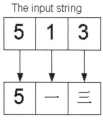

The result

FIGURE

C.3   Translating numbers to Chinese characters

DESCRIPTIONS AND EXAMPLES. The true function returns the Boolean true value.

Usually, you use this function to select one of two choices. For instance, suppose you have a template to generate a link. You do not want to use an image if the browser does not support images. You can define it this way.

```
<xsl:template match='link'>
  <xsl:param name='supportImage' select='true()'/>
  <xsl:param name='link'/>
  <xsl:param name='label'/>
  <xsl:param name='image'/>
  <A HREF='{$link}'>
    <xsl:choose>
      <xsl:when test='$supportImage'>
        <IMG SRC='/images/$image.jpg' ALT='{$label}'/>
      </xsl:when>
      <xsl:otherwise>
        <xsl:value-of select='$label'/>
      </xsl:otherwise>
    </xsl:choose>
```

```
    </A>
  </xsl:template>
```

The default value of the `supportImage` parameter is set to `true`.

C.2.36 *unparsed-entity-uri*

Function: *string* unparsed-entity-uri(*string*)

Argument Position	Number of Occurrences	Type	Description
1	1	*string*	The name of the unparsed entity
Return Value		*string*	The URI of the unparsed entity whose name is given in the first argument

DESCRIPTIONS AND EXAMPLES. The `unparsed-entity-uri()` function returns the URI of the unparsed-entity given in the parameter.

In an XML document, you declare an entity to be unparsed if you do not want its content to be parsed as XML data. You declare an unparsed external general entity by giving a public identifier or a system identifier. The markup declarations you need to declare an unparsed external general entity are the `NOTATION` declaration and `ENTITY` declaration. For instance, suppose you want to declare an unparsed entity called `black-image` that is in GIF format (or notation) with a URI `http://www.wireoptional.com/colors/black.gif`. You will have the following markup declarations in your DTD.

```
<!NOTATION gif SYSTEM>
<!ENTITY black-image
        SYSTEM 'http://www.wireoptional.com/colors/black.gif'
        NDATA gif>
```

To get the URI of this entity, you use the `unparsed-entity-uri()` function like this.

```
unparsed-entity-uri('black-image')
```

The value returned is `http://www.wireoptional.com/colors/black.gif`.

Suggested Resources

Extensible Markup Language (XML) 1.0. W3C Recommendation. World Wide Web Consortium. www.w3.org/TR/1998/REC-xml-19980210.

Extensible Stylesheet Language (XSL). W3C Working Draft. World Wide Web Consortium. www.w3.org/TR/WD-xsl.

HTML 4.0 Specification. W3C Recommendation. World Wide Web Consortium. www.w3.org/TR/REC-html40.

ISO/IEC 10646-1:1993, Information Technology-Universal Multiple-Octet Coded Character Set (UCS—Part 1: Architecture and Basic Multilingual Plane. International Standard. ISO (International Organization for Standardization). www.iso.ch/cate/d29819.html.

Namespaces in XML. W3C Recommendation. World Wide Web Consortium. www.w3.org/TR/REC-xml-names.

Portable Document Format Reference Manual Version 1.3. March 1, 1999. Adobe Systems Incorporated.

Scalable Vector Graphics (SVG) 1.0 Specification. W3C Working Draft, June 29, 2000. World Wide Web Consortium. www.w3.org/TR/SVG.

XHTML 1.0: The Extensible HyperText Markup Language. W3C Proposed Recommendation. World Wide Web Consortium. www.w3.org/TR/xhtml1.

XML Path Language. W3C Recommendation. World Wide Web Consortium. www.w3.org/TR/xpath.

XSL Transformations (XSLT). W3C Recommendation. World Wide Web Consortium. www.w3.org/TR/xslt.

Index

Index

Index

Index

Index

Index

Register
Your Book
at www.aw.com/cseng/register

You may be eligible to receive:

- Advance notice of forthcoming editions of the book
- Related book recommendations
- Chapter excerpts and supplements of forthcoming titles
- Information about special contests and promotions throughout the year
- Notices and reminders about author appearances, tradeshows, and online chats with special guests

Contact us

If you are interested in writing a book or reviewing manuscripts prior to publication, please write to us at:

Editorial Department
Addison-Wesley Professional
75 Arlington Street, Suite 300
Boston, MA 02116 USA
Email: AWPro@aw.com

Visit us on the Web: http://www.aw.com/cseng

CD-ROM Warranty

This CD includes all the self-contained examples in the book. There is one directory for each chapter containing the examples in that chapter.

For Appendix C, the examples for each function and element are grouped separately into subdirectories. Elements and functions with no self-contained examples are not grouped into subdirectories.

More information and updates are available at:
www.awl.com/cseng/titles/0-201-71103-6